JOSEPH SHUMAN
JOURNALISM COLLECTION

POINT PARK COLLEGE

The Bedside
'GUARDIAN'
30

The Bedside
'GUARDIAN' –
30

A selection from
The 'Guardian' 1980–81

Edited by
W. L. Webb

With an introduction by
William Golding

Cartoons by
Gibbard and Bryan McAllister

COLLINS
St James's Place, London
1981

William Collins Sons & Co Ltd
London · Glasgow · Sydney · Auckland
Toronto · Johannesburg

British Library Cataloguing in Publication Data

The Bedside Guardian.—30
I. The Guardian
082′.05   PN6142

ISBN 0-00-216356-X

First published 1981 © Guardian Newspapers Ltd, 1981

Photoset in Imprint
Made and Printed in Great Britain by
William Collins Sons & Co Ltd Glasgow

Introduction

The book you are about to leaf through – for who reads an anthology from one end to the other at first sight? – was brought together from articles written for the *Guardian* newspaper between August 1980 and August 1981. That is not a calendar year, religious or astronomical, but one stemming from the necessity of publishing at a time to catch a book-tide. If you know the *Guardian*, you will assume and rightly that the articles are of brilliant and sometimes dazzling readability. Here and there they are sombre or pathetic or worrisome and always, befitting their provenance, they are set against a background of concern. Some are wildly funny. They, as well as the others, are mostly at two removes from the red hot news. That is just as well for it was not a year in which you could hear much good. Immediacy for most of us came from the box. We were right there, we peered over the shoulders of the reporters and viewed a rag'doll, an arm or leg sticking out of rubble. Blood was the year's badge. Frozen in our fireside seats we attended the occasional execution. At times, the urge to retreat, to get to hell out of the whole mess, was irresistible. So compared with the moving, coloured pictures even a newspaper report or an article written on the report is less likely to exacerbate a sensitive character.

All *Guardian* readers are sensitive characters – it is their definition. I am one myself. We anguish in so many different directions, are convinced of the number one *overwhelming importance* of so many causes we are sometimes like Aquinas's Logical Ass, surrounded by hay and able to eat none. Then we retreat from the insoluble problem. I have leafed through my own journal for 80/81 and find that the instinct for self-preservation has kept me from transferring the more hideous bits of the daily news to it and has made the pages parochial and self-centred. Some pieces of news I have not only omitted from my journal but forgotten deliberately. I crawled inside my journal and pulled down the lid.

The result is I am not really certain what the year contained and as like as not have confused it with the year before which was no better. At some point Russia invaded Afghanistan and some people boycotted the amusingly named Olympic Games. Our Foreign Secretary approached Saudi Arabia on hands and knees. Iraq invaded Iran which was already invading itself, Israel bombed an Iraqi nuclear installation and Syria installed ground-to-air missiles in Lebanon, a country which appears to have ceased to exist. The space race became even more dedicated to Armageddon. England, my England, seemed to break down in a welter of riots that smashed and burned and broke heads and hearts. Even so, the most important news came out of Iran. We had, there, ocular demonstration that economics are not the only cause of revolution! Ayatollah Khomeini with his religious fanaticism put the boot into the whole dreary concept of Marxist historicity – a case if ever there was one of *e malo bonum*.

Of course there were other bits of good news. Inflation came down, if only for the time being. The election of Mitterand to the French presidency was probably good news for Europe if nowhere else. American hostages were released and came home in a ballyhoo the like of which had not been seen since Scotland's football team were sent on their way to take part in the World Cup. The European Space Rocket was tested and worked. Some day we shall have instant bad news (via satellite) from everywhere and cease to look. And so on.

Now I have to confess that the writing of an introduction to a Bedside Book is a tricky business. The avowed intention of such a book is to please and soothe. But lurking behind that bland assertion is the thought that such a book must have something of the effect the lettuce had on the Flopsy Bunnies; and all *Guardian* readers will know what that was. You might wonder, then, if the talented writers whose work is included here would find themselves gratified at being included with soothest syrup, with poppy and mandragora, and coming under the general heading of 'soporific'. Be easy. As one of the breed I can assure you that writers will clutch to them any tribute to their skill they can get. Even if the tribute is barbed or ambiguous we have an innate capacity for seeing the

6

flattering side of it. If you fall asleep while reading this or any of the ensuing pieces (provided you are where you ought to be, in bed) we shall think we did not send you off by boredom but by magic passes.

So if you should have the misfortune to be about to travel from hotel to hotel – where the cupboard-like bedside objects which once held a chamber pot now have only a monoglot Bible, or the New Testament in four languages – take this book with you. Read the good news of Gordon Green and his school. Savour Alexander Haig's invention of a new language in place of the one removed from us by the departure of the unlamented Spiro Agnew. If you want to stay awake (it is sometimes necessary to wait for a bedfellow) turn to Alex Hamilton's Message from my Father, an engrossing piece, ineffably sad but without a trace of self-pity. That will brace you for Remember Forking. Try the poignant An Ill Wind in the Dale. That one ends with a cryptic sentence which might well serve as a motto for our shuddering country. 'If we could live on our losses at this rate we should be doing very well.' There is a mysterious force in that, an ineluctable aptness as if Merlin had said it.

Still, when you compose yourself to sleep remember the best news of all. You will find it in the stark account by Bernard Lovell of How the Battle Lines were drawn for the Space War. Ninety per cent of the space effort is aimed at 'defence'. But a blessed ten per cent is still on the side of the angels. You will remember that percentage, when the space probes voyage on, year after year, one bedside meditation after another. Indeed one of them carries the image of a naked man, equipped with penis and scrotum. A naked woman stands by him, but deprived of her principal reproductive organ – an insoluble problem, I should guess, for the biologists of Aldebaran. That probe, though, brought us the clouds writhing round the red spot on Jupiter. It showed us volcanoes erupting on Io; and as if to emphasise our oneness with the universe Mount St Helens showed us what could be done on the terrestrial front. For it is a truism of the angelic side of the space age that we are seeing more and more the whole earth as our patrimony, our glorious home. Indeed, one

7

of the best ways of getting yourself to sleep – granted *we* have failed – is to put yourself aboard a space probe in imagination and go out, out, away from the news, and news about news, and articles arising from news about news, out to where the silences of the eternal spaces do not frighten or chill but console – even if with nothing more than their indifference. So we may rise from sorrows to news of sorrows, to comments on news of sorrows, to the ending of Sorrow: as it might be by way of angels and archangels, archai, thrones, dominions, powers . . .

William Golding

Alexander the Haigiographer

General Alexander Haig has contexted the Polish watchpot somewhat nuancely. How, though, if the situation decontrols can he stoppage it mountingly conflagrating? Haig, in Congressional hearings before his confirmatory, paradoxed his auditioners by abnormalling his responds so that verbs were nouned, nouns verbed and adjectives adverbised. He techniqued a new way to vocabulary his thoughts so as to informationally uncertain anybody listening about what he had actually implicationed. At first it seemed that the General was impenetrabling what at basic was clear. This, it was suppositioned, was a new linguistic harbingered by NATO during the time he bellwethered it. But close observers have alternatived that idea. What Haig is doing, they concept, is to decouple the Russians from everything they are moded to. An example was to obstacle Soviet ambassador Dobrynin from personalising the private elevator at Foggy Bottom. Now he has to communal like everybody else. Experts in the Kremlin thought they could recognition the word-forms of American diplomacy. Now they have to afreshly language themselves up before they know what the Americans are subtling. They are like chess grandmasters suddenly told to knight their bishops and rook their pawns. If that is how General Haig wants to nervous breakdown the Russian leadership he may be shrewding his way to the biggest diplomatic invent since Clausewitz. Unless, that is, he schizophrenes his allies first.

3 February 1981   **Leader**

The dream time as nightmare

The wrinkled old Hopi Indian from North Arizona sat outside the conference hall in Rotterdam, waiting to hear a case about genocide in Peru. 'I don't want to scare anyone,' he said, 'but in our stone tablets it says that the Earth is about to be destroyed. The whole world will shake and turn red. Then it will turn over and only the ants will survive. Maybe they will create man again.'

It soon became clear at last week's Fourth Russell Tribunal on the Indians of the Americas, as witnesses paraded a grisly catalogue of massacres, betrayals, and broken promises before the jury, that the sessions were not to be concerned solely with violations of human rights or the transgressions of individual governments. The world's most ancient societies were passing judgment on industrialised man and giving a warning that he is about to fulfil their doomladen prophecies.

Spokesmen asserted repeatedly that the fate of aboriginal people, as caretakers of the natural world, was linked inextricably with mankind's survival. 'Indigenous people are the conscience of the world,' declared Oren Lyons, of the Iroquois Confederacy. 'If you kill that conscience, it will mean the destruction of future generations. Technology cannot take the place of life.' Indian civilisation had been based on the study of nature, observed Phillip Deer, a spiritual leader of the Muskagee tribe in Oklahoma. It had no need for prisons, insane asylums, or locks. 'The European people have forgotten their natural way of life. They are programmed to wake up to the sound of an alarm. Only those who understand the original instructions of life will be able to survive.'

The Western Shoshone tribe from Nevada needed no such rhetoric: the United States requires 10,000 sq. miles of their land as a 'national sacrifice area' in which to install the MX missile system. 'Our way of life is about to come to an end,' stated their young representative, Pearl Dann. 'The survival of the natural world is threatened. Land is exploited for economic profit regardless of the consequences.' The Shoshone was one of several groups, not listed among the tribunal's 11 official cases, who were offered a platform to air their grievances. The Dutch organisers, the Workshop Indian Project Foundation, had sifted through more than 40 detailed complaints from North, Central, and South America, in addition to many more from non-Indian indigenous groups throughout the world, six of whom were accorded special evening sessions.

The unfolding evidence began to form a pattern of sustained worldwide assault on the last sanctuaries of aboriginal people, often sited in the most remote and inhospitable areas, to satisfy the increasing demands of industrialised societies. 'God created the world for everyone, not just for a few lucky ones,' lamented a Peruvian Indian whose community at San Juan de Ondores was evicted twice from their land this year, their houses burned, their cattle and possessions stolen, and two of their members killed. A Maori stood with tears in his eyes, holding a facsimile of a 140-year-old treaty with the British Crown. 'We opened the doors to you, but the cupboard is almost bare now,' he said. 'Of the 66 million acres we owned, we are down to 2½ million acres. Japanese companies have leases on our forests. Our artefacts are here in Europe. I feel like screaming my heart out sometimes.'

Britain came in for criticism from several quarters. The arrival of the British in Australia, said an Aborigine, had turned the dream time into a nightmare as his people had suffered genocide beyond Hitler's and Pol Pot's wildest dreams. A contingent of Canadian Indians protested at the refusal of Mrs Thatcher and the Queen to discuss the patriation of Canada's constitution, thereby imperilling Indian rights. 'We never gave up Canada, we still own it,' said a spokesman.

The enforced absence of the Xavante Indian leader, Mario Juruna, from the jury put the spotlight firmly on Brazil's increasingly repressive policies and the activities of FUNAI, the national Indian agency. Evidence was called on the Nambiquarra, who in 10 years have declined from being absolute rulers of their land, to a tiny remnant; on the Yanomami, who are reported to be in a state of misery, sickness, and shock following the invasion of their land by highway workers and commercial enterprises; and on the Aruak and Tukano tribes, whose culture, it was alleged, has been systematically destroyed by Silesian missionaries.

The Russell Tribunal has no power to enforce its indictments, counting on its moral influence to stir the conscience of mankind. Whether or not it succeeds, the discovery of common ties between Eskimos and Tahitians, Aborigines and Navajos, Papuans and Peruvians, has sent up an unmistakable smoke signal. 'For many years we had to crawl and beg,' said Phillip Deer. 'No more are we going to crawl. We're going to die standing up rather than beg.'

3 December 1980   **Stuart Wavell**

God sieve the Queen!

Some talk of Tom Fleming and some of Andrew Gardner but for me there is no wedding commentator to touch Horace, the BBC-2 computer.

Horace was BBC-2's contribution to the Year of the Disabled. By providing instant captions it was hoped he would increase the enjoyment of the deaf and I don't doubt that he did.

One of Horace's own disabilities was that with a vocabulary of only 8,000 words, he had to translate into captions the commentary of BBC-1's Tom Fleming. Mr Fleming is the *vox humana* of the BBC, a commentator lush as plush. His troths are plighted, his toasts are pledged, his churches are 'pale as a bride on her wedding morning'. Mr Fleming, like the true, the blushful Hippocrene, has a purple-stained mouth. Horace's attempts to get all this down on paper, so to speak, read at times like Daisy Ashford and at others Doctor Spooner and, at best, both.

'Heers the seen,' cried Horace, who doesn't spell very well yet pushes on regardless. 'What a po No plee of colour.' Here

is the Archbishop of Canterbury 'in his new cope of silver ma
tee rjul made in nine tin twenty. He has chosen this moment to
ware it.' There is Princess Anne 'wearing an a masing outfit.
Very sump. Shs flat a big firll down the sid.' (I find 'very
sump' one of Horace's more felicitous flights, it wrapped the
whole day up beautifully).

The Queen Mother had 'a cloud of S prays round her face'
while the Queen was 'wearing cre D sheen, sparkling with qui
stls and sapphires.' Horace, evidently a right old softie,
speculated about the contents of the Queen's handbag.
'Certainly eyed think today there might be a po ct hankerchif'
in it,' he offered mistily.

Some of the commentary took on a surrealist life of its own:
'On the right hand sid is where crin ling gi bns had his
workshop, who caufrds so many thins in sid St Paul's' (which
I translate as: On the right hand side is where Grinling
Gibbons had his workshop, who carved so many things in St
Paul's).

By now, according to Horace, the Prince of Wales had
ascended the Redcar pet with the Dew of Edinburgh, Prince
Andrew in n val eun fm, Prince Eddfrd in morning dress and
udder members of the royal fasmli. 'Here,' said Horace, much
moved, 'is a seen that outshines any. We weight for thris gate
moment.' As the bride (or Lady Dja na, Horace called her)
'foamed out of the class coach,' he described the 'hundreds of
jarts of veil,' 'the tiny bodies and gate big skirt,' and the
bouquet in 'white and gream'.

The sub-titles for what Horace called 'the marriage vus'
were pre-recorded. The spelling got better but the reporting
worse. The sub-titles came down pretty sharpish on 'carnal
appetites, sin, fornication and such as have not the gift of
continency,' though the Archbishop, possibly feeling it was
not quite nice, had omitted all this.

I was mildly concerned to hear Lady Diana promise to
marry Philip Charles Arthur George (a slight rearrangement
of the Prince's Christian names) and wondered if she had
inadvertently married Prince Philip. Prince Charles, in his
turn, cleverly promised 'all thy goods with thee I share.'
Impatient of human error, the sub-titles overrode all this and

printed what they ought to have said. The bells were wringing, according to Horace, as the Royal Family made their way home, including a certain Canon Lips who puzzled me for some time until I identified him with relief as Captain Mark Phillips.

Even the parts of London I know well were transformed by Horace into something rich and strange. Fleet Street for instance: 'Past all those one dfl Fleet Street restronts, the printers pup and the newspaper people have tunt auth.' As the 'air to the throne' approached St Clement Danes, I felt my toes tie themselves in anticipatory knots. I began to pray as when, during a pause in the conversation, you see a stammerer about to embark on a word you know he can't handle.

O Lord, don't let Horace say oranges and lemons. But carried away by the 'life garts' and 'keers' and the 'csea of hugh man faces' and the Prince of Wales 'very mucks Amman of the twentieth century,' there was no holding him. 'The bells of St Clament Dames, which say o wnjn js and lemons nu joayn they happy sad to ehe saunts of ln dn' (the bells of St Clement Danes which say Oranges and Lemons now join their happy sound to the sounds of London.')

Buckingham palace is 'insight. The cheers are ever lubber,' cried Horace, breaking down completely and wiping, like Earl Spencer, 'a tear from his aye'.

I myself was holding my po ct hankerchif before my streaming ayes. God sieve the Queen!

30 July 1981   **Nancy Banks-Smith**

Silicon chaps

'Good afternoon, sir, can I interest you in a new brain?' someone asked. After a whole morning spent listening to CBI delegates droning on at their annual conference it seemed like a good idea, especially at only £199 for the basic model, £299 for the one with 'extra memory facility'.

Certainly the most interesting thing at the conference was

the amazing display of technical hardware for the business-man of tomorrow. The New Brain turned out to be a miniature computer. It could be used in the office, at home, or even on a train, so you could work out the repayments on a British Rail gin and tonic. It was small enough to fit inside a briefcase, or even inside your head.

The traditional British picture of a businessman as a boozy old lecher who spends four hours at lunch and the rest of the day pursuing his secretary is clearly going to have to go. For a start, they aren't going to meet any secretaries after the year 1985.

According to a Department of Industry TV presentation depicting the office of the future, the businessman (poor sod) will spend his life chained to a computer which will boss him around all day. It will tell him who to fire, solve his personnel problems, predict his sales graph and even arrange his haircuts. At one point, the harassed bloke shown in the DoI film was faced with a real-life woman, another executive perhaps. A look of glassy-eyed panic swept over him, and he began dementedly asking her what the weather was like in Ramsgate.

Everywhere throughout the Conference there were scores of TV screens, more at times than there were delegates in the hall. The screens nearly all showed data. There was Prestel, Ceefax, Oracle, DataStream, Space Invaders and Galaxian. There were giant 4ft. screens relaying the Conference to all corners of the Brighton Centre, and even in the hall itself, so that speakers could see themselves twice life-size while performing, a narcissism similar to that shown by people who have mirrors on their bedroom ceilings.

They even had devices which simultaneously taped the debates on dozens of cassettes, so that delegates could replay whole sessions in their cars while driving home, a new and terrifying menace on the A23.

There was a proud new British first on display, too – what is claimed to be the most advanced hot-drink vending machine incorporating the microprocessor, so you can now order powdered chicken soup in three strengths, hot or cold, with or without sugar and non-dairy creamer. Yet people say that British industry is not meeting the challenge of the Eighties.

Back on the platform, the businessmen were complaining about almost everything. You can tell how posh a conference is by the decor of the stage. The CBI's was decked out in vast grey sloping slabs, so it looked like the Maginot Line on a wet winter afternoon. On each side, however, there was a magnificent display of exotic plant life topped by mighty bamboos. One almost expected the minuscule Michael Edwardes, dangerously close to this jungle, to be leapt upon by a Japanese soldier who had not been told the trade war was over. In the foyer there was the inevitable Mini Metro. One now realises why it is the size and shape it is; so that Michael Edwardes can reach the pedals.

Actually Edwardes made just about the only decent speech I heard. He was extremely satirical about the Energy Secretary, David Howell, who 'seems to think that Britain is the only country in the world in step. I wonder.' He went on, 'If the Cabinet has not got the wit and imagination to bring the pound down, if they can't find what to.do about North Sea oil, I say leave the bloody stuff in the ground.' This speech, heresy a few years ago, was loudly cheered by the otherwise somnolent delegates.

One can't really blame them for being so dull. Unlike politicians and union leaders, businessmen almost never have the professional need to excite or inspire. Indeed, they seem a trifle embarrassed about doing so. This gives the proceedings a monotonous air, especially after lunch. Now and again someone would try a joke, but they soon gave up. One man, who ran a firm of travel agents, inexplicably pulled off his braces to depict the problems of unemployment. No one tittered or even appeared to notice.

Most of the speeches were attacking the Government. They went on and on about what a rotten government it was, how it was destroying industry, bringing the country crashing down and so forth. One had little sympathy. Most of that lot had done all in their power to get it elected, and on a perfectly clear manifesto too.

Lulled into the arms of Morpheus, I closed my eyes and

tried to remember where I had heard that tone of plangent complaint before. Then it came back to mind: at the Labour conference a month or so ago. It was that familiar traditional sound, the authentic voice of the British whingeing about someone else.

12 November 1980   **Simon Hoggart**

Thatcher's Modern England

I wake up to the news of the monthly unemployment figures. The familiar reassuring voice of Jim Prior tells us that it's going to get worse before it gets better. For the United Kingdom the average is now 10 per cent. In the West Midlands it is 11.3, in Birmingham 12 and in Coventry 13 per cent. Coventry, the proverbial Klondike of the post-war affluent society – the idea of 13 per cent unemployment takes some getting used to. I've heard several people say already, 'we're not used to recessions like this round here' or, 'unemployment is a new experience for us.' It's not quite true. In the last recession, 1975-76, unemployment in the West Midlands for the first time exceeded the national average. The decline of the motor industry, on which one in every six workers depends, has been going on for a decade or more. Rolls Royce had to be nationalised in the 1971-72 downturn, in 1975 British Leyland was taken over and Chrysler baled out, but this time it's far worse. The most apocalyptic of the 'de-industrialisation' schools of thought, the Department of Applied Economics at Cambridge, has predicted that because of its dependence on manufacture, especially metals and vehicles, the West Midlands by 1983 will have become the worst unemployment blackspot in England.

I switch stations. The local commercial station – 'BRMB 261, right in the heart of the Midlands' – is running a feature called Lucky Breaks. The lucky break is a job vacancy for a teenager. Today's lucky lad can be an apprentice joiner. Hurry, hurry, hurry.

17

As I go I'm dipping into Priestley's *English Journey*. He came here to Birmingham in 1934 and wrote 'It looked like a dirty muddle.' Now it looks like a clean muddle. Some people don't like the city centre but I do. It reminds me of Chicago although that is to flatter it architecturally. It seems to me fitting that the capital of the motor industry should have re-designed itself around the motor car. I like the violent irregularity of the skyline, the brash mixtures of old and new, and the confident equation of wealth and concrete. Birmingham is one of the few English cities to have completed its inner redevelopment before the party ended.

Priestley was neither the first nor the last traveller to write the premature obituary of the English class system. In the thirties he was as impressed by Woolworths as people were with Marks and Spencer in the sixties, seeing it as the symbol of a new democracy of consumers. He noted cinemas (of which Birmingham has some marvellously kitsch examples) and dance halls in the way that we note discos and steak houses. He remarked the advent of the buffet pub; now it is the wine bar which is taking over with all the young people drinking a drink called drywhitewine.

Our highest hopes for equality and for classless society were vested in education and for two decades the schools have been in a turmoil of reform. For teachers and children the process of reorganisation has been almost as disruptive as the collectivisation of the farms and a whole generation of pupils may have suffered in the cause. Nor is the aggravation at an end; in Birmingham, like many other cities, the school rolls are falling and the secondary schools are increasingly unable to sustain viable sixth forms: economic logic dictates a third educational tier, the sixth-form college.

Gordon Green is headmaster of Primrose Hill Comprehensive School, King's Heath. He began teaching in 1956 and since that day, he says, there hasn't been a moment's calm in education. But he thinks that the comprehensive principle needs 20 to 30 years to be measured and judged. If exam results had to be compared they must be compared with the whole of the previous systems and not just with the

23 per cent of it which was the grammar schools'. In the old secondary modern schools the curriculum was highly restricted, graduate teachers were a rarity, and the expectations of children and parents equally low. If measured by the number of students in higher education the productivity of the school system had doubled and that didn't mean that standards had generally fallen; for instance the science requirements of the universities had gone up steeply in the last ten years.

The argument about standards, he says, had been going on for a long while before Jim Callaghan initiated the 'Great Debate'. British industry was failing so it turned round and blamed the schools, urged them to go back to the basics and turn out numerate and literate recruits for the factories. Certainly the schools had to be conscious of industry's needs but they had to stop short of vocational training.

What did parents want? They wanted good exam results and they wanted children who weren't capable of academic success to be happy, to make social progress, to be able to read. He would like to abolish the public schools on the grounds that the parents who would do most to press for higher standards are opting out of the system. Social awareness was far greater in the comprehensive schools than it had been in the grammar schools and so was their contribution to the local community. In his own school the social mix had been highly successful. He quotes one of his sixth-formers, a middle-class girl, who had said the other day, 'We all learn to talk the same. Accents no longer matter.'

Gordon Green's school may be a bit of a show place but glancing round it his optimism is hard to resist. Its facilities and equipment are of the best. The teachers seem enthusiastic and the children look happy. Not all schools are as good as this but most of those that I have ever set my eyes on are something like it. Two decades of educational turmoil may have added to the country's problems but it is hard to believe that comprehensive education will not eventually prove its worth; it is, after all, what most other and more successful countries have been doing since the turn of the century or earlier. A visit to a school like this reinforces my belief that the true culprit is a century of educational divisiveness and neglect. Such a quantity of lost time is not quickly made up.

One of the mysteries of England at the moment is that while a great furore is going on about 'the cuts' there have hardly been any cuts yet and the general public has been scarcely affected so far. The explanation is that the battle in progress is chiefly a battle of interest groups. During the seventies there was a vast expansion of employment in the public services and a consequential growth in public service unions.

One leading Birmingham politician, who didn't want to be quoted on this, sees the Labour Party being taken over locally by public sector trade unions. They are using the party, he says, as a means of improving their pay and conditions in local government. Teachers were using their political power to determine education policy and the construction workers (UCAT) were quite prepared, he says, to sell out their private sector members in order to defend the direct labour departments. As for NUPE, it wanted the Council to engage in confrontation with the Government over the cuts. It had suggested even that the Council should resign and fight a by-election against the Government's policies.

If this is what is going on it is not very different from the way in which the older unions of manual workers used their political power to advance their industrial interests. That was why they founded the Labour Party. However, it does make difficulties for local government. In the case of education the question is whether falling school rolls should be taken as a chance to improve teacher-pupil ratios or as an opportunity to save money.

Gordon Green, who plays a leading role in NUT affairs, was quite emphatic when he said that 'teacher employment is synonymous with preserving educational services'. Maybe he is right, but interest groups have always claimed, if they can, that their sectional interest is the same as the public interest. The miners claim that closing pits is against the public interest and makes us vulnerable to Arabs and the railwaymen claim that closing railways is against the public interest and only adds to the traffic jams.

Where the NUT and the educational authorities agree to uphold teacher employment there is the obvious danger that they, as producer interests, will conspire against the interest of the consumers (parents and children) by causing necessary economies to take other forms, for example less school meals or books. The same sort of thing goes on with NUPE and NALGO. A new kind of power structure is developing around the centres of local decision-making and a potentially powerful alliance is forming between the ideological left and the sectional interests of the public sector trade unions.

Inside the Council House is grander even than outside. It would serve for a head of state in most parts of the world. Clive Wilkinson, the leader of Birmingham City Council, shows me the council chamber. It is as solemn as any parliament with its upholstered benches, its marble pillars and arches, its semi-circular dome. When I see a building like this I come to a simple conclusion about local government in England. It should be organised on the principle that there is a place called the Town Hall in which sit the elected representatives of the citizens and that it is they who are in charge of the town's affairs.

The intricacies of local government finance are hard to grasp and people – including me – tend to find it a boring subject. Wilkinson gives me a succinct explanation of Birmingham's dilemma. Its needs are £40 million greater than the £280 million it is permitted to spend. As sixty per cent of the budget goes on education, 55 per cent of that on salaries, in order to make substantial savings it would have to sack teachers. The number of teachers it would have to sack would mean a decline in standards in the schools in spite of the falling rolls. The next big area of spending was services to old people; but how could they cut out meals-on-wheels or home helps to people in their eighties and nineties?

Then there was housing. How could they put up rents and at the same time stop doing repairs? The tenants would riot. If they cut out all excessive expenditures and – if the unions would allow – stopped filling vacancies, then they might save £15 million. They would still be penalised for going over the

Heseltine limit. And the rates would still have to go up by 25 to 30 per cent.

Put like this, by a man regarded in the Labour Party as an arch-moderate, it seemed that the problem which the Government has set great cities such as Birmingham is impossible of political or humane solution. It reinforces my belief that we need a more autonomous locally-financed form of local government.

What is most interesting about Clive Wilkinson is that he has signed the declaration of the Council for Social Democracy. As we are going in to lunch at the Midland Hotel a lady comes up to him, a party supporter, and declares she will follow Shirley Williams to the ends of the earth provided she can be assured that the new party will have nothing to do with the Tories. He asks her how many others feel as she does? She puts it at hundreds.

No one could call Wilkinson a claret drinker. He is a teetotaller. A carpenter by trade, he left school at 15 and became the youngest ever leader of Birmingham City Council at the age of 33. He is 44 and still riding high. He is head of the second-largest metropolitan authority in the country which governs a million people, employs 53,000, and has a turnover of £1 billion. He is king in his own domain, has no parliamentary ambitions, and has everything to lose and nothing to gain.

Birmingham is a city of metals and nostalgia. Wandering around Victoria Square and Chamberlain Square it is impossible not to feel its sense of civic self-importance. The buildings here are worthy and solid, no Gothic follies; the statues recall the golden age of enterprise. It is that vanished entrepreneurial world which Margaret Thatcher would like to restore and so would Neville Bosworth, the leader of the Conservative Group on the City Council. He has the voice of a Churchill although with a Brummagem accent and a similar squat bulldog-like appearance. His father was a district engineer with the municipal water department; he is a solicitor.

Who was Chamberlain? he asks me. Who were Guest, Keen, Nettlefold? Who was Austin? Local businessmen.

Nowadays there were too many big combines and too few individual personalities. We needed to get back to the days when the governor knew all his people by name. The smaller the unit the better it could be managed. Under Mrs Thatcher there was a revival of small business taking place. Was there? 'Yes,' he assures me, 'lots and lots of small businesses – and I mean lots – are springing up, in spite of the recession, gaining momentum. Many of them are using the new technologies.' Where? I ask. What sorts of businesses? 'All sorts, many kinds. Some employing ten or twenty, some only four or five.'

Birkenhead. Fog has made us late. Now the sun is shining brightly. Opposite the gates of Cammell Laird's is the Royal Castle Hotel. The original pub was built in 1640 but it was rebuilt in the Victorian manner in 1898. In a back room a dozen or so shop stewards are waiting for Frank Field, the local MP. Because I'm going to be there – the press! – the Cammell Laird management has refused permission for the meeting to be in the yard. In the chair is a man called Gerry Reeves. He is vice-chairman of the stewards' committee. He is a strong and handsome Lawrentian figure of a-man with a square-cut beard. On the table before him is a pint and the latest issue of the *Militant*.

They have carried out an opinion poll among the stewards for my benefit. The result is astonishing but may simply reflect the weight of the last few days' headlines. It is Labour 43, Social Democrat 17, Conservative 8, Communist 3. What they really want to talk about is the plight of the yard. They've been left to die, says Gerry Reeves; no new order for four years – Merseyside was being used as a whipping boy, to teach the working classes a lesson. We go round the room, Frank and I listening. A sense of being let down, betrayed, is what chiefly emerges. All sorts of explanations and alibis are offered: the industry is a victim of its 'Rolls-Royce standards'; the company overtenders so as to 'devalue the working class'; some of the machinery is pre-war; the Tories are sending all the money out of the country; the Common Market is to blame.

23

Gerry says that he is a one-parent family. He has a son of 16. 'All I can see for him is a life on the dole. I despair for youngsters in this country under this government. This country's going to face a revolution in my lifetime.'

This is not said with much aggression. The entire conversation, which goes on for an hour, is good-humoured, more bewildered than angry, more despairing than defiant. One man chips in and says that it's the same old story; this meeting was called to meet Frank and it's open to all the lads, not just the stewards. But here we are, he says, only a dozen of us. Time was when you could get the whole yard outside the gates at the drop of a hat.

In the bar afterwards I get into conversation with a man called Tony. He is 31, a marine fitter – 'a marine engineer if you want to make it sound posh.' As far as I can gather he is a genuine working-class Tory. He'd recently moved house because the area was 'too working-class, too much the same at home as at work'. He disclaims Gerry and the shop stewards. But he says, 'We've been dragged down, indoctrinated to make us feel that we're no good on Merseyside. I've been made to feel inadequate. We've accepted 10,000 redundancies. It's time for Maggie to recognise that and give us a chance, our reward.'

He then tells me how they make the hole in the stern of a ship for the propeller shaft. 'We use a machine 120 years old. We can still do a perfect job with this but it takes two weeks. A new machine which would cost £500,000 would take three days. But I suppose there's no point if you're only building two or three ships a year. The machine suits us. It's so slow that you can get plenty of overtime and earn plenty of money.'

I don't know whether it's true but that's what he says.

Frank next wants me to meet some shop stewards from the Lucas-Girling brake factory which is threatened with closure and the loss of 650 jobs. The plant has already been hard hit by redundancies and used to employ an average of 1600. These are quite a different kind of shop steward – TASS, ASTMS, AUEW. They could just as easily be middle managers; they

24

*'I think we should choose a
1930's style for the living-room
– in case you're made
redundant.'*

25 July 1980

are indeed a kind of opposition management. They present me with an efficiently prepared dossier, full of detail. There is no way in which any layman could form a useful opinion about their case. How the devil am I to know whether brakes should be made on Merseyside or in Bousanville or Pontypool? They claim that Lucas is shifting its production abroad, in this case to France, using South Wales as a staging post. It is an immensely complicated tale. Their only offence, they claim, is to be the weakest link in a chain of multinational production. They are bitter and angry, worried about their mortgages. Their advice to other Lucas plants and to workers every-where, is: 'Don't accept redundancies, don't give up your traditional rights, don't relax your demarcations, don't be flexible – just look what happened to us!'

Neil Kinnock is here to address a public meeting in Frank's constituency. Afterwards he is guest of honour at the Labour Party's annual dinner at the Al Fresco restaurant. It is a warm, friendly Labour Party occasion. At the meeting Kinnock had paid tribute to the party activists. They were the living Labour Party, he said, repeatedly insulted, called hacks by hacks, offered perfect visions from monetarism to Marxism, yet they fought on for democratic socialism – for the collective ownership of the means of production, distribution and exchange and for collective control through democracy.

Looking around the table I see teachers and lecturers, a probation officer, an electronics engineer, a manufacturing tailor, public officials, railway officials. Nice people with nice manners. The old age pensioners look a bit more working-class. The chairman, Councillor John Croker, a planning officer with Liverpool City Council and a graduate of the Open University, tells me over the Entrecôte Chasseur how furious he is with the 'gang of three'. 'Just as we have won the battle in the party for radical socialist policies and achieved the means for implementing them these people come along and threaten to take away our victory.'

There is too much of past glory about Liverpool. The smell of the sea makes it worse. Economic decline is turning the place into a Carthage. There is little of Birmingham's throb here; the streets are dirty, the people look shabby and depressed. Past and present sit uneasily here. The city centre has an air of work suspended about it. The 'T' has already fallen off the side of the St George's Hotel, a tatty piece of architecture to put so close to the St George's Hall and its adjacent cluster of magnificent neo-classical buildings.

Shades of the Labour Party too. It was here in 1964 that Harold Wilson held his great eve-of-poll rally and afterwards marched by torchlight back to the Adelphi. The cheering crowds that night wouldn't let him leave the balcony of his suite. The Adelphi Hotel is a deserted morgue of marble today. It was here in the early hours of 16 October 1964 that some of us opened a bottle of champagne for the new Prime Minister, the man who was going to build the New Britain.

17 February 1981   **Peter Jenkins**

[An extract from a diary of a journey through industrial Britain.]

Toxteth people

Two singed CS bullets, which burn the skin when touched, and a red cartridge with 'CS gas. Smith and Wesson' on the side, lie on the table of the Charles Wootton Education Centre, in Upper Parliament Street, Toxteth. The centre was named after a black man killed in a race riot in 1919, is run by blacks, and funded with a £20,000 a year grant as a result of Peter Walker's inquiry into the inner city areas in the early 1970s. Now it has been lent to the Liverpool 8 Defence Committee – about a dozen black men and women who saved the centre from burning on the night of the riots and are now devoting themselves wholeheartedly to the downfall of the Chief Constable of Merseyside, Kenneth Oxford.

The bullets are far more important to the committee than the much discussed unemployment in the area, which runs at nearly 100 per cent. High velocity CS bullets were fired directly by the police at crowds during the riots. They were of the type made for use against terrorists and are able to penetrate glass and walls. The police admit using them, but say they were shot on to hard surfaces, to make them explode and release the gas.

The committee regard the shootings as an example of the contempt in which the police hold the black population. This population itself, however, has a deep community pride becuase it has been there for 150 years and is an extraordinarily closely knit and almost parochial society. They regard Chief Constable Oxford as an outsider who, when he came to Merseyside in the mid 70s, started to deal with them in a way they were not used to.

Peter Bassey, one of the committee's leaders, said he told Margaret Thatcher when she visited Toxteth this week that there was no point in giving extra money to the area at present. 'I told her that if they tried to build leisure centres it would only lead to more trouble, because the police would wait around for people and harass them as they came out at night.' The black leaders say they have had unemployment and bad housing for as long as they can remember. They are adamant that it is not that which caused the rioting, even though the local political leaders would have people believe that this was the case. 'It's the police treatment which has become intolerable,' said one. 'They used to give us a slap or two when we were kids if we did anything wrong. Now they beat people up and seem to do it because they enjoy it.'

They are hostile to all the local politicians, particularly the labour councillors who represent the area – 'They regard us as good natured Sambos or savages' – and are highly suspicious of the press, who they say have not tried to report beatings up in the police stations after the riots. Nor, they say, have the press mentioned badly injured black people allegedly turned away from the Royal Liverpool Hospital, and the five people they say were injured by CS bullets.

Yesterday, Phil Robins, the 21-year-old footballer, was out of hospital after ten days' treatment. He thought it was lucky that his chest was as near to being a hard surface as any human being can be or he might not have made such a quick recovery. He said the shots were fired at him from a police line at a range of only twenty yards, as he was helping people choking with CS gas, on the ground. 'It was like a great blow in the chest, and as I tried to get up and turn half round, I was shot again in the back.'

Toxteth is now paying heavily for its hatred of the police. All the corner shops are gone, the bulldozers are out flattening the destroyed buildings, which simply added more ruins to Toxteth's normal air of having just been bombed. There never was any shortage of rubble from the demolished streets around the new council blocks to hurl at the police, but for several nights now the streets have been deadly quiet. The Panda cars have gone and the streets are patrolled by policemen in pairs. The plainclothes men tour in unmarked cars.

On the walls of the education centre are lists of those arrested, with their alleged offences and the solicitors who have been hired for them. No distinction is made by the committee between those taking part in the riots and those who say they were innocent.

Nobody was surprised by the riots, and clearly the Liverpool police's special powers of stopping and searching led to much of the bitterness. 'The anger just built up. You couldn't breathe here, you had no privacy,' said one black girl bitterly. 'They stopped you and made you turn out your handbags for nothing, they hit people and called them black bastards.'

The chief constable has said he will investigate every incident and complaint and when they have been collated, he will make recommendations. Meanwhile, the black community waits for the appearance of armoured cars on the streets and tries to keep its children at home at nights.

17 July 1981   **Jean Stead**

The end of great expectations

When we look back on the youth culture of the past thirty years, what appeared in the 1950s as an exciting and liberating experience – the birth of teenagers, the rise of pop music, the emergence of styles which young people chose as symbols of a kind of elective identity – now seems a less benign phenomenon than it once did.

Of course, even then, newsreel pictures of cinema seats torn up wherever Rock Around the Clock was playing, the screaming girls with tears running down their anguished faces evoked fears of anarchy, warnings of social breakdown. But there was a moment of extraordinary excitement: the sight of indigenous working-class singers on stage, the discovery by the working class that they too were beautiful, that life could be enjoyed, that youth no longer had to be an apprenticeship to drudgery – it felt like a liberation.

The social and economic forces that had permitted this change were felt to be good and positive: spoilsport authoritarian figures were mocked in the popular press, fuddy-duddy bishops, retired colonels in Cheltenham. Life as carnival seemed to be taking the place of life as toil. It looked as if the young were beginning to throw off the old disciplines associated with poverty and work. The old were shocked.

Through the sixties, the process expanded and accelerated. A new generation appeared to enjoy even more ample space in which to express themselves. Even then there were warning signs. The young began to wonder who they were: this was no longer defined for them by what they did or where they lived. But these were the years of sexual liberation, and that overwhelmed every other consideration. Ironically, it is the children of those who were young in Swinging Britain – emancipated from the old repressions and Puritanism, who are now in their teens. Born into an atmosphere of obsessive expectancy and hope, the future seemed to dilate before them.

But the time of excitement and freedom didn't last. It was immobilised somehow; became rigid and constricting. Of course, it was really all about selling things to the previously poor. What happened was that the working class were delivered to the market-place, not as labour, but as consumers. And it did seem like a deliverance at the time: the market seemed the perfect mechanism for supplying the needs of those with money to spend for the first time. It seemed a far more practical and humane way to live than the drab socialist alternative of the postwar years; and if we had any doubts, we had only to look at the impoverishment and greyness of Eastern Europe. It all seemed so straightforward. Everybody welcomed the gains.

To be young was like a holiday from life. It was assumed that the young would grow out of it. They would enjoy a few easy years between leaving school and settling down, and then be reabsorbed into the old networks, the traditional patterns of work and living.

And that did seem to be what was happening. For the first time, even young working-class people spent a year or two bumming around, taking casual work, going abroad; and then they got married, started a family, began to take life seriously. You did sometimes see the elderly Teddy boy in his thirties, but he was felt to be a bit bizarre, with his crepe trousers; and more often than not he was pushing a pram.

Even though there was an increase in crime and delinquency, more broken families, more violence, this was felt to be the necessary price that had to be paid for more open attitudes. The smugness and hypocrisy had gone. This was how people really were; there was no use trying to sweep it under the carpet.

During the sixties it became increasingly unfashionable to ask young people what they did (meaning work), but rather what their tastes were, which music they preferred, what kind of life-style they chose. Not their work-role, but who they thought they were became the main determinant of identity. In other words, the flight into fantasy had begun.

Throughout this whole period, two apparently diverse but dynamically related things were occurring within the working class, which were not given the significance they can now be seen to have had. First, the market-place, following steady increases in real income, seemed to influence wider and deeper areas of human experience. Most of this was presented as the opportunity to buy release from unnecessary work – it was the time of supermarkets and convenience foods, the boom in consumer products, the vast spread of the entertainment industry, the preoccupation with status as an escape from class, which meant that things rather than function increasingly determined the way people thought about themselves.

This process speeded up in the 70s. The market could be seen to invade even non-material areas of life. Children found themselves in a world of expanding fantasy. The child's bedroom – where the old working class had huddled six or eight to a room – became a lonely temple of escape: giant posters of fantasy figures, pop stars and footballers took the place of the real people; with a great frieze of dinosaurs and monsters on one wall, and a panorama of outer space on the other – a beating against the very limits of time and space as they reached out for definition and an identity that was no longer going to be anchored in any significant work.

31

The market-place filled the vacuum with its manufactured excitements – horror films, epics of journeys to distant galaxies, effortless travels through time; and this is as close as many children came to spiritual or religious experience. It is not simply by chance that all this occurred as the economy was undergoing a great shift from its base in primary production, from the hard tangibility of mines, mills and factories, towards non-productive, immaterial and service industries. The detachment of the working-class young from traditional purposes and patterns of work is of course an evolving 'process. It is a long-term change, which continues into the present, not simply something that has happened like an event.

At the same time, from the 50s onwards, the old working class living places were demolished and 're-developed'. The geometric simplicity of the new estates, the tower blocks and concrete slabs looked at first like further important gains. It was believed that people would strike root in these raw new places, just as they had done in the older streets and Victorian suburbs. But beneath the excitement of the new houses and flats, the clamour for the new furniture and equipment they demanded, there were by now less happy voices.

The second important tendency in working-class life at this time – and its dynamic connection with the invasive quality of the market-place was not understood – was a melancholy dwelling on the past, a suggestion that could be heard, in every working-class community, that great losses had been incurred even in the face of the undeniable gains. Twice a week for over twenty years, almost half the adults in Britain have sat down to watch Coronation Street on TV. This experience has reassured people in the presence of the real-life losses they were suffering. It was an assertion that nothing really changed, even though the evidence of daily life told them that so many things were being taken away.

In every working-class district, the middle aged and elderly talked about the end of neighbourliness, the break-up of the old associations, the forfeit of the ties of work, kinship and street – all those things which, we can now see, were connected with the undermining of their once indispensable labour.

People insisted that the human responses to the older poverty had not been things of little worth, to be discarded with the Windsor chairs and Victorian ornament and patchwork rugs. But they were not listened to. These intangible losses seemed in no way commensurate with the material gains, especially as the praise of commodities and hymns to materialism filled the air. What the older people were lamenting was consigned to an area of experience called 'nostalgia', fit for elegiac TV documentaries about change in the East End, but not an issue for political discussion; and politics, voided of its humanity, became more mean and disfigured as a result, as it confined itself to more naked economic objectives.

As time passed, the cities that had been 'developed' came to look ugly and brutal, as if something vital had gone from them. The terms on which the better life had been proposed to the working class began to appear to have been full of obscure penalties and unacknowledged forfeits. In theory, the market-place, as a reflection of free choices freely made, would be all right, if it were possible to start afresh from an ideal beginning with each generation as it made its free choices. But of course there are no generations, there is only continuity. And that is how the market place ceases to be a neutral phenomenon: it becomes a primary determinant on the lives of the young, imposing its imperatives of getting and having. They are born with its exhortations to buy ringing in their ears. Its elaborate displays of merchandise brought to perfection leave them no purpose other than a sustained longing to possess all that is tantalisingly held out to them.

As long as there was money enough to give the illusion that the penetration of the market-place into areas where it should have no place could be compensated by buying, the losses went unnoticed. It is only at times of recession, when the dynamic is interrupted, that the extent of the dependency of millions of young people on the products of the market-place can be assessed. The golden cloud of the consumer society of the 50s and 60s is dissipated; and what is left is a wasteland.

For the poorest, it is disastrous. They, like everyone else in society, have had the same needs kindled, the same wants goaded by the shrill insistence on buying all the things that

33

have become indispensable, are identified with life itself. There is no longer any question of self-discipline, self-control. The orgy of buying has been built precisely on the breakdown of these things. Above all there is no counter-balance to the idea of work as a means to reward or as a role in production. The anchoring of people in a sense of function, of having indispensable labour to offer, helped to prevent the development of too lopsided a human being, in spite of the relentless compulsion to spend money and amass things. But the damage done to labour and its sense of worth has destroyed that equilibrium in the young; and the roots of their identity have struck in the kind of cargo cults that have come to surround material products. Schumacher, in Good Work, 1979, said: 'The basic aim of modern industrialism is not to make work satisfying, but to raise productivity; its proudest achievement is labour saving, whereby labour is stamped with the mark of undesirability. But what is undesirable cannot confer dignity; so the working life of a labourer is without dignity.'

If this is true even of much work that remains, how much more true it becomes for the inheritors of an extinguished sense of functions. Their sense of superfluity is complete. So although unemployment is in part the cause of recent disturbances, it also goes much deeper; and the young scarcely recognize it, because they have never known the energising experience of doing and creating anything in which they have something of themselves to offer, a contribution to make. Nobody has ever demanded anything of them but passivity and subordination.

The cry of rewards, free offers, prizes, gifts, that have issued from the market-place for thirty years has served to conceal the opposite of these things – the draining away, the emptying, the distraints on the working class. Just what these losses add up to we can begin to see in the rioting in those former working-class areas: not only the loss of the sense of worth from necessary work, but the loss of morality in those poor, proud, stoical working communities, the loss of the human comforts of the formerly poor. There has been a gutting of the substance of the old working class; above all, the surrender of that sense of a shared predicament that united people in the face of pain, suffering and death – enduring human values. All this has been usurped by the power of money and the promise of what it can buy.

These children of the poor have been brought up to the kindling of their appetites, and the suppression of their unwanted, redundant abilities, and then they have been denied access to all the things they have grown to depend on. Even the connection between effort (work) and achievement (pay) has been broken for many thousands of them. The dependency on the market-place remains, but the supply of what they need has arbitrarily dried up; arbitrarily, because the shops are no less full than they have always been. The images of looting disturb so, not because people are getting something for nothing, but because they have a doomed dreamlike quality of individuals reaching out vainly for something they feel has been denied them or taken away from them; only they no longer even remember what it is.

This new, modernised version of poverty – where people grow to depend on the market-place, and then are denied the money to fulfil that dependency – offers a sharp contrast with the testimonies of that older poverty, where people united against cruel material privations and discovered the possibilities of the human consolations they could offer each other. This is not, of course, to argue for that older poverty. That would be absurd: looking at the great shopping malls and pecincts, who can doubt that there is enough for everyone to be properly clothed and shod, sheltered and nourished and warmed. But the looting has this other, symbolic dimension: a gesture of despair, a blow, however unwitting, against the causes of the curious unacknowledged captivity in which they have grown.

The destructive power of the market-place lies in this, that it has robbed even the poorest, those who appeared to have nothing, but who had still managed to evolve a human response to their condition. This is as true of the migrants from East Bengal or Jamaica, who had developed skills to deal with the poverty of their societies similar to those of the indigenous working class. But we have all been lured by hopes and promises of something better, and have been induced to set aside those skills, which become relevant in the changed context. All the children of the poor have been given over, in good faith, to the influence of the market-place; the consequences of which we are now living through. It hasn't provided the promised freedoms, but a new kind of subordination. This is why it is not a racial problem in its origins, even though it too often becomes one, because of the large number of the children of migrants among the poor, because of the clouded issues, the absence of the will to look at the way we live and to ask why we live so, the lack of any real desire to understand.

The equilibrium has only been maintained until now by the growth in incomes, which has to a certain extent smothered the sense of loss in people's lives. The violence we have seen in recent weeks is the ultimate reason why no one in the West can seriously imagine an economy in which growth ceases, even though that growth may be cancerous, created as it has been out of our human substance.

The violence we are living through is in itself a response to the violence done to our humanity. It is a reaction to the suppression of skills and the stimulation of appetites, the weakening of the power to do and create and give and the fostering of passivity and impotence, the subverting of long-term goals in the young by the lure of momentary gratifications. The working class has been cozened out of the best qualities that sustained them, the old tolerance and humour and humanity; and the whole of our society is the poorer for these losses, they are not confined just to those who have suffered them.

The most profound effect of the invasion of the market-place is that nobody ever discusses the kind of society we want any more. The values of money and the lack of it have usurped all other categories of good and evil. The creation of wealth is the closest we come to a spiritual idea. If it makes money, it must be good, whether it is the most debauching horror-film, a staple food, the sale of arms, or the priority for rich tourists in world capitals that cannot decently house their own population.

The meaning of the moment of liberation in the fifties becomes more clear. It has led through time to an even greater subordination. That is what the riots are about. It is no good saying, as Mr Whitelaw did last week, that looking for reasons for rioting comes dangerously close to finding excuses. It is too important an issue to be suppressed. The effect of the market-place and its messages to our children have been deeply damaging: it speaks to them beyond parents or teachers, beyond the churches, beyond morality or wisdom.

The moral, spiritual, and finally, human content of our society must not be determined by cold economic processes which ravage people's lives in this way, which are so barren and reductive that they strip the young of everything but a cluster of unsatisfied appetites, an identity pared down to a sense of their blackness or whiteness; and offers them no function, no contribution, no making or creating or giving anything of themselves. Jobs as occupational therapy are not enough.

The lone unemployed youth sitting in a shopping precinct in a midland town put it to me most succinctly: he shrugged, gestured to the people moving urgently among the climbing plants, the marble and the piped music, and he said 'Looting, everybody does it all the time, but they do it with money; looting without money, what's the difference?'

20 July 1981   **Jeremy Seabrook**

Cashing in on The Boom

The nuclear shelter industry is expanding with a prodigality almost reminiscent of the proliferation of sandbags, window tapes, and Anderson shelters before the outbreak of the last war in 1939. Some manufacturers are cheerfully predicting that a shelter from a nuclear storm, military or civil, will raise the sale value of a house in the same impressive way that central heating did at a time when avoidance of discomfort was a more dominant factor than avoidance of death and mutilation. An estimated 300 firms are now offering nuclear shelters made from steel, steel-reinforced concrete, and plywood sandwiched between glass-reinforced plastic, and with a series of equally various (and largely unprovable) claims. Their cost ranges from about £500 per head for a prefabricated shelter using glass fibre to £2500 or so a head in more sophisticated shelters built on the site.

Dafal Limited, which produces a range of shelters, including the Churchill Mark IV for four or more people at between £8000 and £10,000, unveiled the shelter yesterday and held the first of a series of seminars on nuclear protection and civil defence at its headquarters, based emotively enough at Hastings, the site of the last successful invasion of Britain.

Mr Graham Rattenbury, the firm's chairman and managing director, is the retired owner of a concrete firm who has built a nuclear shelter at his home in Kent. He said that the number of inquiries received in the first two weeks of the firm's life added up to £9 million.

Mr Rattenbury said: 'I feel that, on the basis of my experience, half the population realise the necessity for nuclear defence and realise something can and must be done. The other half are deeply apathetic and completely lacking information on this subject, and this is the vast educational task which our company has.'

The task will obviously be pursued with some vigour. Mr Rattenbury associated himself with the remarks of Sir Miles Clifford, the monocled ex-Marine who opened the seminar with a brutal brevity which left Ronald Reagan sounding like a vacillating pinko.

'I have watched Russian activities for many, many years with increasing concern and today I regard it as the most evil and cold-blooded despotism since the Third Reich – more dangerous, even, because it has overtaken NATO, and our American partner and ultimate umbrella, in both nuclear and conventional weaponry, in the air and on the sea,' said Sir Miles.

'It is plain that the claim that this amazing escalation is for self-defence would not deceive a child of six. The nuclear threat grows nearer, and the need for guard against it is imperative.'

38

Dafal is anxious to avoid any impression that nuclear shelters are only for the rich. Mr Rattenbury reported that the company hoped to plough back some of the profits into shelters for the general public.

Certainly, his fear that the industry will soon be a crowded one is justified. Work is already in progress on the first of London's communal shelters, being built at Chiswick by Allguard Shelters, a British company which is starting to sell space in the shelter to the public. Fifty-six people prepared to pay £1800 each will get protection which is claimed to be sufficient to withstand all the effects of a one megaton bomb. 'A shelter of similar quality for a family of four would cost in the region of £20,000,' a representative of the firm estimated. The shelter is being constructed underground, as recommended by reputable makers, with steel-reinforced walls, floor, and ceiling. The main entrance has two steel armour doors, plus an 8in. reinforced steel and concrete blast door.

Like Dafal, Allguard is sniffy about the competition. Dafal says it is one of the few companies with the professionals (McAlpine) behind it to do the job properly. Allguard representatives say that their shelter came about after the efforts of the firm's two directors, Mr Joe Stanley and Mr Andre Coleson, to protect their own families from nuclear attack had been foiled by lack of surrounding expertise. They bought a site at Chiswick, near their homes, and solicited tenders for the design and construction.

The claims and the promotion gimmicks of some shelter-makers verge on black comedy. Dafal yesterday had the Beauty Queen of Kent, a Miss Nuttall, showing its seminar guests around a mock-up of the Churchill Mark IV. Inside was a family of four (friends of employees at the firm), a British bulldog called Dora, and a tankful of edible Japanese carp, which looked like goldfish but which, said Mr Rattenbury, 'symbolise the fact that edible food will have to be grown after the fallout'.

Near Tonbridge, a 28-year-old unmarried dentist, Mr Nigel Sudworth, is coming to the end of a seven-day solitary stay in a shelter designed by Design For Defence Limited, who will present Mr Sudworth and a full report on his monitored experience at Brighton on Monday. Mr Sudworth is expected to leave the shelter tomorrow. He had a spell of high blood pressure earlier this week, though it was back to normal by yesterday. 'He puts it down to frustration,' said Mr Stephen Dargavel, marketing director of Design for Defence. 'He has rested over 10½ hours a night and is not used to it. He thinks he is so rested and fit that he wants to be up and at it, and is frustrated because he can't be.'

4 October 1980   **Dennis Barker**

Requiem for a rodent

When the last guinea pig bites the dust there remains the ultimate problem: where to bury it. When Pearl, survivor of a dynasty of guinea pigs that stretched, like the great Chain of Being, from the mighty boar warrior Lollipop (who used to attack cats) and from the first guinea pig earth-mother, Lily (gravid thrice yearly, waddling about with her burden of fecundity like a white hot water bottle on legs in the days when all the world was young, or at least the children were): well, as I was saying, when Pearl emitted his last, despairing squeak and fell into his final bed of hay, I glumly took up my spade, and reflected once again upon the transience of being and the mournful conundrum of death, and found a bare patch of soil and stood poised for the first thrust of the blade into the dust to which we all must return when . . .

'You can't bury him there,' said a voice. 'That's where you buried Ruby.'

It was an awful moment. Ruby had been the last death but one, or possibly the last death, and the reason the patch was bare must have been that he had been but freshly buried there, and the marigolds planted in memoriam over his final resting place had not yet sprouted. And suddenly this small suburban garden seemed not a haven of shrubbery, tiger lilies and old mouldering tennis balls but a charnel house veneered with carnivorous green.

The violets sheltered the earthly husk of a dearly loved cat;

40

rabbits lay end to end under the plum tree; a barbary dove was planted under the gooseberry bush; a climbing Josephine Bruce began where the first guinea pigs had (so to speak) left off; there were gerbils and zebra finches strewn like broad beans between the roses, and I dimly remember posting the goldfish into the ground head first down a hole made with a dibber.

I don't know what happened to the mice. 'Are you sure we even had any mice?' I asked my daughter.

'Sure,' she said. 'But we didn't really have a hedgehog or a toad. We don't even know if they're really dead. And Topaz wasn't really ours either. He just turned up.' Topaz? What the hell was Topaz? ·

'You can't bury Pearl there, either,' said the voice again. 'That's where you buried poor little Coral.' 'All flesh is grass,' said I. 'We'll dig up the lawn.' When the Last Trump sounds and the dead awaken, it'll make a terrible mess of the garden.

The problem was never one of mortality, but rather of fruitfulness. One invests in a rodent at one's peril. Dowered by nature with an urge to replicate matched only by the oyster, which releases its young into the world uncaring and by the millionfold, in the hope that one or two at least will thrive, the average household pet rabbit, guinea pig, hamster or gerbil carries within his mighty loins enough seed to plant a lawn six feet deep with his dead progeny.

We began with a guinea pig, and bought a tiny rabbit because he looked lonely. The rabbit stayed tiny for about a week, and then began to commit Hunnish practices upon the cat next door. It didn't seem right, although we should have left him to his fearful perversions. But we bought a female rabbit and within six weeks the garden was teeming with dear little pink and white bunnies that everybody in the street adored and nobody actually wanted. We neutered the buck.

Meanwhile we had imported a sow guinea pig and she and her spouse and five miniature white cavies were grazing on the lawn, all heads and tails in identical orientation.

'I can't buy them from you. There's no demand for guinea pigs,' said the man at the pet shop who sold them to us. 'I'll take them from you for nothing, as a favour, like.' I think he fed the babies to his rock python but I've never dared ask.

'You must love animals very much,' said a friend respectfully when she arrived. On her next visit she left a pair of gerbils and a pair of zebra finches and vowed that they were in all cases sterile, infertile, asexual, impotent, far too old, and quite probably all of the same gender. And then some fool (probably me) introduced a little nest into the zebra finch cage.

By the third clutch, our local department store was making a weekly delivery of white, pannicum and spray millets, canary seed, cuttlefish bone, sand, charcoal, and crushed oyster shell.

'Got lots of birds have you then?' said the driver when the zebra finch tally alone (there were also canaries, doves, orange-cheeked waxbills and some delicate little green birds that turned out to have been dipped in dye) reached a majestic 32. 'Do you want some?' said my wife. 'Whew!' he said when he saw them. 'How many can you spare?' 'Take the lot,' she said. He took all the ones that didn't have arthritis.

The years now seem to have been a cavalcade of death. The gerbils were no trouble: if the young ones died the parents ate them, and by the time mother and father gerbil had cloned three crops of babies, a man who worked in an institute came and took a batch or two away ('I'll see they get a good home') and I never dared ask him what sort of institute.

One by one the rabbits and guinea pigs fell prey to the ills the flesh is heir to: tumours, heart attacks, epilepsy, and prolapses of the anus. Vets used to wince when we walked in the door. A cat relieved us of four birds. A canary died of shock. Mice came and went like summer showers. I hardly noticed the toad. The goldfish gave up the ghost after years of vacuity and suddenly there was no need to cultivate greenfly.

And now Pearl is dead, and in the last possible resting place in a garden replete and groaning under its burden of cold little bodies. After the cascade of fecundity, the house seems empty: all we have to care for are two kittens, a dove, a canary, and five arthritic zebra finches.

Only, in the wake of grieving upon the interment of a guinea piglet nursed from birth through the years of travail with cucumber peel and sunflower seeds to its final coronary, the survivors don't, momentarily, seem like living beings at all. They just seem like nine more potential holes in the lawn.

14 May 1981   **Tim Radford**

Mrs Thatcher rules, OK?

Seven days after the Budget and the earth is still trembling. There has never been a week quite like it. A Prime Minister publicly denouncing her Cabinet colleagues and forcing them into equally open submission, a senior Minister semi-publicly challenging the way in which a Prime Minister runs her government, the Conservative Party rumbling ominously in the background and at Westminster on Monday night erupting into an unprecedented revolt. Yet at the end of such a week the Lady was unrepentant.

There is no immediate threat to Mrs Thatcher from within. Indeed at the end of the post-Budget week it is harder to see how she is to be got rid of than it was at the beginning. The revolt of the Gang of Wets came to nothing. It subsided before it had begun. Theirs was a soggy front. A Thatcher aide was able to say with pleasure, 'We've whittled them down from six to three.'

What happened was something like this. Several of the rebels who last autumn prevented the Thatcher-Howe axe from falling upon another £1000-million-worth of government expenditure (let us call them the Novemberists) had been engaged in making Budget representations to Sir Geoffrey Howe. They were behaving exactly in the manner of outside interest groups, requesting meetings with the Chancellor or corresponding with him. One of them was Mr James Prior. On Monday of last week, the day before the Budget, Mr Prior again saw Sir Geoffrey. What he had already read in the Sunday papers was confirmed and worse than confirmed; the representations of the 'Wets' had had no effect whatsoever, had been totally ignored.

Only at this stage did the leading 'Wets' compare notes. Three of them – Mr Prior, Sir Ian Gilmour and Mr Peter Walker – considered resigning. They decided against. The Budget was signed and sealed, too late to change it now. To have stabbed the Chancellor in the back on the eve of his Budget address would not have gone down well in the Conservative Party. It was more important to stay and fight again from within. The possibility of Mr Prior's resignation became known and on Wednesday, the day after the Budget, he rearranged his day in order to make himself visible at the House of Commons and even issued a denial of the resignation rumour.

Meanwhile, the Cabinet had met. That was on the Tuesday morning. Only three Ministers openly opposed the Budget. That is an important fact. They were Mr Prior, Sir Ian and Mr Walker. It was subsequently reported that Mr Francis Pym, Lord Carrington and Lord Soames had also voiced their opposition. Some reports added Mr Whitelaw's name to this list. The reports were untrue. Mr Whitelaw did not speak up against the Budget; he was suffused by one of his hot flushes of loyalty. Nor did the Admirable Carrington on this occasion speak out of turn; his head was well down. Lord Soames's ample mouth was kept shut.

Who had falsely leaked the proceedings of the Cabinet? The silent 'Wets' suspected black propaganda by zealous Thatcherites. In any event it gave her her chance. At the *Guardian*'s lunch at the Mansion House she rounded on her critics, the guilty and the not guilty. The Whitelaws, Carringtons and Soameses were angered at being so collectively traduced. So was Mr Pym. A usually cautious politician, it was he who launched the counter-attack, questioning the lack of Cabinet discussion and consultation which went into the making of the government's economic strategy.

By now, however, Number 10 knew that it had the enemy divided. The suggestions for new modes of economic decision-making within the Cabinet were given short shrift by the Prime Minister. Dissident ministers were ordered to support the Budget publicly at the weekend. In effect it was an ultimatum: speak up or get out. Mr Whitelaw spoke up, so did

Mr Pym and Mr Prior; Sir Ian Gilmour issued a terse statement to the Press Association. Only Mr Walker was unheard from, Mrs Thatcher had cracked the whip.

The dissidents' next objective is to bring about a change in government policy by July. They are fearful of the consequences of delaying until the autumn, the economic consequences and the political consequences for the Conservative Party. Their chances of success seem slight. Mrs Thatcher, as this week has shown, has established a Prime Ministerial despotism of a formidable kind.

She works within a narrowing inner circle. Mr John Biffen has not been seen at breakfast since his astonishing and brilliantly entertaining television performance on the Sunday after the débâcle with the coalminers. Mr John Nott, or Nit, as he is known within the camaradarie of the Thatcher Cabinet, is removed from the centre of economic policy-making and is seldom to be found in the kitchen these days. The breakfast cartel is down to three – Sir Keith, Sir Geoffrey and the Prime Minister. 'She is disappearing into herself,' said one of her colleagues.

Cabinet government has all but been suspended. Here is an insider's account for the new Bagehot (Revised Thatcher Edition):

Q: How does she operate?
A: I don't know.
Q: Was the Leyland decision taken at Cabinet?
A: No.
Q: British Steel Corporation?
A: No.
Q: What does come up to Cabinet?
A: Nothing.
Q: So what do you all do?
A: Waste time.

This mode of working is officially described as her 'executive style of government'. To be sure, policy questions are fiercely disputed in the Cabinet's 'E' (Economic) Committee among the members of which are Mr Prior, Mr

Walker and Lord Carrington. Amazingly, Mr Pym is not a member of it; nor is the Leader of the House, and the man she put in charge of co-ordinating the presentation of government policy, to be counted among her intimates.

Her method of working has been called into question by the accusations she made against her own Cabinet at the Mansion House. She claimed that those who were most critical of the extra taxes in the Budget were the most vociferous in demanding the extra expenditures. Yet it was Sir Keith, single-handed, who added £900 million to Sir Geoffrey's borrowing requirement with his hand-outs to British Leyland and the BSC.

The other big spender was the recession – Mrs Thatcher's recession, Sir Geoffrey's recession. They say it is not their recession which came as an international surprise. That is not true. The world recession did not make its impact on the British economy until into the second half of 1980. The manufacturing output was already falling at twice the rate forecast by the Treasury last April. Both the CBI and the all-party Select Committee are clear about this, the chief blame attaches to the government's economic policies. Of the Thatcher-Howe £5000 million overshoot on public borrowing the 'Novemberists' were responsible for £1000 million only.

Revenge for what happened in November was one of the ingredients of her Budget. To attribute it to monetarism is to pitch it too high; she was possessed of a simple, housekeeper's indignation. Of course, you couldn't spend more than the housekeeping, that would be *immoral* – the word she used at the Mansion House; how dare those toffs, with their acres and their butlers, lecture her on good housekeeping? She'd show them.

Her visit to Washington was an important event. She had been seen off by the miners. U-turn was in the air. Mr Pym had spoken of 'adjustments' and Mr Biffen of 'flexibility'. Ideology, a strange perversion for the Conservative Party, was no longer in fashion; the process of 'de-Thatcherisation' had begun – or so it seemed.

Then came the excitements of the Washington visit, the

bands playing on the South Lawn of the White House, the talk of Budget cuts and 'supply-side fiscalism'.

Credibility, especially her own, was another consideration. She was hoist by a speechwriter's phrase. 'The pound in your pocket . . .' 'We shall cut prices at a stroke . . .' '*This* lady's not for turning.' It sounded good at the time. As one of her friends explained the problem: 'If the Government had failed to hold to its course in this Budget we would be bereft of all credibility.'

So pride too – inflexible pride – was a factor in the Budget equations. Pride, idealism, revenge – they weighed as heavily as the money aggregates. All of this will fuel concern, already growing within her own party, about Mrs Thatcher's Prime Ministerial style. The faithful down in the grassroots still applaud.

Those who watch at close quarters are less impressed. The Iron Maiden act is beginning to look too much like Bette Davis playing Queen Elizabeth. No politician has spoken so frequently and firmly in the first person since General de Gaulle, yet she is no de Gaulle.

Sometimes it is as if she is not the Prime Minister at all but still Margaret Thatcher, conviction politician. She attacks public expenditure as if she were not responsible for it, inveighs against bureaucrats as if she were not in charge of them, treats her Cabinet as her enemy and distances herself from it. Probably she fancies that she can appeal to the people over the heads of the politicians and not be counted in their number. It is the old populist trick of running against yourself. She has been almost two years in the job, in charge of the compromise industry called government, and yet she remains rhetorically intact. Some might say that rhetoric is all that remains, which is why she clings to it.

For now she is beset by troubles. Her party, which she tends more carefully than she does her Cabinet, may not love her for much longer. She has quarrelled with all her friends at once, no badge of political skill. Industry is up in arms against her. If industry has no confidence in her policies, who can? The CBI has been spurned, almost humiliated. The Industry

Department is doing nothing to advance the case of manufacture; Sir Keith is too ashamed of what he has done for Leyland and the BSC to urge more aid for the private sector. The competence of the Government is in question, and the competence of the Prime Minister; very little confidence remains.

May will not be a merry month for the Government. Higher charges and price increases will hit pockets. Local government elections promise to be disastrous. Union conferences may reveal a revival of militancy. Trade union negotiators will study the Retail Price Index but their members will be more concerned with beer and tobacco, and these days, petrol. Mrs Thatcher has probably forfeited the working-class constituency she won in 1979, the 11 per cent swing to the Conservatives among the skilled workers. The regressive injustice of the Budget will rankle, unemployment could cease to cow and start to anger.

Her Budget is designed to revive the economy by curbing inflation, reducing borrowing levels and interest rates, devaluing the pound. But the taxes she has levied, the unemployment she has set out to create, and her refusal to aid industry's competitiveness, are as likely as not to push borrowing interest rates higher once more, dragging up the rate of exchange and further deepening the recession.

The weight of opinion expects the vicious spiral not the virtuous one. More cuts will be needed if the strategy is to work at all, deep ones if there is to be much of a tax-cutting harvest by election time. It is to be doubted whether the Government has the strength or skill to carry through such a strategy: degeneration into an all-round crisis, political and economic, is possible by the summer or autumn.

Yet there she stands in the last ditch, gallantly dug for her by her Chancellor. She is unmoved and seemingly unmovable. The intriguing happenings of the past week are only the beginning of a new chapter, not the end of the story. She will take a great deal of turning yet. We are left wondering whether she will prove capable of it.

18 March 1981   **Peter Jenkins**

Information Incorporated

Yesterday's issue of the *Neue Zürcher Zeitung* published an interesting article entitled 'Bestätigung des deutschen Schwerbehindertengesetzes' and for the whole of this month both Mercury and Mars are too close to the sun for observation. The selling price of *Time* magazine in Portugal is 85 escudos and road works on the M6 may continue to cause delay between Wednesbury and Walsall. A great deal, in fact, is happening this week. Today is the 243rd anniversary of the birth of George III, tomorrow the Easter Law Sittings end, and Saturday is the anniversary not only of Lord Carrington's birth (he will be 62) but of the D-Day landings in 1944 under the late General Eisenhower. When it is midday in London it is only 7 a.m. in New York, owing to the earth's rotation on its axis, which inclines to the vertical, with respect to the sun, at an angle of $23\frac{1}{2}$ degrees. To revert momentarily to the roadworks, they are happening all over the country, not least on the M4 between Feltham and the North Circular Road. Sussex, meanwhile, are playing Somerset at Hove.

Most newspapers, by definition, set out to provide information but there is a tendency, lately embraced by honoured colleagues at *The Times*, to classify information in three senses: the sense of the news which is happening now or happened yesterday, and the background thereto; the sense used by Mary Kingsley, writing in 1897 ('The next news I was in the water') which refers to an essentially anecdotal, ephemeral, or predictable event, a jotting, as it were, in a notebook; and the sense which was discouraged by the Geneva edition of the New Testament (1557) in the heading to the First Epistle of St Peter: 'Salutation in Christ is no newes, but a thynge prophecied of olde.' There may be value in the distinction. For example, Thursday next week will be the Feast of St Barnabas (category 3) and there can be no question that roadworks, if not at Wednesbury then elsewhere, will impede traffic (category 2) on that day, as indeed they will again when the 151st anniversary of the death of

George IV falls due on 26 June. There is, however, an argument, which we find compelling, for directing attention to information in category (1). That is not to say that jottings, or thynges prophecied of olde, deserve no place in the chronicle; merely that we would find it hard to summarise in a few words Le Monde's analysis yesterday of the current situation of the American Negro and that we have come, wrongly perhaps, to equate roadworks rather with normality than news.

4 June 1981   **Leader**

Package flight to the knife

Alongside all those colourful invitations to exotic places like Bath and Bond Street, British Airways offices round the world are about to offer brochures for the most expensive and painful package tours in the business.

A traveller from Tokyo can have 22 days in London, with full board, for the knock-down price of £10,550, including a couple of new heart valves. ClinicAir, says the brochure, brings you to Britain 'for the finest medical care at guaranteed prices'. In some cases this 'may be combined with a holiday or business trip'.

The packages have been put together by BA and American Medical International, which runs a string of private hospitals in Britain, including the Harley Street Clinic and the Princess Grace hospitals in central London. It is planning to have half a dozen more.

Dr Stanley Balfour-Lynn, chairman of AMI (Europe) told a press conference to launch the scheme that the 60 or 70 doctors involved were all 'top consultants from London teaching hospitals'. They had agreed to reduce their normal private practice fees so that the costs of the packages could be held down, he said. But the doctors, not surprisingly, have insisted that this should not be revealed to patients by giving a breakdown of the package costs, because their British-based patients will be paying the full rate.

The package price for a heart operation is only £9350 if the patient is coming from Malta, or £9750 from Kuwait. A hysterectomy patient arriving from Athens – 18 days in London – will pay £4150, and for stripping varicose veins (one leg, eight days) the cost for a traveller from Singapore is £3200. Prices for treatment at hospitals in Windsor or Harrow are lower.

The numbers of Middle Eastern patients arriving for treatment in Britain's burgeoning private hospitals have dropped sharply, so the medical companies are keen to find new sources of business.

27 November 1980   **Hugh Hebert**

A wire from the shire

It's funny (writes J. Arthur Composite, our occasional correspondent on the Conservative back benches). You spend almost all your adult natural in politics, and after a time it seems just a blur. The moments you remember are the moments everyone remembers: the night with Sandra when Kennedy was shot, the night without Sandra when John Lennon died. How awful, how amazing, you said then; and yet the really amazing thing is what happens around you, day by day, cushioned by familiarity. If someone had told me twenty years ago that my spell in Parliament would see America lose a war against little yellow men and a President drummed out of office for crookery, with only Frank Longford having a decent word for the chap . . . if they'd prophesied old Alec and old Ted . . . if they'd said a Canadian and an Australian would run *The Times* with the bally establishment lying on its back, and that in February 1980 Mrs T would be packing her bag to snuggle up to Ronald Reagan whilst poor Michael was wandering round Glasgow for the telly waving his stick. If anyone had put that in my 1960 almanack I'd have booted them all the way to the funny farm.

People in the tea-room on Wednesday were saying the

ghastly thing about politics is that they're always the same. Get across the miners and you'd better abandon ship; a lesson of history, my son. But I don't know what the lessons of history are, except that I keep waking up in the middle of the night in a muck sweat feeling puny and frightened because I don't understand, and I feel so bloody helpless trotting out the nostrums of the day handed down by whoever happens to be the Great Party Panjandrum.

What do I still believe in? Nothing that seems the least bit coherent. I believe in the people I know at home and in the constituency. Good people who make things and grow crops and rush about when a lame dog hits a stile. They're nice deep down, like when I was a lad. They want enough work to make themselves tired of an evening, as small a tax bill as we can contrive and all the damned benefits they can get. They want their streets swept and their schools heated and a video recorder on every hearth. And why not? That's exactly what I've promised them at seven elections.

I've always stood up on the platform and said: Look here. You know what I stand for and someone brighter than me at Central Office tells me that if we merely control M3 or roll back the frontiers of the state or establish cash limits, then everything will come up roses. I've never said that there is no magic potion and that the clever stick in Smith Square is only old Keith stubbing his toe on the Philosopher's Stone again. I couldn't say that, you see, because it's not political. Politicians have to trot round pretending they've got all the answers. Next time, I know, it will be my sacred duty to warn against the Dragon of Socialism, and help make Britain safe for liberty and Sir Albert's dukedom. I might even start to get temporarily excited when the briefings arrive. There are some jolly funny turns in the Labour Party these days (though not in my constituency since we sicked the poly off next door when those boundary wallahs came around). But do I, here and now, actually believe all the palaver about Worthing as the new East Berlin? Not for a second, because Michael is truly the most Tory old buffer I know. A fine man with the extended metaphor, I grant, but give him a problem with details attached and he'll shuffle it over to someone who understands detail: Jack Diamond or Alan Bullock, one of those Council for Social Whateveritis fellows. You're a long way from the Long March with that lot.

It's the unreality of the whole shooting match that gets me down. Either keep Britain free for a million years. Or ten years to the Marxist millennium. You'd think they weren't all mortal politicians who knew that they might get the heave-ho at the next election because something they can't cope with – like an Arab in a nightshirt blowing up Saudi – turfed them out. You'd think they would just keep quiet and get on with the job. Instead it's all masterplans in the long term and falling over your bootstraps tomorrow. If Labour gets a Gallup boost, then Clive finds a new scheme to make Moss Evans King. If we get ahead, then Margaret falls down the pit with her mouth open. If it's so jolly important we win next time, why don't we start trying to score a few points?

I register what I see at the weekends. Half the High Street shutting up. Half the Rotary Club banging on my door. Sandra's brother saying his socks cost twice as much as your average Korean's. Decent men I've known for decades trooping into the surgery asking for a job. That Liberal bookseller candidate looking like the cat in the cream, inquiring after my ticker. Well, I tell them all, we're doing an awful lot more to help than you might think listening to the PM. Cars, steel, coal, punk rockers cleaning beaches. You can see how hard poor Keith is working, I say. But somehow it doesn't sound so hot when there she is again next minute on the goggle box doing her Asbestos Ayatollah bit. People don't give you any credit that way because they feel they're suffering. People think it's her fault.

As a matter of fact, I think it's her fault, too. The lady was an accident. Kick Ted on the first ballot, we said, and then she was out of sight. And of course we went along because she seemed so damned certain, and even fiercer than Sandra at the woman scorned bit. But now my chums in the team room really hate her. When one of her toadies started talking about 'the courage to change her mind' last week, we just beavered off.

Everyone knows it's a shambles and I keep thinking back

over those two decades. Perhaps things are only amazing because you can't see farther than your nose. What does the Labour organisation in my constituency add up to? Three men and a Trot. What do I feel when I meet our people? Sheer bloody apathy and a lot of miserable excuses. Some of the superbright men you bump into in London – silks and things – don't see the problem. But I see the problem. I'm in politics to do my best to make people happy. That's what politics is about. And I've had two years of making people very unhappy. That's not what politics is about. I can never recall a time when it all seemed more of a charade, when you felt the ice was closer to cracking. Nothing to be done about it, of course. You must be loyal to the Leader until she's an ex and you can Khrushchev her in the lobbies. But, golly, sometimes I think that's the only thing I've got left to look forward to.

23 February 1981   **Leader**

The Tory party takes freight

During the House of Lords debate yesterday at the Conservative Party conference an intense woman who seemed to be angling for a peerage kept referring to Lord Boyd-Carpenter as Lloyd Bored-Carpenter.

One could see what she meant. Actually, it was quite a lively debate, by Tory standards, with speakers passionately urging each other to rally behind this crucial motion committing the Government once and for all to do whatever it thought was best.

Alas, we time-travellers had been spoiled, coming straight to Brighton from the 'Blackpool hallucinations' (as someone put it yesterday) without a break – roughly like going from a riot to a prayer meeting.

Inevitably, the cultural adjustment took some time. By lunch-time one had accepted the fact that there would be no emergency motion congratulating the Vestey family on extending free collective bargaining to the tax system, and adjusted to the tradition whereby the patron saint of Tory conference procedure is the Boston Strangler.

Then there is the language problem: the need to go from polytechnic militant to the languid vowel sounds of the Tory Toffs on the platform.

Why, for example, was the lady mayoress presented with 'a buckey of flarse'? Didn't she normally get some roses? What did Lord Thorneycroft mean by 'the end of the dye'?

'Thenkoo, Lord Thorneycroft,' says the chairman. Conference supported the privatisation of BR freight, but also took freight over Mr Benn's plans for the Lords.

It is an awesome thing to behold what Mr Benn does for up-market adrenalin. Yesterday he got far more references than Disraeli, Churchill, Salisbury, or Ted Heath (the only one present) and almost as many as the Incumbent herself – though not as flattering.

Tory conferences being unselfconscious, speakers are able to warn that Labour would turn the Lords 'into a rubber stamp' (no laughter) and declare passionately: 'We want freedom and we want it, among other things, to appoint hereditary peers if we wish.' In Consett they talk of little else.

Yesterday morning Mr Norman Fowler, the thrusting young Transport Minister, struggled to get a libertarian peroration out of transport (and failed – you try it). And there was warm applause for the return to the rostrum of two of the party's Big Stars – Mr Norman St John-Stevas and William Hague, who a few years back was the first child in nappies to address the conference (William, not Norman). He is now at Oxford and seems to be reading Clichés.

The pressing post-prandial question was, of course, Heseltine: would he be able to pull off his annual triumph yet again when this year it was coming so soon after the O'Toole Macbeth?

There were bound to be comparisons. The Environment Secretary's difficulties were increased by the fact that not all Tory conference debates are as boring as they are meant to be. It became plain during the local government debate that there was actually some debate taking place (complete with heckling) between the defenders of the town halls like Sir

'Tag' Taylor and a lynch mob crazed beyond endurance by their excessive business rates.

Mr Heseltine got through the tiresome responsible passages first. He eloquently described how he had 'rolled back the frontiers' on building regulations, Parker Morris standards (cheers) and something called performance statistics. But it was heavy going. He lashed Mr Benn with a piece of rhyme which overshot its cash limits by several syllables. Mr Heseltine got his standing ovation but it was touch and go. The Cabinet strategy is working. His material is getting him down.

The next topic was civil defence, which precipitated a mass flight from the hall in search of emergency rations of tea and gin.

8 October 1980   **Michael White**

A trillion and one things

You can get a genuine horn eighteen inches long at Harrods. For £19.75. Not the kind you blow, by the way, but a shoe horn, once a genuinely fearsome offshoot from the poll of an Aberdeen Angus. But who'd want one that long – a man on stilts? People who don't like to bend down, said the Harrods horn buff. If it wasn't Angus, he added, it was definitely an edible quadruped.

These by-products of the beef industry were selling well to tribes of women in pleated skirts, belted jackets and pudding-basin felt hats. Apparently many have men in their lives – Harrods phrase – who won't, or can't, bend down.

Touched by the pathos of it, I turned away, and eagerly awaited the choice of two young Commando types in high heels, scarlet jumpsuits and German helmet haircuts. They scanned the bow-tie section. Dress bows of the made-up variety that the Duke of Windsor abhorred were displayed at £18.50, but some 'to tie on yourself' at £7 struck a sturdier, self-reliant note.

It was a near thing but another customer, in leather from

wishbone to merry-thought, put them off by saying, 'He *used* to wear bow-ties. I remember going through his drawers and throwing *out* bow-ties.' The Commandos wavered, and opted instead for Famous Church's Slippers at £17.95.

I pressed on through the Man's Shop, past Continental silk scarves, Regimental and Old School ties and a £375 Cashmere overcoat, turned right by the Gannex raincoats at £75, and down the stairs. My priority was a haircut, plus some pampering of the beard as a double treat, and I expected Harrods to make a production of it, like the Jane Austen character who travelled to town for a similar purpose.

The omens were good. The barbershop is through a green jade sort of pub, where you build up to opening time with cheesecake and apple-pie and kleinesprach in German.

In the barbering temple I claimed an introduction to the beards buff. The vestal at the cash register said '*All* the staff are *fully* trained.' She gave me a ticket, and within six minutes of my number coming up, I was back paying £2.50. Before I could object, I'd been turned from a Cavalier into a Roundhead. I told my taciturn operative I felt odd. 'You would do,' he said with grim satisfaction, 'after wearing it long.'

To my relief, he didn't insist on demolishing my beard as well. He dabbed it a couple of times with a stiff brush, grunted, 'It lies wrong,' tossed the brush in the sink and let me go. More or less in shock, I returned to the pub and was given a large Scotch. By 'given' I don't mean it was free, but that somehow payment doesn't put you on level terms with Harrods.

I brooded. I thought of wearing a deerstalker till it grew again. I looked for the silver lining: presumably I now looked like a regular Harrods customer, one of those who'd use a long shoe horn. I could roam the famous store without being charged with vagrancy. Harrods is said to stock 1,000,000,000,000,000,000,000 objects. I might buy one – a suit of armour, an Aztec toothpick, a platypus puppy. I set off for the pet shop.

Ordnance Survey should do Harrods. There are maps but you get no contours. I took advice on the route from Perfume and Fragrance, where the troops behind every shimmering redoubt are kitted uniformly in sugar pink, and mostly redolent of a novelty called Valentino.

A soldier of the line, not only sugar pink but sassy, remarked that she could direct me anywhere in Harrods, because she'd taken an exam to get the job, like taxi drivers when they do 'the knowledge'. Her directions were clear and simple but, distracted by the bakery waft, and the sight of cakes made to look like Dougal, and a racing car, and beds with marzipan mice inside, I lost my way again.

Once in the Food Hall, under a suspension of hams and tongues and salamis, I ricochetted about like a pinball. 500 sorts of cheese, 4lbs of fresh Beluga for £532. Queues for salmon at £10.50 a lb. China Black-Brick Tea with a gazebo in sur-relief. Several varieties of sea salt. Venison sausages 88p – I bought a pound as a talisman.

After many vicissitudes, via Body Tops and Monet, Bridal, Spode, Knobs and Knockers, Electronic Games and Power Play, I came at last to Pet Shop. Well, it must have shrunk. No platypi, not anywhere there, though there were some handsome fish. But few warm-blooded creatures except rodents, cats and dogs.

Before me a man paid £102 for a King Charles Spaniel, then I asked Pets what chance of a Sealpoint Siamese kitten? 'None,' she said. 'They go mad in here. It'd cost you about £140. We could do a Blue Persian for £100.'

In the Lending Library you pay £30 a year, and take out one book at a time. 'Daily if you like,' added a Librarian. They keep several copies of each title, mostly unjacketed until they're sold second-hand or twenty-second-hand, at half-price. On the shelves there were 39 copies of Mountbatten, Hero of Our Time, 37 of The Duchess of Windsor, and 15 each of Prince Philip and Jack the Ripper.

In Pianos, you could have a Bechstein Grand for £13,600, a Bluthner in pyramid mahogany for £8,950, or a Wurlitzer for £812. A Harrods pianist was tinkling Black Witch on a Hoffman priced at £3,300. He said I could have the Harrods tuner come round for £12.

Crossing the furniture departments on the third floor is like

58

a trek in an abandoned civilization. You could exercise a horse there, using sofas as jumps. You could make assignations, conduct interviews, pass military secrets – any enterprise demanding absolute privacy and freedom from interruption. The satraps sit like carved figures behind huge desks opposite one another.

The gem in this overlooked crown is Fine Art. Romney's Lady Hamilton as a Bacchante bares her breast above a tag of £18,500. In a deeper recess is Reynolds's Miss Montgomerie at £28,000. A lovely early-nineteenth-century Dutch hand-made sailing ship waits in a sombre corner for an owner with £3,900.

Outside is Putai, the Chinese God of Laughter, in polished wood. And well he may laugh at the company he keeps: Three Graces in Carrara at £2,150, a bronze eagle on a stump at £8,750, an implausible bust of Napoleon. Most grotesque, a Frankenstein of design, is a set of buffalo horn furniture about a hundred years old for £5,900.

I totted up 24 horns to the sofa, 18 to a chair, and 12 on the rocker – scalloped at the ends. If I were Harrods, I'd cut my losses and make 108 long shoehorns of them, and sell them off at £50 apiece.

I never found the Aztec toothpick, but there was the suit of armour – sixteenth-century German, with handaxe, for £1,250 – cheaper than my favourite Bonsack bath at £4,000, or the Harbilt Golf Trolley at £2,750, but still more than I had on me, with lunch still to get.

Harrods has any amount of restaurants and they're all full of Fairy Godmothers wanting to put their feet up. In a self-service I took ham quiche and a glass of California red wine, chambre up to the drinking temperature of tea.

My table companions were an excellent family from Tunbridge Wells, cosmopolitan schoolteachers who treat Harrods like Mexico or South Africa, as an exotic sightseeing trip. They'd bought nothing, but came for the decorations, based this year on a clown motif. They spoke enthusiastically of nursery schools in Soweto, where they'd been surprised to see the children had black dolls.

They were probably from Harrods, I thought, and went to

check dolls in the Toy Kingdom, where the rocking horse is
£499. They could manage two in the Doll Boutique – a little
plastic one at £2.95, and a cloth Fisher Price model at £6.95.
This one had a tartan dress – perhaps the influence of the
House of Fraser.

Before I left I tried to get up under the dome, which carries
ropes of bright lights outside. But I was told it was forbidden
even to staff. What guilty secret could it enclose? My mole
told me it was packed tight with rubbish even the Arabs won't
buy.

30 December 1980   **Alex Hamilton**

Unsettling Mr Benn

'Isn't it *awful* about *Benn?*' said the lady jogger. 'I mean, he's
quite mad.'

'But you spent eight years marching for CND and Benn
wants nuclear disarmament.'

'That's as may be,' said the lady jogger, thin-lipped.

'You're anti-market and Benn wants out.'

'I dare say,' said the lady jogger, frowning.

'And the other day you said you'd give anything to see
Ulster vanish in a puff of smoke. Benn only wants to withdraw
our troops.'

'Possibly so,' said the lady jogger, 'but the man is mad.
Good heavens, don't you read the papers?' And she jogged off,
crossly.

Curiouser and curiouser, said Alice. Living on these British
Isles, we are all perfectly free to campaign for our beliefs, yeah
upon the very streets. We may march up and down for
anything we wish, we may protest in our thousands in
Trafalgar Square, sit down in Piccadilly, stand up outside
Downing Street or shout from soapboxes in Hyde Park. In
my time I have myself marched and protested and signed
petitions for troops out of Ireland, more aid to the Third
World, more industrial democracy, and equal rights for

women, black people and gays. I have also marched or protested against nuclear weapons, the Common Market, private education, and the House of Lords. Some of you must have been there, too, because there was ever such a crowd.

We thought, then, that They were listening. The Labour Party, that is, because most of us were loyal Labour voters. The kind that Mrs Shirley Williams praised at her Blackpool mini-conference last week, and how we all loved Mrs Williams. But at Blackpool we learnt – if we had our ears open – that They had never been listening. They had only patted our heads and made agreeing noises and said comforting things about freedom and democracy and righting wrongs while they got on with the real business of the Party, which was to make it look as much like the Tories as possible without actually losing our votes. Because, though I, for one, have always marked my cross for Labour, what I was really doing was all they allowed me to do – vote *against* the Tories.

Indeed, I had more or less forgotten there was any more positive way to vote Labour until Tony Benn stood up at Blackpool and actually gave voice – on a real platform and in front of real politicians – to all my beliefs and principles. Well, you would have thought the skies had fallen in. Not only did the Centre not hold, it broke cover and ran in small circles, frothing at the mouth. How *disgraceful* of Benn to blow the gaff. How contemptible to air such views in *public* where the voters could hear. Argument, anger, conflict? It's not right to worry our pretty little heads with such things. I tell you, sir, the man's no gentleman. Why, he talks *in front of the servants*.

The Gentlemen of the Press recognised the crisis, bless 'em. To a man (well, to a *Morning Star*) they charged in to bolster the *status quo*, bellowing of brawls and disaster, emitting dire warnings of splits and collapses and rudderless driftings to chaos. Nurse Rachets all, they waved their scalpels and tried to lobotomise Benn. He's mad, he's lunatic, he's dangerous, he's raving. Operate quickly, nurse, and shoo him back to the cuckoo's nest.

I tell you, it made me feel a little odd. I kept looking over my

'It's very convenient, you can join by credit card and at the same time write everything they stand for on the back of it.'

27 March 1981

shoulder, wondering when they were coming for me. Was it folie à deux or could anyone join in? If Tony Benn was round the bend, was I ga-ga, too? In any European country (outside West Germany, that is) we would both be considered perfectly normal citizens, a trifle dull perhaps, but with our hearts in the right place. But cross the Channel and, whoops, here come the men from the funny farm. What can it all mean? Why does our socially-permissible political spectrum run from right-wing Tories only unto liberals with a conscience? Why does one whiff of anything more Left set all True Brits to shouting 'go back to Moscow'? Why do people I know with impeccable left-wing theories suddenly start convulsing at the sound of Tony Benn's voice? Has he green teeth, body odour, scurf? Dirty fingernails?

The fault, I fear, lies in ourselves, that we are underlings. All very well, as private citizens, to espouse the same causes as Benn. All very well to march about keeping our freedom muscles flexed, our consciences supple, our eyes alert for instances of exploitation and injustice. Very cosy to talk at parties against privilege, make jokes about the public schools, air our impeccable credentials as deeply caring citizens, equal to anyone and better than most. But, by God, we *are* British. At heart, we know our place in the hierarchy. We are rebels who stand against injustice and for change to remedy injustice, whether in Ulster or in the Third World, whether for the working man or for disadvantaged blacks. But we only *stand* for it. We don't wish to be pushed *into* it, thank you very much. Stop jostling over there, would you? D'you realise, you almost had me unbalanced for a moment? Filthy, ill-mannered Trots.

A *Times* leader summed the whole thing up very neatly last week. Mr Callaghan, it pronounced, should bow out of the leadership, to be succeeded by Mr Denis Healey as the head of a party that was safe for right-wingers to live in and for sensible, moderate people to support. The left, thus thwarted once again, would permit Labour to get on with the proper business of an opposition party. And so say all of us.

I must admit there was a moment there, in Blackpool, where I thought change might be possible, but the newspaper headlines soon reassured me. Fancy thinking that just because you'd bought nuclear weapons, you could stop buying them. Fancy believing that if you sent troops to Ulster, you could get them back again. Imagine being so naïve as to think that joining the Common Market means you can leave it. Imagine imagining that just because people mantled the House of Lords, people could dismantle it.

It was wrong of Mr Benn to unsettle me, I see that now. It was right of Mrs Williams to ask me to ask myself why the Labour Party was only percentage points ahead of Mrs Thatcher's Conservatives. I had thought the answer was that Labour voters couldn't tell one from t'other but I see, now, the error of my ways. Mrs Thatcher's role is to do wicked things and our role as loyal Labour voters is to stand beside her, telling her how wicked she is.

I am, it is clear, a very slow learner.

9 October 1980 **Jill Tweedie**

Big Mal and the malcontents

Mr Terry Venables, manager of Crystal Palace (bottom of the First Division) is now favourite to take over as manager of Queen's Park Rangers in succession to Mr Tommy Docherty, former manager of Chelsea, Rotherham, Aston Villa, Oporto, Manchester United and Derby, who was dismissed as QPR's manager, for the second time, last week. Mr Docherty's name has, of course, been linked with Manchester City, who last week said goodbye to their controversial coach, Malcolm Allison, a former manager of City and also of Plymouth Argyle (twice) and Crystal Palace. City, last but one in the First Division, are now expected to launch their bid to regain their place among football's elite by recruiting John Bond, manager of Norwich City, last but two in the First Division.

Mr Allison's dismissal, along with that of Mr Tony Book, the City manager now expected to join Swindon, in succession to the recently dismissed Bobby Smith, followed only a week after a boardroom assurance that their jobs were safe 'barring a disaster'. Their fate is thought to have been sealed by City's defeat at the hands of Leeds United, who recently brought Alan Clarke from Barnsley to replace the former Burnley and Sunderland manager, Jimmy Adamson, sacked after Leeds had fallen to the foot of the First Division. Mr Adamson's dismissal followed repeated demonstrations against him by supporters, some demanding the appointment of Mr Geoffrey Boycott, interspersed with boardroom declarations of unmitigated confidence in him.

A successful manager needs to keep the confidence of his board, of his supporters, and also of his players. The fact that so many managers nowadays seem incapable of satisfying this triple test could well be due to the undemocratic procedures under which they are appointed, in which neither supporters nor players have any direct say. The sensible course, surely, would be to open up the appointment at Manchester City to an electoral college, in which all three groups could be represented. There might be, say, a 40-30-30 breakdown between board, supporters and players; or a breakdown of 30-40-30; òr perhaps a weighting of 50-25-25. The voting system should not be decided by the board alone, but by a special conference of all the groups affected, which – to allow time for delegates to be mandated – might conveniently meet in January. And where better to hold it, in the circumstances, than Wembley? Who knows, a resurgent Malcolm Allison might recapture two jobs for the price of one.

14 October 1980   **Leader**

Solid citizen

The most powerful man in Poland operates out of a hastily converted bedroom – No. 63 – at the top of a rundown sailors' lodgings, the hotel Morski, here in Gdansk. The bed has gone, replaced by a small secondhand desk. The wardrobe has become a filing cabinet, the wash basin a giant ashtray. A plain wooden cross hangs on the whitewashed wall.

Solidarity took over the building this autumn during the illegal strike and now 50 paid workers and a further 110 volunteers are busily creating the first free trade union movement in the history of international Communism. Crude protest posters and mimeographed underground newspapers, still, technically, illegal, are being produced by hand in the basement.

Walesa, a short, stocky man with a massive moustache, a polo-necked sweater and a crumpled suit, bounds upstairs shouting to friends. He promises two minutes' discussion. Instead he talks non-stop for more than two hours, chain-smoking cheap cigarettes, opening his own post, answering his own telephone and haggling with other officials all at once.

'I am not afraid that the Russians will intervene,' he says, 'and I am not afraid if they do.' That is his style, the carefully balanced 'on the other hand, but . . .' Thus his talks with the prime minister were 'good and bad'. They discussed 'everything and nothing'. Now he believes there will be a compromise in the Supreme Court row over legal pressure to force the union to recognise the 'leading role' of the Communist Party. 'There is no other possibility except confrontation,' he says. 'If we strike from November 12 it will be the newest kind of strike in the world.'

The idea is a series of rolling, one-day, regional strikes. 'Once we start we can keep it up for a year or more – we will go on until we succeed,' he says. It is a dire threat in a country whose economy is falling apart and whose people go to bed cold and hungry.

But Walesa's emphasis is on construction. Sometimes he sounds more like a prime minister than a rebel union leader. 'We need technological aid from abroad on issues like agriculture, engineering and building. We need foreign experts to come in and point out our mistakes and advise us how to solve our problems. Our people are clever and educated. They can learn. We do not want any more foreign indebtedness. We will be asking for extended credits on the money we already owe and suggesting that some debts should be cancelled. We are poor but proud and we need all the help anybody can offer us – including money. We do not like to ask but if anybody feels friendly he should help.'

Asked whether all this should be done through Solidarity or the government he shrugs. 'At the moment our relations are not good but we hope they will improve so we can help them. For the moment, aid should go both to Solidarity and the government.' It appears that Solidarity sees itself playing, in practice, the role that unions have always played, in theory, in Communist countries. It hopes to represent the direct interest of the workers and also to involve itself actively in the search for better management, higher productivity and improved output.

Asked to list the intellectual advisers to Solidarity, Walesa cites first, people around Cardinal Wyszynski and the Catholic

66

establishment, second, those around Tadeusz Mazowieki, editor of the liberal Catholic paper, Link, and third, the Kuron group of dissident intellectuals.

And what provoked the wave of strikes this summer? 'The Pope's visit must have had an influence. Then there was the bad weather and the harvest failure. Finally there was the memory of other years of revolt – of 1956, 1970 and 1976.' In his own case Walesa was sparked into action by the mass shooting of strikers in Gdansk in December 1970. 'I will fight for the right even on my knees. I wanted a memorial to the dead. I have been fined many times and held without trial again and again by the police for organising memorial demonstrations. A year ago I said at such an illegal protest that I would build a monument for the tenth anniversary of the killings next month and there would be no arrests for those who attend that ceremony. So it will turn out.'

Sacked from his job in the shipyards for such outspoken subversion, Walesa made contact with dissident intellectual groups. This summer he climbed over the gates of the Lenin shipyards after the strike had started and found himself adopted as its leader.

'Now we have more than ten million members and that does not include peasants. I don't really know how many people we have. Almost everybody I suppose. As for the old, Communist unions – we do not even notice them any more. They no longer exist. People say those unions are genuinely trying to liberalise themselves. But they have only a tiny handful of members left to do anything with.'

Walesa is aware that splits have developed inside Solidarity and that he is sometimes criticised as a compromiser and a fudger. He does not complain. 'It is good to have different tendencies in the movement. If we all had to say the same thing together that would be merely the old style. As the chief I have to balance all these people. I must. It is my job. So do not give me labels – moderate or militant – I have to change day by day. Sometimes I have to calm the radicals. Other times encourage the fearful.'

Yet Walesa claims that he is not a politician. 'I am a union man and not a socialist. My religion helps now – it has helped all my life. A man without religion is a dangerous man and without my religion I would be a dangerous man. I go to church every day of my life and on specially difficult days I pray the "Queen of Poland (the Virgin Mary) help us".'

Talking about the form of society he wants, Walesa agrees with Solzhenitsyn's criticisms of the West as well as of Russia. 'He wants both systems improved. He wants everything for the human being. Each system, Socialist, Communist or capitalist, must be a humane one; for the people, with the people. That is my view. I ask, what fault of mine is it that I am born a Pole and you are English? Why should I go hungry while you have plenty?

'Change must come in England too, you know. You are too rich and too comfortable. People ask if this is a Polish revolution. In certain circumstances it could spread across the world. The world is not perfect. I have never been abroad, but even now I can tell you what is wrong in your country.' Aware that his enthusiasm has carried him over the top into apparent arrogance, Walesa stops and smiles. 'When we have finished here I will come and help you out with your problems.' Then he leaps from behind the desk, offers cigarettes, shakes hands and bounds off down the stairs, his bodyguard trailing disconsolately behind.

6 November 1980   **John Torode**

The mouse that nibbles at freedom

'Here you are – Mysia,' said my guide to the Polish literary scene. This particular cultural monument was an anonymous, indeed unlabelled, building conveniently facing Party headquarters across a rather gloomy little triangle: the Central Office for Control of Press, Publications and Performances – in short, the censor's office in Mysia Street.

When I asked her what Mysia meant, I thought she said Mouth Street, a mishearing that sent her into such howls and snorts that a militiaman came looking round the corner to see what was disturbing the peace. What a pity, I said to Tadeusz

Konwicki the next morning, that it wasn't Mouth Street. Well, he said, Mouse Street is just as good. Little mice in the attic, nibbling away at our freedom.

Poland has an intermittently brilliant cinema, a theatre as rich in imaginative innovation as any in Europe. There are good novelists, like Jerzy Andrzjewski, Kazimierz Brandys and Konwicki himself, who is about to become better known to us with the publication by Faber of his two latest novels, still officially unpublished in Warsaw. Poland has its Nobel Laureate, Czeslaw Milosz, and in Zbigniew Herbert one of the finest poets of our time, many of whose works are available as English poems of rare authenticity and fidelity, through the generous bilingual subtlety of Milosz himself. And it has this miserably embarrassing institution, set to watch over them and their readers.

Talking to Polish writers I found that few of them had much to say about the censor. It wasn't fear or anything like that; many of these were men and women whose bravery had been proved well enough in adolescent encounters with the Nazis as well as in later dealings with the Stalinists. It was more distaste, or simply boredom.

Jerzy Surdykowski of Zycie Literackie in Cracow, was unusual in knowing something about the man who had censored him. His censor was a very hard-working fellow – he'd had two heart attacks – and was of a distinctly literary bent. He had not only marked cuts in Surdykowski's story about the strike in Gdansk (he'd mostly disliked the suggestion that the strikers had quickly and efficiently been able to take over the running of the city, organising a blood donor service, for example); he had actually added romantic invocations to alter the tone: 'People of Gdansk, think what you are doing! No ships are being built; the yards lie idle' – that sort of thing.

Readers of Solidarity Weekly last month were able to get an even closer insight into the psychology of the censor, when the paper published an interview with one, by Barbara Lopienska. He emerges as a rather vain young man, quite motiveless, except for a curiously punctilious loyalty to what he usually refers to as 'the firm' he served for three years – not

69

so much to its aims as to its efficiency which he thinks remarkable by comparison with the generally 'schlampig' (sloppy) nature of Polish office life. He is now a sociologist, and preferred, as they say, to remain anonymous.

Anyone could join, he said, so long as they had a degree and passed the interview; there were geographers, political scientists, philologists, some people who'd graduated in journalism; and it was becoming 'a feminised profession,' said this censorious sociologist, full of graduate housewives.

He thought there was no particular psychological type. There were some 'keen devils', guarding the leading role of the party with the censor's pen, and some 'chess players . . . happy to make a fool of the journalist whose words they're playing about with.' But most, he thought were like him, 'people who can't make up their mind what to do' and who join not least 'because it's good money at the beginning. I got 4000 zloty (a month) in 1974; but it doesn't go up much – my mate who's worked there for seven years still only gets five grand' (about £74).

His other motivation was that he'd wanted to be a journalist, to write, and he thought he might learn a thing or two with 'the firm'. 'If you've got a lively mind,' he adds rather nauseatingly, 'working in censorship tends to make you more radical, if you're not a complete cynic.' ('I'm a liberal really,' he added later on. 'I went through March' – the student demonstrations of March 1968 – 'with my dignity intact'). However, he decided that writing was too much like hard work.

But he'd quite liked 'the firm', liked his boss ('direct, no bullshit, no clichés: he said that censorship had existed throughout recorded time'); and there was a certain social cachet attached to it – all that access to virgin information and ideas: 'I got on well at parties. The girls were starry-eyed; blokes from ordinary offices didn't stand a chance.'

For people outside that charmless world the old censorship meant a kind of spiritual maiming and shaming of two or three generations of journalists and of all but the strongest minds and spirits among Poland's poets, novelists and scholars. It would be good to be able to report that the censors' mean old instruction books were closed now. Certainly they had retreated into a sort of nervous idleness over the last year, and the new draft censorship law, as described to me by Jan Josef Lipski, Solidarity's chief negotiator with the Government, would have curtailed the censor's powers considerably.

What's left of that draft law still contains such valuable new safeguards as a right of appeal to the supreme administrative court; it's still a genuine advance. But, the mice have been at it since the Russian written offensive of early June and the subsequent Party plenum, and some of its definitions – as to what criticisms might constitute an attack on Poland's alliances or an offence against the state – have been made ominously vague by official redrafting.

The result is that the network of independent, unlicensed publishers who have grown up since 1976 have repudiated the law: they say they do not intend to conform with its rulings which by vagueness leave them open to crippling fines, 'because of the need to protect cultural values, and in view of the universal social acceptance of the work of the independent publishers.'

Acceptance they certainly have, and some of the best lists in Poland now, especially that of Nowa, presided over by Mierek Chojecki, that imp with the face of an ikon, who has done time for his enterprise and isn't likely to buckle under the censor now. Not that he doesn't owe the censor something: for example, Gunter Grass, the complete text of Herbert's Pan Cogito poems, George Orwell, and the remarkable diaries, crucial for an understanding of modern Polish literature, of Witold Gombrowicz, Poland's own cunning exile, something between Joyce and Bulgakov, and author of that great expressionist novel, Ferdydurke.

Among its other successes are two novels by Konwicki. The Polish Complex carefully explores the spiritual hangover which his country's bitter history has bequeathed to its best sons and daughters: the dilemma of a nation pulled between east and west, forever trying to find out what it means to be true to itself. (It is striking, incidentally, how many of the best writers are exiles even in their own country: Konwicki,

Herbert, Milosz himself and many others, come from Lithuania or Lvov, now in Soviet territory.)

The other novel, A Small Apocalypse, is the stuff of Polish nightmares, set at some time in a disastrous future. A blocked Warsaw writer, who once mattered but is now bogged down in midlife crisis, is approached by a party of his confreres. They have learned that Poland is about to be absorbed as a state of the Soviet Union. It's necessary that a dramatic sacrificial gesture should be made: self-immolation is suggested. They've looked around and decided that he is the most appropriate subject. The writer wanders the streets of Warsaw crucified by his dilemma.

It's necessary to remember, however, what remarkable things have been done above ground as it were since last August. The journalists' union produced a notably brave and dignified statement in response to hardline criticism the other day, and seem to have been able to protect several of their members who were under threat of dismissal. And astonishing things have been appearing on the Polish stage.

I will describe just one of them – Jerzy Sito's verse play Polonez – because it places the Polish crisis so dramatically in an historical context that makes it plain that this is a Russian crisis too.

Sito is a great Anglophile, a friend of Al Alvarez, translator of Shakespeare and a passionate student of the English metaphysical poets; a big collection of his translations of them, the harvest of 15 years' work, is due to appear in Polish this month.

I had forgotten that I had already met him once. Then as I stood outside the green door of his house in Saska Kepa on the other side of the Vistula, I had a strong *déja vu* feeling. I had been here before, on a bitter night in the miserable February of 1969. We had talked in a depressed way about the production in the previous year of Mickiewicz's play Dziady which had been shut down after demonstrations had greeted some of the anti-Russian speeches in which this nineteenth century nationalist classic abounds. Most of decent Poland then was suffering a hangover from its country's formal part in helping to close down the Prague Spring and licking the

6 April 1981

wounds suffered in its own anti-semitic, neo-Stalinist purges in that year.

'Who can tell,' I wrote after that trip, 'when Poland's "insommia of the conscience" will become intolerable again, or another romantic epic upset the political applecart?'

And now here was Sito, himself, rocking Poland with his own extraordinary play, faithful in every historical detail, about how certain misguided conservative Polish 'patriots', alarmed by Poland's new constitution of May 3, 1791, invited in Russian troops ('Illustrious guarantors of our sovereignty,' as the rhetoric of the time had it) to help them occupy the country and squash this dangerous democratic nonsense.

The rest of the play concerns the treachery of Catherine the Great, who connives with the equally disturbed Prussians in the partition of Poland, and with the dismal behaviour of some of the Polish intelligentsia and aristocracy, and the corrupt parliament.

One climactic scene shows the assembling of the parliament, the Sejm, convened to rubber-stamp the new, counter-revolutionary order. As the members arrive the secretary of the Russian embassy reads to the Ambassador the list of bribes (all taken from the actual archives) received by each MP except for four just men; their names he hands over on a separate list to the general commanding the Russian forces of occupation.

In the production which played to packed houses in Warsaw and then at the Wrocaw Theatre Festival, the exits not only of the parliament chamber on the stage but of the theatre itself were guarded by Russian soldiers – in their fine eighteenth-century costumes; it's a very grand production. So is the new one which has just opened at the Slowacki Theatre in Cracow.

Surely it's not necessary to labour the way in which this play suspends history like the sword of justice over all the actors in the play now going on in the theatre of contemporary politics in the eastern half of Europe? One bit of resonance I can't resist mentioning, however. The reactionary 'patriots' who brought in Catherine's troops called themselves 'the Targowice Confederation'; the group of hard-liners who harrassed Mr Kania and the 'renewal' line before the central committee Plenum called themselves 'the Katowice Forum'. It's strongly rumoured in Warsaw that when Kania rounded on his critics and challenged them to vote, a voice – perhaps his – was heard to say: 'It's time to settle this Targowice Forum business once and for all!'

It's not hard to sympathise with Mr Kania, or to see that some restriction of the freedom to publish and be damned may seem the least painful hostage to deliver to his powerful critics in return for some lessening of their pressure, and acceptance that Poland, once more, is 'different'. But it is hard to see how people who have been living on a diet of things like

Sito's play or the rich fare coming from Nowa are going to accept anything like the pettiness of the old restrictions.

There is no easy way forward for the new Polish society, but unless after all someone does bring in the bulldozers, the way back too is closed.

1 July 1981 **W. L. Webb**

Rolling round the monde

The notion of a shadow cabinet does not exist in France. Either one is President Giscard or one is wholly other than President Giscard. The London correspondent of *Le Monde* has therefore had to find a French term both to describe Mr Michael Foot's administration and to explain its status. The term he has chosen is *'cabinet fantôme'* and his definition is: *'c'est-à-dire l'organisme parlementaire suprême de l'opposition appelé à succèder eventuellement à l'équipe gouvernementale.'* Care must be taken in translating this back into English and perhaps even in reading the original French. To describe the Opposition front bench as an organism would not come naturally even to the most withering of its Conservative detractors. He would be more likely to say the gentlemen opposite or that gang over there. *Appelé* to the English has a messianic meaning more appropriate perhaps to other potential leaders of the Labour Party than to Mr Foot. The supreme organism is not 'called' in the sense that a postulant monk or Jehovah's Witness might feel himself 'called'. Indeed in spite of the reputation which the French language has in this country, its words do not necessarily take on a metaphysical meaning. *Appelé* in this case means little more than designated. *Le Monde*, however, has run a slight risk with its readers' perception of British politics, for General de Gaulle was undoubtedly *appelé* in both senses.

Succèder eventuellement. Here is another difficulty. To suggest that the supreme organism will 'eventually succeed' the governmental team requires a prescience which *Le Monde*, shrewd and well-informed though it is, would hesitate to claim. Yet *eventuellement*, though an ambiguous word, does correspond more closely to 'eventually' than to 'possibly'. *Le Monde* may have intended to suggest that the organism will 'possibly eventually' accede to government, and one can fully appreciate that in any language such a thought would be cumbersome to express. In the interests of mutual understanding, however, it would have been better to leave the French in no doubt about the inherent indeterminacy of the British electoral system.

Some of the misconception which *Le Monde* may inadvertently have caused is fortunately removed by its phrase *cabinet fantôme*, which will convey to Frenchmen, as it does to the British, an entity not fully possessed of a corporeal nature. (Nineteenth-century German philosophy, with which readers of *Le Monde* are likely to have a passing acquaintance, gave much thought to this notion of being and becoming.) If in the end there lingers in the French mind some doubt about the eventual succession of the supreme organism, *Le Monde* may faithfully have mirrored the state of affairs in *l'Albion perfide*, without inviting too much confusion about M. Benn, *l'ombre rouge*, et M. Rodgers, *le fantôme sans responsibilité*.

13 December 1980   **Leader**

The moment of surrender

Real power in France will be handed over in furtive privacy on Thursday morning, in a room at the Elysée Palace with only Mr Giscard and Mr Mitterrand present. Mr Giscard will remove from his neck (or maybe his wrist) the secret code for pressing the right buttons to fire France's nuclear deterrent.

In a patriotic television broadcast earlier this year, Mr Giscard had explained that he alone, unaided and unadvised, would take the nuclear decision in the room called 'Jupiter' under the Elysée. Nobody will know what he says to Mr Mitterrand in the half-hour meeting, only a few weeks after he had said in the election campaign that Mr Mitterrand, in

*'What worries me about
Michael Foot is that deep down
he might prefer the Booker
Prize to the Leadership of the
Labour Party.'*

22 October 1980

addition to all his other shortcomings and his association with
the Communists, lacked the qualities of a statesman. Mr
Mitterrand, a recent convert to the nuclear deterrent, has not
said if he will act with equal solitude.

The handover of the code was the only precisely known fact
about the ceremonies yesterday, because the event has no
precedent. Mr Giscard will be waiting for Mr Mitterrand on
the inner steps at 9.30 in the morning. Will Mr Mitterrand be
on time? He is normally between one and three hours late at
political meetings and party conferences. Will he have the
Garde Républicaine all the way from his home in the Rue de

Bievre? Asked for details, Elysée officials said they were no longer in charge and Socialists said they had not decided.

Later, the 'presidential liaison group' at Socialist headquarters announced the first reform of the new Administration. The Marseillaise, slowed to funereal tempo by order of Mr Giscard, is to be restored to its revolutionary jauntiness – as from Thursday morning, when Mr Mitterrand reviews the Elysée guards. The new President will drive down the Champs-Elysées in an open car to the tomb of the Unknown Soldier under the Arc de Triomphe, before paying a call on the man who made his victory possible, the Gaullist mayor of Paris, Mr Chirac. Socialist mayors will give their staff a holiday to take part in provincial rejoicing, but Gaullist and Giscardian mayors have made no such decision.

In a different kind of power transition, vanloads of documents have been leaving Elysée and ministerial offices all week, bound for discreet storage, the incinerator, or the shredding machine. 'Only personal notes and irrelevant matter,' officials explained, and Socialists appeared to be resigned to the obliteration of incriminating material, ranging from Bokassa to the 23 years of Ministry of the Interior files about everyone on or near the Left.

Tonight, Mr Giscard will make a farewell broadcast on all three channels and tomorrow will lay his last wreath at the Unknown Soldier's tomb. On Thursday evening the new President 'invites the people of Paris to come with him' to the Heroes' tomb at the Panthéon to pay homage to the Socialist leader, Jean Jaurés, and the Resistance hero, Jean Moulin.

It is announced from Socialist headquarters that later 'the President will walk up the Rue Soufflot while the orchestra of Paris and a choir of 150, conducted by Daniel Barenboim, will play the Ode to Joy'.

19 May 1981   **Walter Schwarz**

Palma days

The Tea Dance for the Golden Days pensioners at the Bahamas Hotel, Majorca, was well under way. Free sangria flowed and the old people on the dance floor were bopping with abandon to this year's sequence dance craze, The Cheeky Birdy. Waving their arms in the air they made clacking birdbeak gestures with their hands, flapped their wings, patted their knees, wiggled and danced around to the thumping Dutch pop song that they request over and over again, drawing them all out on to the floor.

Intasun's Golden Days Holiday Club is one of many firms arranging long-stay foreign holidays for the over-55s. In the winter a pensioner's holiday costs as little as £47 a week for the first month, and the longer they stay the cheaper it gets, down to £28 a week. It is a booming section of the holiday industry. About a million people over 55 in the CDE socio economic group took all-included package holidays in Spain or Malta last year, and more this year, according to the British National Travel Survey. Many of them stay for three months, to avoid the worst of the British winter. Another million old people take more adventurous, non-packaged winter holidays.

For many pensioners, it is as cheap, or cheaper than staying at home, and facing winter fuel bills. If they want, they can arrange to have their pensions paid to them abroad, though most of those I spoke to were letting their pensions accumulate at home, so they could use the money as a down payment for next winter's holiday. With all meals provided, warmth, company and entertainment, it's an attractive proposition.

Two couples from Accrington had just come off the dance floor, and reached for their ice-and-lemon-packed sangrias. They were part of a group of twelve from Accrington, who had taken long winter holidays for the last seven years, all in Spain. Norman Hebson was a retired foreman at the Ewbank carpet sweeper factory, and he and his wife Anne were full of praise for this year's holiday. 'We've had one or two before

that have been a bit rough,' she said, 'but this is the best –
spotless bed linen, towels changed every other day in our
bathroom, good food, and plenty of it. . .' she went on listing
its glories. 'We go back a week before the bowling season
opens, and that sees my husband through to October.'

She and her friend Nellie Briggs, whose husband used to
work in a Christmas card factory, described how they spend
their days. 'We have breakfast at eight, then we go walkies at
nine, don't we?' Anne said. 'We walk round to a bar, have a
drink, and walk back again. We stop at Jaws bar at the bottom
of the hill – Jaws is where everyone goes – to get up the energy
to walk back up the hill to the hotel, in time for lunch. Lunch
is always nice, a choice of two main dishes – meat or liver or
kidneys or fish or salads, for instance. Then we have our siesta
until four.'

Nellie Briggs went on: 'Then it's our afternoon walkies
again, and back into Jaws for a coffee and cognac, and then we
get changed for first dinner at seven.' In the evenings there is
entertainment provided by the hotel every night, usually the
same English cabaret artiste, Barry Jordaine, combined fire-
eater, magician, hypnotist, and singer. Three nights of the
week, the Golden Days guests have their own old-time and
sequence dancing in another room. 'We're usually in bed by
ten, absolutely knackered,' Anne Hebson said, and they all
laughed.

They also get two free trips and two half-price trips
included in the deal. They had a trip to Palma flea market, a
barbeque in the hills, and a visit to Val de Mosa monastery
where Chopin and George Sand stayed. Being more
enterprising than most, the two couples had also hired a car to
take them round to other parts of the island off the very well
beaten tourist track. 'It was wonderful – a Talbot Chrysler,
polished to piddlyo,' Anne Hebson said.

Lena Pow from Bristol used to work in a laundry and her
husband was a welder until he went blind. They had been
staying at the Bahamas Hotel for seven weeks. Last year they
had nine weeks in the Rio Park in Benidorm during the
outbreak of Legionnaire's Disease. 'People were very silly
about that,' she said boldly. 'We didn't panic like some, and

we stayed and had a lovely holiday. We save every penny the rest of the year, don't drink or smoke or go out, so we can have these holidays. It's like being a queen, waited on hand and foot. At home my husband just sits, but when we go away he comes to life.'

They first went abroad in 1971, to Moscow. 'We loved that, caviar with every meal, and opera or ballet every night. It doesn't seem so popular now, but packages to Moscow were all the thing then.' They have also been to New York, and up the Hudson, 'We didn't like that,' Capri, Rome, and Venice which they did like. They are hoping for California next year, where their son is a plumber in Santa Barbara.

It has been an extraordinary ten years for them, after a lifetime of hard grind. 'I worked my fingers to the bone in that laundry, and now we're enjoying ourselves,' she says. 'We all notice the old people in places like this are much better at enjoying ourselves. After all, this is all we've got. We may not be here next year so we'd better enioy life minute by minute.'

Golden Days employs a couple for the season to organise dancing for the old people. Vivienne and Jim McFarland came out to the hotel in October. They get free board and lodging, and a bit of pocket money. In the summer they work the holiday camps in England – last year it was Butlins at Minehead – and take the winter abroad. They have no home, and no roots, and live out of their suitcases. They are hoping for a cruise job to see them through next winter. Vivienne used to work for Rolls-Royce, and Jim was at British Leyland in Coventry, when they took up ballroom dancing, and got themselves the requisite teaching qualifications.

'Sequence dancing is what they all want,' Vivienne said. 'The old-fashioned kind is barn dances, the St Bernard's Waltz and that, but they want something more up to date. One of the favourites right now is what we call the Bahama Dance, to the record 'Viva L'Espagna'. Three nights a week we do the dancing, and four mornings we run an English library for them.' People complain, she says, that the Spanish dance floors are too small for that sort of thing. 'And so they are. They're built for intimate smoochy European dancing. The

Spanish waiters laugh at us, but I get used to that. The waiters hate our tea dances. It's siesta time, and they're a bit disdainful.'

This company has forty reps in Majorca. Old people present special problems. They have had six deaths since December. The area manager explained that they can get the body and bereaved partner home within a few hours. All the old people have to have health insurance, and a high proportion of them need hospitalisation some time within a long stay. 'It's partly that they panic if they get something even minor wrong with them. But the insurance covers all that.'

'And, of course,' said Vivienne McFarland, 'you always get the one or two professional grumblers. I suppose they enjoy grumbling.' Just then a gloomy-looking old man came and hovered over us. 'It's not fair,' he said. 'Everyone's getting free sangria, but my wife's a diabetic and she can't drink alcohol. Why can't she have a free bitter lemon? It's not really fair, now, is it?' With a quiet sigh the area manager got up and bought him a bitter lemon at the bar.

The brochures for holidays like these advertise Palma, though the two main tourist centres are in fact several kilometres either side of that still reasonably charming walled city. The Bahamas Hotel is in Arenal, the world's first mass package tourism spot. Driving mile after mile along its desolate and destroyed sea front is a depressing experience. Intasun's area manager said apologetically: 'This is where they made all the mistakes in the beginning. The rest of the world should have learnt from this.' But, looking at developments still going on in the rest of Spain, Greece, and other parts of the Mediterranean, it doesn't look as if the lesson has been taken to heart. It is a kind of shanty town of none-too-crisp-looking high-rise hotels, crammed one against another. I don't know how they contrive to produce such glowing photographs for their brochures.

The sun makes the place look better, but there is no doubt it is more horrible to the eye than any English seaside resort. There is nothing old, nothing charming to break the unremitting concrete and tatty vulgarity of the strings of souvenir shops, bars, discos, restaurants, crammed up against one another, and for such miles at a stretch; Souvenirs Darling, Bavarian Dancing, Henry VIII English Pub with English Food, Bar Dusseldorf, L'Angel Blau Souvenirs, Rhodes Snack Bar, Zorba's Disco, even an English sign reading Minerals, everything plastic and concrete, and most of it crumbling a bit.

The hotel was at the far corner of all this – a fact much appreciated by those who had been in the thick of it in previous years. 'At least there's a bit of green up this end, a few trees to walk through. We didn't like the last hotel, partly because there was just nowhere to walk,' one of them said.

The Germans have almost as firm a grip on the place as the British and amongst the old people there was clearly some antagonism towards them. Anne Hebson started on that theme quite early on in our conversation and the others were keen to join in. 'They're pigs, real pigs. I've never seen anyone eat the way they do. I'm a big eater, but I couldn't put away a fraction of what they do.

'And they're up to all the tricks. We watch them. One German this morning ate six boiled eggs, yes, six! They need nosebags, not plates. And they steal. They take tea bags, sugar, rolls, and packs of butter out of the dining-room. Just yesterday we saw one German woman ask the waiter for something, and soon as his back was turned she emptied the fruit bowl into her bag. The waitress saw her and made her empty her bag out. It was full, choc-a-bloc, with food.'

Another woman joined in, 'The way we see it is it's not fair on us. If they eat like that the hotel will have to put their prices up next year, and we'll be paying for it. We tell on them when we see them at it.'

The gossip became more general. 'And what about Mr Goatee?' someone said. The others roared with laughter. 'He takes pockets full of figs, every time figs are on?' Someone else added, 'Not surprised. That's probably where he gets his stamina from. He'll never see seventy-five again, I shouldn't think. He's been here all winter, always after the ladies. He gets them right against a pillar, you know. He has a lady for a few weeks, and it's all lovey-dovey, tears and bye-bye and

83

sniffing when they leave. But once one's gone, he's off with another the very next day!'

'Viva L'Espagna' was playing again on the dance floor. 'We're off to sunny Spain . . . Viva L'Espagna!' Out they went on to the floor, brown and glowing, clapping and swaying, until a large lady sank to her chair in a corner, fanning her flushed face with a huge flamenco fan. 'In all my very hard-worked life,' she said, gasping a bit, 'I don't think I've had such a good time.'

13 April 1981   **Polly Toynbee**

The West's Arabian beach-head

In the cool of the early evening one day last week the royal clans of the Gulf gathered in the desert to watch that most sheikhly of spectacles, a camel race. There one could see a representative selection of the 10,000 or so men who rule Arabia – the Al Bu Falah of Abu Dhabi, the Al Maktum of Dubai, the Al Thani of Qatar, the Al Bu Said of Oman, the Al Khalifas of Bahrain, and, of course, at least one prince of the House of Saud.

On the flat grey sands at Al Wathba, near Abu Dhabi, it was suddenly possible to really grasp the amazing fact that half a dozen families, with a fringe of poor relations, control the destinies of one of the richest, most strategically important, and potentially most dangerous areas in the world.

The resonant romance of their names, the black of beards against white robes and silk cloaks, the camels padding past, seemed to roll back the years to the days when these men, or their fathers, were lean and hungry war chiefs, successful sheep herders, or shrewd exploiters of tatty one-dock ports.

But then there are also the paunches, the flash of gold Rolexes, and the setting sun's rays glinting on the polished carapaces of Mercedes, Rolls and Buicks. And, a few miles away, the magic towers of Abu Dhabi, a modern city created from scratch in little more than ten years, aggressively interrupt the desert horizon.

Everybody knows how old and new clash and mingle in the strange realm of the oil sheikhs, but it is still weird to see, or to hear, how 'traditional' ways persist in places that twenty years ago hardly had a telephone but which have now become command posts of the world economy. The occasion that brought the clans together in Abu Dhabi last week was a case in point: the marriage of the Abu Dhabi ruler's third son, Mohammed. (The camel race was just one item in a week of celebrations.)

There was the usual mind-boggling heaping up of gifts, copper trays loaded with gems and the like.

But the most interesting aspect of the marriage was a dynastic twist straight out of the Muslim history books and to do with that staple of Islamic monarchical politics, the rivalry between younger and older wives expressed through competitive pushing of their respective sons. Abu Dhabi already has a designated crown prince, yet Mohammed, first son of the ruler's favourite wife, has now contracted an extremely advantageous marriage with a girl from the senior branch of the family. Could this mean, muse the gossips, that the succession is not quite as clear as it was a week ago? That at least is the talk in the new Intercontinental coffee shop; but what Sheikh Zayed thinks, he is, as usual, keeping to himself.

With stories like these in mind, one cons the comings and goings of Arabia's ruling families, and meetings like that at Al Wathba, not only with nostalgia and with the critical curiosity we all reserve for the very rich, but with apprehension, and even fear. For the real question about Arabia is not whether it is, or could be, a target of Soviet attack by conventional or subversive means, as sometimes General Haig and even Mrs Thatcher, who will be seeing for herself in a few days' time, seem to suggest.

The real question, when looking at the Arab royals, is whether there are, somewhere among this crowd of camel fanciers, falcon buffs, video addicts, and family intriguers, enough men of ability and foresight to steer their countries towards true stability – a course that will inevitably demand that they progressively yield wealth and power. The further question is whether even the best men in the ruling families, assuming they have or will come to the fore, can handle such a transition. 'What we ask ourselves every now and again, when we have time to look up from our desks,' one Western diplomat in the Gulf said, 'is whether these people can survive.' This is what is meant in London or Washington when it is said that the real threat to the States of Arabia is 'internal' – the possibility that political evolution will fail: and then, of course, you can wheel on your Soviet scenarios, although even here there are optimists who argue that certain kinds of radical political change would not necessarily jeopardise Western interests.

Those 'western interests' are obvious enough, but the facts bear rehearsal. The royal elite of the six conservative states of the peninsula rules an area as big as the United States but with an indigenous population which, at something over six million, is less than that of Greater London, with another five million foreigners sucked in by the wealth.

Those are the negative superlatives. The positive one is that together, the states – the big league is Saudi Arabia, Kuwait, and Abu Dhabi – produce around fourteen million barrels of oil a day, about a fifth of the non-communist world's oil supplies. More than the proportion, there are the reserves, about a quarter of the entire world's. More than the reserves, there is the fact that the Gulf oil strip is the closest the West now has to a 'reliable' and 'controllable' major oil supply outside its own national territories; more than the 'reliability' of the region itself, there is the influence, in particular, of Saudi Arabia, on other oil producers.

Again, as important as the oil itself is the buying of Western goods, which has become one of the central transactions of the world economy, and the Arabian investments in the West, which are massive. No wonder Western leaders wince at the mere thought that the Gulf states, and above all Saudi Arabia, might be 'lost'. Taking territory along with resources, such a denial would mean, even if Soviet influence was not paramount, in the words of one British ex-military man, that 'the game would be over, old son'. All this may have a certain logic, but there are certain other and more fruitful ways of looking at the same facts.

The desert around Al Wathba, for instance, is probably not too different from the areas in Arizona and Nevada in which the US Marines and army have been intermittently, and not too discreetly, practising an Arabian intervention over the last ten years. Their planners have thrown down their pencils many times, and their problems are easily appreciated in Arabia itself, where the gross difficulties of major intervention – unprotectable oil and water installations, nightmarish logistics, the sheer viciousness of the terrain – are all too apparent, even before you bring up the political impossibility of acquiring the facilities in the region that might make the military problems more soluble.

Then there is the contradictory bundle of purposes that the intervention concept drags along. Conventional deterrent to Soviet attack, 'trip wire' force to signal nuclear readiness, intervention force to deal with coups or civil wars and rescue local regimes, intervention force to coerce local regimes, occupation army for the oil zone – take your pick.

All have different military and political requirements and effects and the result is a messy, dangerous policy area that nobody in the region wants to touch with a bargepole. Many might agree, in the words of a Bahraini minister, that 'a strong signal of resolve' to the Soviet Union could help governments – a little – to solve their real problems, which are internal and fraternal. Nobody, on the Western or the Arab side, has solved the dilemma of how you make political military noises at the Russians without creating the military capacity to get them, and those being 'protected', to take you seriously.

But this dilemma over the military connection is not the only one the West has dumped on the rulers and inhabitants of Arabia. The contradictions that oil sheikhs now face, and which they must resolve if they are to survive, are contradictions which the West played a dominant role in creating. The interventions which matter have already happened. To stick with the military metaphor, the Gulf littoral from Kuwait to Dubai constitutes the Normandy beaches of Western technology and capitalism.

In an astonishing achievement, the West has flung itself on to these arid shores, ferrying in, like a military expedition, every item of what it has built, from the nuts and bolts to the very labour which has carved out these beachheads. The result is a chain of manic municipalities from the head to the foot of the Gulf, with another chain cutting across the waist of the peninsula through Riyadh to Jeddah – a giant T-shaped urban grid, laced together by super highways and jet routes, and feeding off Kentucky Chicken and Australian lamb.

The Saudis are rounding off the business with two new industrial cities, and, in a final refinement, the whole network is being computerised, so that it can control the population and machines it has amassed. The new Saudi computerised intelligence system, for instance, is believed – like everything else around here – to be one of the most advanced in the world. It is being installed by the same government that bans associations and clubs of any kind and which recently closed a women's group in Riyadh, apparently on the grounds that the women were 'laughing too much'.

That is only one of the more comical examples of how the Gulf has become a sort of zoo of strange behaviour, of muddled styles and purposes. What is obvious, in the end, is that it has been the West which has – more or less – dictated the rate at which the oil has been lifted, and it has been the West which has – more or less – in its frantic anxiety to get the oil money back, dictated the rate at which the oil revenues have been spent and therefore the vast 'development' which has distorted and punished the social fabric of the peninsula.

It was the West, too, which played a large part in the creation and definition of the regimes which rule the peninsula. Only a decade ago, Britain was still deposing 'unsuitable' rulers, and only two decades ago, the United States was putting its weight behind Feisal in his struggle to get rid of Saud. The West still wants all the same things – suitable rulers, both oil and development on its own terms, and, to cap it all, 'stability'.

But what has really been emerging, obscured by all the talk of rapid deployment forces and the sociological guff about 'patriarchal structures' and 'transition', is a realisation that the West's demands are as contradictory as anything else in Arabia.

Among those with sense in the peninsula, including some members of the ruling families, the view is taking hold that the way forward must be towards representative government, peninsular unity, and a radically more rational economic policy, and that must mean changes in Western as well as local policy. Otherwise, the mad social chemistry of the region will eventually produce precisely what the West, and the beleaguered princes of Arabia, fear – an explosion.

15 April 1981 **Martin Woollacott**

Letters from a fainthearted feminist 1

Being the continuing correspondence of Martha, a striving woman of mature years, to a younger Sister, her 'polished female friend'.

Dear Mary,

Sorry I haven't written for a while, but back here in Persil Country the festive season lasts from November 1 (make plum pudding) to January 31 (lose hope and write husband's thank-you letters). I got some lovely presents. Your useful *Spare Rib Diary*. A book called *The Implications of Urban Women's Image in Early American Literature*. A Marks and Sparks rape alarm. A canvas Backa-Pak so that the baby can come with me wherever I go (a sort of DIY rape alarm). Things I did not get for Christmas: a Janet Reger nightie, a feather boa, a pair of glittery tights.

Looking back, what with God Rest Ye Merry Gentlemen, Good King Wenceslas, Unto Us a Son is Born, We Three Kings, Father Christmas ho-hoing all over the place and the house full of tired and emotional males, I feel like I'm just tidying up after a marathon stag party. Our Lady popped up now and again but who remembers the words to her songs once they've left school? We learnt them but, then, ours was an all-girl school, in the business of turning out Virgin Mother replicas. If I ever get to heaven, I'll be stuck making manna in

89

the Holy Kitchens and putti-sitting fat feathered babies quicker than I can say Saint Peter. Josh, on the other hand, will get a celestial club chair and a stiff drink. If God is a woman, why is She so short of thunderbolts?

I went to a fair number of parties dressed up as Wife of Josh but, to tell you the shameful truth, it was my Women's Collective beanfeast that finally broke my nerve. One wouldn't think one could work up a cold sweat about going as oneself to an all-woman party, would one? One can. I had six acute panic attacks about what to wear, for a start. Half my clothes are sackclothes, due to what Josh still calls my menopausal baby (come to me, my menopausal baby) and the other half are ashes, cold embers of the woman I once was. Fashion may well be a tool of women's oppression but having to guess is worse. In the end I went makeup-less in old flared jeans and saw, too late, that Liberation equals Calvin Klein and Lip Gloss or Swanky Modes and Toyah hair but not, repeat not, Conservative Association jumble. Misery brought on tunnel vision, I swooned like a Victorian lady and had to be woman-handled into a taxi home. Quelle fiasco.

That same evening, the blood back in my cheeks, I complained to Josh that I was cooking the three-hundred and sixtieth meal of 1980 and he said move aside, I'll take over. Coming to, I found myself, family and carry-cot in a taxi driving to a posh restaurant. Very nice, too, but Josh was so smug afterwards that I felt it incumbent upon me, in the name of Wages for Housework, to point out that his solution to the domestic chore-sharing problem had just cost us fifty quid, and if he intended to keep that up, he'd have to apply for funding to the IMF. Bickered for the rest of the evening, Josh wittily intoning his Battle of Britain speech – you can please some of the women all of the time and all of the women . . . but you know the rest, ha ha.

I had hardly recovered from these two blows to the system when Mother arrived to administer her weekly dose of alarm and despondency. How can I *think*, she said eighteen times, of letting my Daughter drive van, alone, to Spain? Do I *want* her to be raped, mutilated and left for dead in foreign parts? It is my duty to insist that a *man* goes with her. I point out that Jane is a large, tough, twenty-year-old rather more competent than me, Mother and Mother's Husband put together and Mother leaves room in huff. I then had a panic attack about Jane being raped, mutilated and left for dead in foreign parts and insisted she took a man with her. Like the Yorkshire Ripper, for instance, shouted Jane and left room in huff.

Myself, I blame British Rail. Does Sir Peter Parker realise the mayhem caused to family units all over Britain by pound-a-trip Grans intent on injecting overdue guilt into long-unvisited daughters? Josh's Ma trained over, too, apparently to make sure I wouldn't grass on Josh if he turned out to be the Yorkshire Ripper. Ma, I said, what alternative would I have? Even the sacred marriage bonds might snap, given that one's spouse was a mass murderer. Marriage bonds maybe, she said, but I am his Mother. Then she said would I give Ben away, I said what else could I do and she said you could stop his pocket money. She did. Ben, I said, glaring at the stick of celery that is my son, if I hear you've murdered *one more woman,* no sixpence for you next Friday. Well, now they've arrested someone who's got a wife and a mother. Keep your ears pinned back for the feminine connection.

Ben's friend Flanagan stayed most of the holiday. He explained that he had left home because his mother had this new boyfriend. How difficult it must be, I thought, for adolescent boys in the midst of the Oedipal Dilemma to have alien males vying for their love-object's favours. Flanagan said he couldn't stand the way his Mum bullied her boy-friends and now she had chucked them both out because of her women's meetings. You're as bad as the NFers, he told her. I can't help being a boy, can I, any more than if I was black? But you are black, I said, and black is beautiful. Yeah, except I'm white, he said. Flanagan's Dad is white, said Ben, so why shouldn't Flanagan choose? What am I, anyway, a racist or something? With that, they both pulled on jackets covered with swastikas and went out. At times like this, I am so grateful for the baby. Dear thing, he's hardly a boy yet at all.

You probably won't read this letter until mid-January – I read in the papers that your lot had gone to Rome to picket

Nativity Scenes. My goings-on here on the home front must seem very trivial to you. Ah well, we also serve who only stand and whine. – Yours from a hot stove.

21 January 1981   Martha

The rise of meritocracy

The new greenery of Arabia is perhaps the single most startling aspect of the assault on nature which oil wealth has made possible. Every city of the Gulf and Saudi Arabia is stuffed with trees, flowers, and radiant turf, as if the whole peninsula were engaged in a competition in the conspicuous consumption of shrubs.

But the green of the trees leads you out of the cities, and away from their beautification by what must be the most expensive parks departments in the world, to rural and agricultural schemes that poignantly illustrate the central problem of the Gulf States – the intense artificiality of their new economies and therefore of their societies.

Along the road from Abu Dhabi to the inland oasis town of Al Ain, trees struggle under the sun, bedded down in mounds of imported soil and sustained by hosings from water trucks. This part of the Emirates reminds one of models arranged in a sandbox, and each village seems to come out of the same kit. Brown and yellow shophouses, always in neat sets of three. A nice fancy mosque, a school, and one-storey family houses laid out on a rectangular grid – all of it brand new, and shielded from the desert by still more trees.

But it is difficult to see what the villagers do, apart from live in the houses, send their kids to school, attend the mosque, and admire the trees. It is like Noddy's Toytown, with a mayor, and a policeman, and roads, and stores – and not a vestige of productive work in sight.

Suddenly, there's a golden fluff on the desert, more amazing than the trees. Fields of wheat stretch out between the road and the mountain ranges of Oman. Miniature rainbows dance as the light catches the sweep of the sprinklers. This government scheme produces wheat and potatoes for the Al Ain area, but the costs of turning the sand into something like a Mediterranean landscape are incredible.

Aside from quantities of valuable water from the shrinking reserves underground, there is the pumping equipment from Germany, the combine harvesters and tractors, the manure from Pakistan, the fertilisers – it hardly makes for a cheap loaf of bread. And the manning of the scheme is symptomatic, too – the field workers are Baluchis, and the technicians and experts are Tunisians, Egyptians and Palestinians.

'It's good wheat,' said one of them, rubbing an ear of it in his hand, 'but – you see the problems?' And he waved at the red desert beyond the wheat and the trees – the armies of dunes silently and ominously deployed against the thin green line.

In fact, some of the agricultural schemes, in spite of their costs, have been relatively successful. But that expensive, fragile green in the desert still stands as a symbol of the way governments in the region, aided and pressured by Western industry, continue to fly in the face of social and environmental realities. The price that they are paying, and will continue to pay, is a heavy one, and money is the least of the penalties.

The Gulf States began by importing the means for their upper classes to live in luxury, and then by bringing in what was necessary for their ordinary citizens to live in relative affluence. They topped that with the importation of expensive weapons systems for their small but lavish armed forces, and with the building of petro-chemical and other industrial complexes. The incredible spending on 'infrastructure' – roads, ports and airfields – reached a sort of climax this week when King Khalid of Saudi Arabia opened the new airport at Jeddah, which is, of course, the world's largest.

Saudi Arabia's third economic plan will involve the spending of $250 billion in a country where a new school is already being opened every two weeks. In that country, and in the richer Gulf States, anybody of passing intelligence can go abroad to be educated if he wishes, and this enlarged class of graduates is now returning to complicate further the strange class system that 'modernisation' has created.

Economic and educational change in Arabia has created an upper class which is an uneasy mixture of royals, plutocrats, and technocrats. There is a tension building between the latter and the first two groups. Flooding back from America and Europe now, and particularly into Saudi Arabia, are large numbers of well-educated young men.

Most of them will take good civil service jobs, although not quite such plum positions as their sparser predecessors of the Yamani generation. In such jobs they are bound to meet and resent royal obstinacy or foolishness and to clash with the avarice of the overlapping top business class.

One such graduate confessed that it sometimes took him an hour to explain to his minister – a prince – the simplest of schemes, only to wait while the old man mused his way to an arbitrary decision for or against. Such technically trained men also include, at least in Saudi Arabia, a new and more sophisticated kind of military officer educated at Western military academies and staff colleges – and that could also have its implications for the future.

But the potentially more serious divide may well turn out to be between these three groups and the rest of society, ranging from a locally educated middle class to what remains, in some states, of a population which could be termed either rural or lower class. And the catalyst could be a popular irrationality which these governments have done much themselves to create.

The featherbedded life of citizens of the richer oil states has been often described. A Kuwaiti with a middle grade civil service job, for instance, will dress in the morning in Dishdasha (robes) laundered by Koreans, will be served at breakfast by his Thai maid (who may also double as his mistress) and with coffee at the office by a Keralan Christian.

There he will be advised by a Palestinian before lunching at a restaurant presided over by a Swiss chef, and driving home past construction sites where sweating peasants from Baluchistan and upper Egypt will be adding to the splendours of his city under the direction of choleric men from Yorkshire.

With honourable exceptions, his job may well be a non-job, set up, like his cheap petrol, his subsidised house, and his free annual holiday abroad, by his government in order to keep him happy.

As one weary Englishman said: 'Show me any ministry in the Gulf States, and I'll tell you what it is – 400 dumbos drinking coffee, and three Palestinians working like dogs.'

Welfare statism of this scale and lack of discrimination is producing, many intelligent Arabs themselves believe, a class that is losing sight of the relationship between work and reward, that is incipiently anti-foreign, and yet which lacks the drive to push its way forward on merit. It is wide open for an ideology which would purge it of its unease and guilt without materially reducing its privileges.

The youth of this alienated middle class and confused, if materially comfortable, working class is already showing signs of going in the most likely direction – towards political Islam. Kuwait University, for instance, has been almost taken over by pro-Islam groups.

As one professor there said: 'People are looking for a goal. True, they have money, but then what? In three years I have seen a change among students that I can hardly believe, in dress, in approach, in everything.' In Saudi Arabia, a journalist said: 'The scale of development is so immense and the ignorance of the people so catholic that you are going to get, at the very least, constant tension between the modernisers and the religious right.'

It used to be thought that the enormous expatriate army which labours throughout the peninsula, at every level, to keep its complex technology and administration functioning, could be a direct factor in political crisis. In particular, the many northern Arabs, including Palestinians, were seen as a potential political threat. It now seems more likely that, if the expatriates do play a part, it will be a passive one – as an object of resentment in a new kind of political struggle between modernising masters and reluctant populations.

Whatever the elements of irrationality or racism in popular resentment and protest in the Gulf States, its basic thrust can hardly be dismissed. Something monstrous has been set down

95

in the Arabian peninsula – an enormous battery of Western-type facilities that could never, unless with the most radical modification, be serviced or controlled by the peninsula's own people.

Saudi Arabia's prospects may be better, with more people, and, by the meagre standards of the peninsula, more non-oil resources. But her wealth and her problems are correspondingly greater, and fears about Saudi Arabia's future are by no means confined to Western pessimists. In all the lesser states, there is a whistling through the teeth when Saudi Arabia is discussed. It is on the lines of 'If they make it, we all will, and if they don't, we all go down.'

Shrewd Arab observers note the increasing divorce rate, the frustrations of the Saudi middle class, the rocketing growth in the video market, the use of alcohol and drugs. They also see a royal family big and diverse enough to contain radically different groups, and armed forces whose nature is changing with expansion and re-equipment.

In the fort-like suburbs of Kuwait, a city which has always believed in working out the odds on the future, television aerials of immense height and complication top the stubby skyline like a hairpiece. The Kuwaitis, most sophisticated of the peoples of the Gulf, tune to every station within 500 miles. As always, they want to be the first to get the news – good or bad.

For the region of which they are part it can only be said that the formula of the last twenty years, a vast development which, while it has benefited citizens, has also by-passed and even emasculated them, is beginning to reverberate with danger signals. The question is now whether the two parties which devised that formula – the West and the Gulf's Royal governments – are ready to try to change it.

16 April 1981   **Martin Woollacott**

A country diary: Kent 1

Have you seen the ghost? Have you see the monkey? Strange
questions asked in a disused quarry. Unwittingly I was back
on the orchid hunt. There were enthusiasts around with
rumours of sightings of the rarest orchids, and I could not
avoid getting caught up in the general air of excitement.
Evidently, the wet spring has made this an outstanding year
for the rare flowers, and the arc of hills around us was one of
the most promising locations in the entire country. Wisely, no
one would say exactly where they saw them, merely waved
hesitant hands over large areas of the map indicating beech
woodlands in the far distance in the most general way
possible. There was no need to search for the more common
species. They were clustered round our feet. In that small
quarry heavily used by local children as a playground there
were five species, standing up proudly from the patches of tall
grass. Man orchid going to seed; Common Spotted ranging
from pink to pure white; Fragrant orchid in loose spikes;
Pyramidal, a much deeper purple, just appearing. A grassy
track through the adjacent woodland was lined with them,
many species appearing side by side, creating hybrid forms.
An accidental diversion through the woods produced the
bird's nest orchid, a small inconspicuous spike of brown
growing direct from the bare ground beneath the trees. That's
one of the pleasures of orchids. They seem to come and find
you when you're not really looking. Among all these treasures
was a white flower freshly opening, smelling like meadow-
sweet. The dropwort, for such it was, was abundant on the
slope above. Yet this is the only place I have ever seen this
flower. The occurrence of such flowers always puzzles me.
They are so variable in time and place. Standing here you
would think orchids and dropwort were as common as rock
roses.

26 June 1981   **John T White**

Letters from a fainthearted feminist 2

Dear Mary,

How my heart raced when I read your last letter and learnt that your Women's Sub-Orgasmic Therapy Group has been discussing little me. Or rather, as you more discreetly put it, 'my type'. Such a relief you all concluded that 'my type' is not really neurotic *as such* but is merely 'an organism appropriately adapted to a restricted environment like a crossopterygian fish.' Well, ta ever so, sister. A man once told me his wife never cooked *as such* and another man confided that he didn't have sex *as such*. I couldn't bring myself to ask as such *what* in case the answer was too boggly but I do know I'm not at all like a crossopwhatsit fish, even as such.

Personally, since you're not asking I think people, who keep talking to cushions, as you say your group does, are already well on the road to the bin and no as such about it. And I'd be glad if you'd inform the next cushion you converse with that this particular organism will shortly leave its restricted environment and hit them all over the head with its appropriately adapted handbag unless they stop discussing it instanter. As for you, be warned. One of these days I may be forced to telephone the News of the Screws and reveal to a stunned public that behind Smash Video-Porn and Vegans Against Sexism and Lesbians for the Whale and Women Pavement Artists' Workshop and Wages Due Very Small Grannies in Hair Nets there is only you and Mo squatting on overdue library books at 2 Sebastopol Terrace with an old Imperial you ripped-off back stage, the night you raided the Miss World contest. So watch it.

My friend in America sent me this really depressing article, all about how the whole country is awash with wonderfully warm, highly educated, deeply brilliant and purposefully independent women who come home from their executive jobs and spend the night sobbing in their lonely beds because they can't find a single man who isn't either gay or being mobbed on all sides by hundreds of other wonderfully warm, highly educated etcetera women hungry for their annual quickie. At least, I think the writer meant quickie but you never know with Americans – one came into the pub the other day and asked for a mushroom quickie, which was the cute way he pronounced quiche.

And the article went on that when these men do decide to marry, they 'marry down', which means they get themselves hitched to dumb blondes well below them on the evolutionary ladder, which must take some doing. Of course, that's a typical mcp ploy, making sure you're top dog by picking a pussy cat of very few brains with whom to exchange vows of eternal domination-submission, but we have to remember that though American men are God's gift to no-one, all those warm, wonderful women are also American. That means most of them spent most of their time verifying their perceptualisations, relating to their authentic selves, demanding positive ego-reinforcement, diagnosing their Irritable Bowel Syndrome (IBS) detailing their Pre-Menstrual Tension (PMT) and then telling everyone to have a good day. No wonder the sexes are drifting apart. Never mind. If things go on this way, Americans will shortly stop producing little Americans, the whole race will vanish from the earth and we can all breathe a sigh of relief.

And another thing, Mary, before we bury the Gestalt hatchet. I'm sure it's very nice and unselfish of you to say you're working on your feelings with the aim of becoming a truly caring and accessible friend but, to tell you the honest truth, I prefer the old uncaring, fairly inaccessible you I know and love. OK? As for me, I have been taking lessons from old Mother Nature who is all around me, especially in Ben's room. There amongst the luxuriant flora and fauna – curls of dry orange peel, banana skins, stale jam crusts, half-bottles of festering milk and cups containing tea leaves half as old as time – two of God's little creatures live and have their being. Ben won them three years ago on Hampstead Heath and brought them home, two goldfish in a plastic bag. Ever since, they have swum round and round in a green and slimy bowl, hardly ever cleaned, hardly ever fed. I have threatened to call in the Hunt Saboteurs to spray lemon in his eyes. I have vowed that the Animal Liberation Front will vivisect him in his bed but all to no avail. Yet do the wretched fish protest? They do not. His friends' goldfish, treated properly, have all given up their little goldfish souls a long time ago. His flourish. Their scales gleam, their fins waggle, they are clearly in the pink.

Same applies to the Gerties, Ben's white mice. Sunk in Stygian gloom, their only pals the gaping goldfish, nothing to do all day but hide their heads in straw and they're happy as clams and what, for heaven's sake, have clams to be happy about? Plants are the same. Leave them in draughts over radiators, their earth as dry as Arizona and what do they do? Put out shy little shoots and coy buds. Start to care, bustle around them, give them doses of plant food, chat to them and they reward you by turning brown and passing away.

There's a lesson there for us all, Mary, and especially for me. Neglect is Good. Care kills. And that is my new life plan for Josh. He didn't come home at the weekend after all. No sooner had I transferred the contents of Sainsbury's to my pantry and the fridge had produced enough ice to sink the *Titanic* than I got his cable. Can't make it back Thursday, bringing Irene. So Ms Boss is now Irene, is she? Well this is my new scenario. 'Hullo Irene. Hullo Josh. Have some green slime. A little stale fishmeal? I'm off to beddy-byes, goodnight Irene.'

Yours from a whole new space,

11 March 1981   Martha

Born-again America

Five young couples, the men dressed in dark three-piece suits, their wives in long scarlet dresses, stand close together, their heads nestling over five coloured microphones. 'After the Civil War,' one of the young men intones, 'General Robert E. Lee went to a church in Washington and knelt down next to a black man to pray. Someone asked him why. General Lee replied: "Why not? The ground is level at the foot of the cross."'

The group begins to sway and croon: 'The ground is level at the foot of the cross.' Three thousand people packed into the redbrick Baptist church in south-west Virginia sit raptly in their pews.

The American South has spawned many mass movements and many varieties of Christianity in its time. Here in the Thomas Road Baptist Church in the small town of Lynchburg, the South is launching a new kind of evangelism for the Eighties. A revivalist crusade over liberal humanism and the permissiveness of the Sixties and Seventies, a movement which transcends the racial divisions of past generations and reflects the mood of anger, impatience and self-doubt which afflicts so many Americans.

Ironically, the evangelical movement poses a threat to Jimmy Carter, the first born-again Christian to occupy the White House for a long time, who himself came to power as an outsider preaching the traditional virtues of strong and decent families in a strong and decent America.

The new movement combines the technology of computerised mass mailings and television broadcasting, the so-called electronic church, into a national political campaign. Its fury is directed against equal rights for women, homosexuality and abortion. It demands a restoration of prayer in public schools and a militarily supreme America which must outspend and outgun the Soviet Union.

Perhaps the surprise is that it has taken so long for evangelists to move into the national political arena. In the 30 years since Billy Graham first made born-again Christianity into a mass media affair, other charismatic preachers have spread their influence across the country. But only in the last five years has religious broadcasting grown in leaps and bounds, and only in the last two years has it started active lobbying for specific political changes.

Rev. Jerry Falwell, the founder and pastor of the Thomas Road Baptist Church, is at the crest of the new wave. A friendly man with a double chin, a smile which frequently

101

turns smug, and a plumpish figure, he has the manner of a successful salesman rather than a charismatic leader. But there is no doubt that he commands enormous loyalty from his followers.

In the 24 years since he started his church in what was then the Donald Duck Bottling Company's headquarters, he has seen his empire grow rapidly. His Sunday morning services are broadcast on 304 stations in the US under the title *The Old Time Gospel Hour*, with the entire cost paid by millions of contributions from viewers. He has started a secondary school called the Lynchburg Christian Academy, and a Liberty Baptist college with more than 2000 students. There is a total ban on alcohol, cinema, and rock music and all male students wear ties on campus. Immediate expulsion awaits any student who enters the room of a member of the opposite sex at any time.

Other evangelicals have also started universities and TV programmes but Mr Falwell was picked by a group of right-wing politicians eager to forge a national movement. A combination of hellfire preaching, bigotry against intellectuals, financial huckstering, and super-patriotism is an old mixture in American politics, particularly in the Bible belts of the South and South-West. But television has given it a new dimension.

Howard Phillips, a former Nixon aide and organiser of the 'Conservative Caucus', Paul Weyrich, a leader of 'The Committee for the Survival of a Free Congress', Robert Billings, an Indiana Republican, and Ed McAteer, a former marketing man for Colgate Palmolive, were the core. They persuaded the Rev. Falwell to found an organisation last year, called The Moral Majority.

It now claims to have the support of 72,000 pastors around the country. They say they have already registered three million new voters, and hope to bring the total up to four million by the time of the election. This is what worries the Carter people, and many liberal candidates in this autumn's Senate elections, including Gary Hart of Colorado, John Culver of Iowa, George McGovern of South Dakota, Alan Cranston of California, and Birch Bayh of Indiana. If these five were defeated, for example, all chance of ratifying the SALT Treaty would be dead.

Besides Moral Majority there are other Christian lobbies such as the Religious Roundtable and the California-based Christian Voice which produces a Report Card on the way Congressmen have voted on fourteen key 'family issues'. The cards are sent to ordinary citizens and newspapers, and can have important influence, resulting in one paper carrying photographs of various Congressmen under the headline Saints and Sinners.

Being a clergyman is no guarantee of immunity against the Report Card. Only one of the six clergymen in Congress scored more than 50 per cent on this morality rating. Mr Falwell has made it clear that even a born-again Christian is not safe from His wrath, if he does not vote correctly. The most recent victim of the Moral Majority's campaign was John Buchanan, a Baptist minister. A Republican member of Congress for the past sixteen years, Mr Buchanan alienated conservative Christians by taking moderate stands in support of women and blacks. That was enough to bring out 2500 volunteers from Moral Majority who went from door to door in the Republican primary in Birmingham, Alabama this month, 'educating voters on the moral issues' as their local organiser put it. Mr Buchanan lost.

Rev. Falwell is strongly against President Carter because of similar stands. But he says he does not endorse individual candidates on the grounds that he would 'weaken his cause' if he did. 'Although I'm certain that Jimmy Carter is not the political Messiah for this country,' he said in an interview in his large, dimly-lit office with its yellow stained-glass windows, 'I'm not at all sure that Mr Reagan is. Besides,' he admits with some honesty, 'I don't want to alienate myself from half the population of this country.'

He puts great emphasis on Congress, mainly because it is more important than the Presidency on most of the issues he cares about. His 'laundry list for the Eighties' includes constitutional amendments to ban abortion and permit voluntary prayer in schools, defeat for the equal rights amendment, stiffer penalties for pornography and drugs, no national health

doorstep? Nevertheless, they are also silly. I can't explain how, they just are.

And so will you be if you insist on training yourself in Caring. You've got it wrong, Mary. Women should care a bit less so that men can care a bit more. Daily, I conduct my own one-woman in-home classes. Martha, I say to myself, today you will not care that the floor needs scrubbing, the sink is blocked and we're down to two fish fingers. You will not care that the roses are unpruned and the cats unwormed. You will ignore Ben demanding who's pinched his Biology Project, Jane moaning about how boring everything is and Mother just moaning. Don't care was made to care, my father used to say, but he meant me, not him.

Before my new leaf turned, I worried about everything. Starving Ethiopians, gulls in oil slicks, mugged old ladies, badgers, apartheid, Sri Lankan workers on tea plantations and the bits that fall off Suffolk villages when juggernauts drive by. You name it, I've cared about it. My cheeks have fallen in, my teeth are falling out, I've got white flecks on my nails and a twitchy sciatic nerve and still Ethiopians starve, gulls get oiled and bits fall off Suffolk villages. Whereas Josh, who only cares about the MLR and the state of his shirts, blooms.

Yes, Josh has finally returned. He and Ms Boss – or Irene, as I am now instructed to call her – zoomed back from Brussels on Thursday. They were high on travel, I was low on Home sweet home. Irene must be at least my age but then so am I, so that's no advantage and as far as coiffures go, I'm still cantering up to the starting post. Josh remarked on how small and dark the kitchen looked, Irene said everything was delightful. Delightful home, delightful baby, delightful to meet delightful me. She said Ben was delightful too, and even I, who gave him birth, know that delightful he isn't.

I stuck three frozen pizzas in the oven and she said how delightful home cooking was, after hotels. When I said could do with some hotel cooking myself, she gave me an understanding chuckle, put her hand over mine and d me she knew I didn't mean that because home-cooki and motherhood was the most rewarding career of all. What conversational exchange was left after that? Tisn't, tissn't,

'What variety is it?'

19 August 1980

tis? I wanted to say why waste your time then, rushing off to foreign parts with other people's husbands and getting four million pounds a year, if boiling nappies is your heart's desire, but Josh gave me one of his looks.

All through the meal they both chatted merrily on about macro-economics and private equity investments and people called names like Hoofy van Winkle and Jay Bee. Mind you, Irene was most polite. She kept leaning over to include me. Hoofy, she'd say, is the MD of IBD International. Had I noticed, she'd say, the pre-Budget 5 per cent over base rate and oh and yes and would you believe it, I'd say. What stick do I have, Mary? All I hear about is the 10 per cent rise in brassicas and that's only the price of cabbages in fancy dress. If home-making is so deeply rewarding, how come no women who aren't doing it want to hear about it? You don't, do you? I just keep telling you because it's good for you.

I mean, take two of my aunties. Mother rang about them last week. So sad about Aunt May, she said. Always so neat, *lived* for the children and Uncle John. Now she's gone peculiar. Came to see Mother, stared at her for a while, said 'I want my tea,' stuffed herself with scones and cake, said 'I want to go now,' and went; waddled off, says Mother, fat as a house, her hair all over the place. As for Aunt Myrtle, she spends all her waking hours packing. She packs, Uncle Eddie unpacks, she packs, Uncle Eddie unpacks. Mother puts on her compassionate voice and says it's senile dementia and they ought to be put in homes.

I say it's getting what you want at last, or trying.

Those two old ladies have looked after other people all their lives and now that they're looking after themselves they're instantly called dotty and put in homes. I said to Josh, the night he came back, would he put me in a home if I ate cake all day and packed, like Aunties May and Myrtle, and he said (compassionately) that he supposed he'd have to. Still, he'd brought me a very pretty nightie edged with Brussels lace and we retired to have a good time in it. We might have done, if Ben hadn't knocked on the bedroom door in the middle, asking could he have £3 for an all-night movie and where were his Converse All-Stars and did I know the baby was crying. Good idea, your Sub-Orgasmic Group, Mary, but what happens once you are orgasmic? Ben is what happens. I'm sure he's already done it himself but clearly it's never crossed his mind that Josh and I do it too or why would he rattle the door and shout Mum, it's *locked*, in an informative sort of voice. Can he still think step-fathers are just step-*fathers*?

Which reminds me, I got a letter from Ben's father yesterday. He says he's writing a book entitled The Flasher's Guide to Feminism, but more of that in my next. – Yours, frustrated,

18 March 1981   Martha

The end of a lovely affair

Those positioned high in the eyries of the creepered balconies could watch both matches – and the contrast could not have been greater. Miss Wade, for the last 'serious' time, gave us her full repertoire of grunts and groans and inner turmoils and haughty despair. Miss Barker, as ever, swayed dainty and delicate and dangerously on her usual tightrope, only keeping her balance with that great whooshing scythe of a forehand.

At the end the furrows on Miss Wade's tanned leather forehead were ploughed straight and deep. In future she would only play for fun. Thank heavens for that. Her dress was appropriately piped in purple as a nation mourned for the final time. They'd been together now for twenty years – and now, to all intents, Britain's affair with their arrogant yet ever vulnerable favourite, their nice-nasty, infuriating beloved Virginia, was finally over.

Over the way, Sue Barker, the heir apparent for so long metaphorically accepted the heavy hometown burden with a smile that lit up the day as the photographers inveigled her to pose with both little fists triumphantly clenched up alongside her ears as though, Lord help us, she was Dave Boy Green who's just kayoed a hired bum in the third.

As Virginia sighed a huge sigh and ferociously zipped up her rackets, hands up who didn't whistle deep for memories of four years ago when we stood to serenade her with 'For she's a jolly good fellow!' as she took the golden biscuit from Her Majesty? So tumultuous was the nation's noise that Virginia said afterwards, 'I couldn't hear what the Queen said to me, but it was just great to see her lips moving.'

For all the blind, blinkered and often boring patriotism that England and Wimbledon smoke-screened around Miss Wade each year, she was for much of her time just about our leading international sports girl. And a real original. She would rather go down spectacularly than win ordinarily, seemingly preferring to lose a brilliant rally than win a point by an unforced error.

Some years ago the American poet Galway Kinnell sent over a hymn of praise and devotion to Miss Wade's lion-like appeal: 'She was,' he wrote, 'the last amateur in the big time, the last utterly human player . . .

'She pursues absolute tennis, tennis which by its inner necessity will not only do that gross thing, win, but will also be recorded and remembered stroke by stroke, much as a great championship chess match is remembered.'

Precisely. Now, for England, it is very much 'Miss Barker to serve'. Let's hope she knows what she is in for.

26 June 1981   **Frank Keating**

A show for the European theatre?

I have been teaching and peace-working in the United States for five months, and the scene is frightening. Middle America has got itself into a Suez mood, and Reagan was floated to power on a tide of Know-Nothing nationalist sentiment unloosed by totally irresponsible media.

The burden of it all is this: America has been humiliated, first in Vietnam, then by a bunch of Iranian fanatics. America is being pushed around. The American armed forces are falling apart. The Russians have stolen a lead in arms. No one pushes Americans around. Reagan is going to stop that and go for US superiority. US technology is still the Greatest, and now it is time to use it. The first Commie or wog to get in Reagan's way and – WHAM!

This surge of nationalism is combined with an utterly unrealistic, indeed isolationist world-view: it is a sort of psychological isolationism armed with nukes. War is, always, something for export – 'over there'. It seems that few Americans, outside the liberal enclaves, understand that in any superpower conflict the North American continent will share in the common incineration.

I found three things especially frightening. First, there is an ugly hysteria about oil. Americans have been sold the notion that the Persian Gulf is an American sea, and that the Russians are poised to cut their jugular vein.

(Yet the US has huge stock-piles of oil, little over 10 per cent of US oil consumption comes from the Middle East, and this could easily, with benefit, be saved by a little conservation.)

Europeans are chided for being slow to prepare military interventions in the Middle East. We are now being asked to harbour in Europe (and contribute forces to) the US rapid deployment force of 100,000 men poised to defend the jugular vein. From the standpoint of the Middle East, 'defence' and good old imperialist aggression look much the same.

Second, there is an ugly desire to push Europe around, to bring the NATO states into more obedient clientage (paying more for their 'defence'), and to harden all East-West oppositions. During the long Polish crisis of this winter it became clear that the NATO hawks actually *wanted* Soviet military intervention in Poland. They were panting for the Russians to come, so as to legitimate a huge upping in military expenditure, and so as to confirm their own worst-case ideology. They need Russian actions of a kind to justify their own.

Third, and most threatening, is the confirmation of that process of the 'deep structuring' of the armaments race which I argued in *Protest and Survive*. Like actors summoned to cue, there enter now on the world stage Vice-President Bush (from the CIA) and General Haig, from NATO Command.

Democratic opposition to Haig's appointment centred on his seamy record in the Watergate affair. Less was said as to his role as the architect of the NATO 'modernisation' project. Haig has been not only a theorist of 'theatre war' but has actually directed a dry run for such a war in NATO's 'Wintex' exercises of 1977. As Supreme Allied Commander, Europe, he then signed the order for a NATO first nuclear strike to 'convey a decisive escalation of sufficient shock to convincingly persuade the enemy' to withdraw. More was to be split in this strike than a mere infinitive. The General nominated as targets five airfields in East Germany and five in Bulgaria, and three each in Czechoslovakia, Poland, and Hungary, as well as sundry troop assembly and supply areas for further strikes. Russia was not to be struck, the first time around.

This is the man who now is architect of US diplomacy. According to this scenario, after this first ('persuasive') strike, the President and the First Secretary will get together on the hot line and will agree to call the whole thing off. Everything that walks or grows or flies or swims on this planet will be at the mercy of the decision of two panic-struck silly old men.

And now General Haig's loyal successor, General Rogers, comes forward to sell us the neutron bomb. The cuddly, chuckling general was afforded prime TV time to explain, with a glint in his eye, how he, as a military man, needed (oh, so much!) this sweet piece of hardware, because he could then put it down among the enemy software, but in safety, only a few hundred yards in front of his own. But, of course (chuckle, chuckle) it was only a 'deterrent': the whole point of making it was that it would never be used.

The stench of those megadeaths, only a little way ahead of us in the future, is beginning to drift back into our present time. We begin to rise from our seats, in the European theatre, and make for the exits. But each time we try to move, in West Europe, the exits are blocked by those monstrous SS-20s. Have you noticed how they are multiplying, if not on the ground, then certainly in the Western official hand-outs? And multiplying perhaps they are. United States militarism looks so ugly at the moment – and its diplomacy so irresponsible – that it is possible for some in the Western peace movement to forget that Soviet militarism is ugly also. The upthrust of weaponry is reciprocal: the hawks continue to breed each others' hawks.

Last autumn I spoke at a large and friendly meeting in Manhattan's Riverside Church – a church with an outstanding record of work for international reconciliation. In a smaller discussion meeting afterwards, a well-briefed Russian (I think a Georgian) announced himself as secretary of the World Peace Council. In an eloquent and peace-loving statement he commended me for my correct delineation of the aggressive strategies of NATO, but then explained, very patiently, that I was mistaken in calling on the Soviet Union also to halt deployment of SS-20s. After all that I had said about NATO's menacing strategies I would surely agree that this was 'quite impossible'? The SS-20s were absolutely 'necessary' for the Warsaw powers' 'defence'.

I told him that he was arguing as a nationalist and not as an internationalist; that his arguments were the mirror-image of those of NATO apologists; and that, very certainly, the Soviet Union could take unilateral action, today, to halt or to reduce their SS-20s without endangering its security one iota. Moreover, no action would contribute more to the strengthening of the peace movement (and its arguments) throughout all Europe than this.

I think it is of great importance, at this moment of growth in the Western European movement, for us to keep steadily in view the strategy (however difficult) of bringing pressure upon *both* sides to disarm. I shall oppose Cruise and Trident whether or not the SS-20 is dismantled: these are evil and they bring us into greater danger. But our movement cannot succeed unless we can break, somehow, across that divide, and call forth reciprocal responses from the East.. To allow the Western peace movement to drift into collusion with the strategy of the World Peace Council – that is, in effect, to become a movement opposing NATO militarism *only* – is a recipe for our own containment and ultimate defeat. This will also meet with a refusal in those parts of Eastern Europe (Czechoslovakia, Poland) where much public opinion is utterly jaded with official 'peace-loving' propaganda, and where state-sponsored Peace Committees have never, throughout their whole 30-year existence, fluttered an eyelash in protest against any action of Soviet militarism.

The European Appeal insisted upon the need for lateral exchanges between citizens, by-passing the organs of the State; and insisted also upon the necessity for open exchanges of information and proposals between East and West. This entails a clear general commitment to the cause of civil rights and open communication in the East. Only in this way can the tissues begin to heal across East and West. Peace and democracy have to go together.

I wish I could write more fully about the initiatives now

being taken by individuals and groups in East and West Europe and in the US. But the *Guardian*, hospitable as it is, is not our organ: for this you must read the *END Bulletin*.

END has been around for less than a year. It is not in competition with CND or any other part of the British peace movement, but seeks to provide a European dimension to the work, with various specialist task groups furthering lateral exchanges. The size of the operation is already far greater than the initiators can cope with. END has now opened a London office (6 Endsleigh Street, WC1 0DX) to service some part of this work. But the opportunities on every side have outrun our exhausted treasury. (If this were a commercial I would add that we have launched an appeal, and cheques should be made out to 'European Nuclear Disarmament', but this would trespass too far upon this column's courtesy.)

The least movement of NATO is lavishly funded. Mr Nott is about to launch a deafening media operation to convert the British people to the cause of the missiles. Every penny of this is funded out of our own taxes. But to do the least thing to promote the cause of peace, we can do no other than tax ourselves.

23 February 1981   **E. P. Thompson**

The Begin revolution

Menachem Begin has reverted to type. Not so much to the terrorist Begin of Arab propaganda and selective British memory, but to Begin the disciple of Vladimir Ze'ev Jabotinsky, the prophet of muscular Jewish nationalism that bred the Irgun Zvai Leumi and the Herut movement.

The Prime Minister is schizophrenic – Begin the demagogue brandishing a mailed fist and Begin the statesman craving respectability. During the June election campaign the first Begin submerged the second in a wave of intimidation and mob oratory, ethnic resentment and personality cult.

The intoxication of victory, however narrow, has perpetuated the change. The blitz on Beirut was its first expression. It was opposed by the two ex-generals in the outgoing Cabinet, Yigael Yadin and Ariel Sharon. The army could point to no strategic justification. Begin willed it, and Begin could not be denied.

This revolution has polarised Israeli society, less between Western and Oriental Jews, than between fundamentally different conceptions of a Jewish state. Visitors detect a degree of mutual hostility between the two camps they have never found before. Half the country feels not just that it lost an election, but that its way of life is in danger.

For all its compromises and paternalism, the Labour movement, which ruled Israel throughout its first three decades and dominated the pioneering years of the state, was rooted in the Liberal-Socialist tradition. However reluctantly, it came to terms with a rival claim on Eretz Yisrael, the ancient homeland. David Ben-Gurion embraced the partition of the promised land.

Menachem Begin never did. The emblem of Betar, the Herut youth organisation, to this day flaunts 'both banks of the Jordon' as the Jewish patrimony. For Begin, Palestinian nationalism is a fraud. The Palestinians may be allowed autonomy, but never sovereignty. There is no place for accommodation. The Jew must be proud and mighty. Concession is weakness, criticism is either anti-Semitism or Jewish self-hatred. If the world must be defied, so be it.

Opposition is seen as treachery. Israel remains a democracy; Begin the statesman rejoices in that. Parliament flourishes, the press is free. But Herut's innate authoritarianism is asserting itself. Within the public sector, independent voices are being suppressed. The two deputy governors of the Banks of Israel, a counterweight to the Treasury in economic policy-making, have been dismissed. The governor is expected to follow, to be replaced by a party nominee.

Ministers are waging a guerrilla war against the Israel Broadcasting Authority, whose charter is modelled on that of the BBC. Yoram Aridoer, whose electioneering economics was second only to Begin's mass appeal in winning the Likud a second term, refuses to be interviewed by Israel Television's financial correspondent, whom he charges with being antigovernment. The director-general of the broadcasting authority, Josef Lapid, recognises this as an attempt to dictate a choice of specialist reporter and is resisting, fortified by the knowledge that he was appointed because of his right-wing views and can hardly be purged because of 'bias'.

Begin constantly evokes his doctrinal origins. He is a son of Betar, the commander of what Irgun veterans call the 'fighting family', the founder of Herut, which increasingly sets the tone for the Likud block of parties and factions.

'Herut,' Ezer Weizman wrote in his recently-published memoirs, 'was a tiny preserve for an endangered species'. The former defence minister, who was in the movement but never of it, depicted Herut as 'Menachem Begin's sculpture park', with a statue of Jabotinsky as its largest and most imposing monument.

Jabotinsky died forty-one years ago, yet the more you observe Begin, the more you listen to what he says, the more you are convinced that Vladimir Ze'ev remains his inspiration.

Last week Begin paid homage at Jabotinsky's graveside on Mount Herzl in Jerusalem. 'Western Eretz Yisrael is in our full control,' the Prime Minister proclaimed, 'It will not be divided again. No part of its territory will be handed over to foreign rule or sovereignty. We believe the day will come when the two parts of Eretz Yisrael will establish peacefully, in agreement and understanding, an alliance of nations, a free confederation for co-operation.'

It was not a foreign policy pronouncement, or signal to King Hussein, who happens to reign over 'Eastern Eretz Yisrael', it was a rededication to the ideals of the master, an act of appeasement to the blessed memory. The other bank of the Jordan had not been forgotten.

Jabotinsky was not simply a right-wing nationalist. His Zionism, like that of the Labour movement, grew out of European soil. But its progenitors were twentieth rather than nineteenth century.

Schlomo Avineri, professor of political science at the Hebrew University, analysed Jabotinsky's thought in an essay published last summer in the *Jerusalem Quarterly*.

'Jabotinsky,' he wrote, 'was a polished European gentleman towering above other Zionist leaders between the world wars in his cultural attainments, sensibilities and intellectual horizons . . . No Zionist leader could rival his accomplishments . . . poet and translator, essayist and novelist.'

Begin has stayed true to his teacher, with one major exception. Jabotinsky was a secular nationalist. He would have winced at Begin's skullcap, at his frequent invocations of divine will, and above all at Begin's theocratic partnership with the religious parties, including one (Agudat Yisrael) which does not even acknowledge the legitimacy of the Jewish state.

The greatest irony is, however, that Begin has fallen victim to the same contradiction as Jabotinsky. Their dogma rests on Jewish power. In Jabotinsky's heyday, the Jews of Eretz Yisrael were few and weak. He sought to persuade imperial Britain that its interests were identical with that of Zionist self-fulfilment.

In the 1980s Israel has the strongest army, navy and air force in the Middle East. Yet it remains dependent, not on the British but on the United States. Begin, encouraged by the campaign rhetoric of the Reagan administration, is seeking to persuade Washington that American and Israeli interests are identical. The haste with which the Prime Minister accepted last month's ceasefire with the Palestinians at the crack of an American whip demonstrated that Washington, too, was not so persuaded.

4 August 1981   **Eric Silver**

The Kremlin and Cold War II

Moscow is enjoying its mildest winter for years. For the past fortnight no fresh snow has fallen at all. Pavements which in February and March are usually a mass of slush, interspersed with lumpy ice where thawing snow has frozen overnight, are smooth and dry. Instead of having to keep your eyes on the ground and your face inclined against the wind, pedestrians can look up at the façades and domes of this handsome city in unaccustomed winter sunshine. Marvellous though the weather was for the thousands of delegates who were in town for the party Congress, it seemed unsuited to the prevailing mood. Five years ago President Brezhnev could tell the previous Congress: 'The world is changing before our eyes, and changing for the better.'

His optimism was justified. Western politicians who talk endlessly about the Soviet Union were at last talking to it. Some even bothered to visit the country. Mr Brezhnev had had three summit meetings with American Presidents in the previous four years. He had signed one strategic arms limitation treaty and was in the middle of negotiating another. Under President Nixon and Dr Kissinger the United States had accepted the concept of strategic parity with the Soviet Union.

Of course there were disappointments. Relations with China were going from bad to worse. In the Third World the United States was still highly competitive. Egypt had asked the Soviets to leave, and the Americans were eagerly filling the gap. In Chile a potential friend had been overthrown in a military coup.

This time the picture looks very different. An American retreat towards a more rigidly anti-Soviet posture which first became evident in the middle of 1978 has culminated in the election of a President whose attitudes go back to the days of the Cold War. His vocabulary, with its accusations that the Soviets 'lie and cheat' and are bent on annexing the rest of the world into a single Communist state, has not been heard from the White House for 20 years. Even as the party Congress was under way, this man was announcing the biggest increase in military spending in history, and thereby inevitably challenging Moscow to follow suit.

No wonder that Mr Brezhnev sounded glum as he called the world situation 'rough and complicated'. In a rare reference to the cost to the Soviet economy of military spending, he said that the slowing down of détente and the new arms race 'are no small burden for us as well'.

Beyond the sphere of relations with the United States, the outlook is little better. Poland is in turmoil, with 'the pillars of the socialist state in jeopardy', as he put it. China has begun to destroy the legacy of Mao but its foreign policy is still fiercely anti-Soviet. In Afghanistan what was intended as a limited police action has become a quagmire. In Africa and Latin America there has been little of great cheer, and Mr Brezhnev passed over these two continents in his speech with barely a mention. The non-aligned movement which was once a potential beacon of hope for Moscow has turned against it over Afghanistan, and was dealt with in a single paragraph.

Faced with these awesome difficulties, Mr Brezhnev and his comrades took one overriding decision. They felt they must restore a dialogue with the United States. It is hard to find anyone in the diplomatic community in Moscow who does not feel that Mr Brezhnev's offer of a summit meeting was sincerely meant. It was a serious, perhaps desperate, perhaps – in the present climate in Washington – futile effort to get arms negotiations going again before the nuclear race reaches a stage of technical sophistication which will make attempts to verify agreements impossible.

Everything else pales before this Soviet priority. It was noticeable how little space Mr Brezhnev devoted to his relations with France and West Germany, who had been so civil to him over the last two years when President Carter began to turn away. Now Mr Brezhnev seemed to forget about them in his effort to stress that Soviet-American relations have to be the centrepiece of détente.

If this Soviet insistence on dialogue with the United States was the most striking theme of the Congress, there were other strong impressions, from both Mr Brezhnev and the other Soviet representatives who spoke. No one could claim that this Congress was a place for open and honest discussion or a forum for a wide-ranging debate on the Soviet Union's future. But there were hints of a greater sophistication in handling the problems of trade unions, consumers and national minorities. Mr Brezhnev touched, however obliquely, on many social ills – alcoholism, vandalism, corruption, and crime. Economic difficulties were not ignored.

Party Congresses provide the only opportunity for five years for party leaders from every region of the country to speak publicly in the capital. Reading their speeches in *Pravda* is tough going, but a useful reminder of a point which is usually ignored in the West. This is a highly centralised, but not a monolithic country. Its different republics are far more diverse than the East and West coasts of the United States. In climate, culture and language this is the world's most varied state.

Slowly and hesitantly the Soviet Union is undergoing a political modernisation. Admittedly Mr Brezhnev and his senior colleagues made it clear at this Congress that they intend to die in office. Not only are they not preparing for the succession, it seems quite possible that they are not even thinking about it. But the West's natural focus on the succession at the very top may be obscuring the fact that there is a growing body of foreign policy advisers in their forties and fifties who are much better educated and better-travelled than the present men in the Politburo.

They have worked abroad as journalists or diplomats, and provide a far greater stratum of expertise than was available a generation ago when the Soviet Union had had diplomatic relations with only a handful of countries. These men know the West, Eastern Europe and the Third World. They work in the Central Committee, the Foreign Ministry or academic institutions like the Institute for the Study of the World Economy and International Relations, the Institute for the Study of the US and Canada, or the Institute for the Study of the East.

A new theory seems to have emerged among Western hawks that these people, because they are too young to have fought in the Second World War, may be more 'adventurist' and more likely to risk world peace and nuclear war than veterans like Mr Brezhnev.

First of all, the theory is founded on weak demographic ground. Although they themselves did not fight in the war, many of them lost fathers and in some cases mothers among the 20 million Soviet citizens who died. It will be at least another 15 to 20 years before the children of the postwar baby bulge, whose links with the war really are weaker, reach senior positions.

15 August 1981

Even then the theory of 'adventurism' rests on nothing but a hunch. It is just as likely that people who have lived through the relatively good years since the war, and have enjoyed a gradual increase in prosperity, will be more materialistic and less willing to risk everything than those who went through the 1930s and 1940s.

Private talks with the new pool of foreign policy advisers – who help to write Mr Brezhnev's speeches, or write commentaries in the Soviet media – certainly suggest a sense of realism and the limitations of Soviet power in a complex world. They admit, for example, that they will not be able to split Western Europe from the United States in any foreseeable future. Of course, they will play on differences for tactical and diplomatic reasons in the hope of minimising the arms race, at least in Europe, but they have no illusions about the deep political, economic, and cultural ties across the Atlantic.

They know that Soviet relations with China will take years to repair, if they are ever repaired at all. In the Third World they know that the end of political colonialism has not produced the automatic dividends for Moscow which Soviet politicians expected 20 years ago. They admit frankly that the Third World is unpredictable. In Iran some argue that Khomeini will be succeeded by another Islamic regime; others put their money on a secular national bourgeois government led by President Bani-Sadr or someone similar. In either case they admit that Iran showed that not everything which is bad for the Americans is good for the Russians.

They admit that Afghanistan was more costly than they anticipated. One relayed the comment he had heard from Soviet army generals who had come to Moscow for the Congress – 'Our soldiers don't have any work to do. You have these people in the villages by day, and at night they get out guns and shoot our men.' Shades of the Vietnam war.

Some are disparaging about the 'barrack-room socialism' they find in countries in Africa whose revolutions are hardly more than skin-deep. Others complain that the cost of aiding their friends is high (a complaint shared by many ordinary Russians).

These new doubts about involvement in the Third World have to be measured against the relatively few benefits the Soviet Union gets from it. The Soviet Union exports no capital and earns no profits. It is almost entirely self-sufficient in raw materials and imports few essentials from the Third World. Its relationship is not that of a classic imperialism, but rather a series of marriages of convenience, in which Moscow mainly provides arms and technical assistance in exchange for nothing more valuable than temporary political influence and, occasionally, military facilities. Even in Eastern Europe, where the Soviet role is more strictly imperial, the economic costs are high. A major factor restraining the Russians from going into Poland is the knowledge that they alone would then have to pay its bills.

In short, among the widening ranks of Soviet officials who are aware of the complexities of the world, one finds little of the appetite for expansionism of which they are so often accused. What they share with the men at the very top are old Russian attitudes – a desire for docile buffer states on their borders and a deep fear of encirclement.

Washington's acceptance of parity in the 1970s was important for them psychologically. Now they feel indignant at the non-ratification of the SALT II treaty, not because they think the new Administration is really concerned about its detailed provisions, but because they feel the new men in Washington 'resent the image of parity and want to re-assert American supremacy', as one official put it.

8 March 1981   **Jonathan Steele**

The writing on the wall for Reagan

The capital cities of the republics of Central America are surrounded, for the most part, by huge volcanoes. Some are smoking and have half the crust torn away to reveal a red hot internal lake of fire. Others are quiescent, silhouettes on the skyline. Eric Wolf, the great anthropological investigator of

Central America, called his book on the area *Sons of the Shaking Earth*.

Today the seismic activity is mostly political. The entire isthmus is absorbing the reverberations of the great Sandinista upheaval in Nicaragua in July 1979 that swept away Somoza. In almost every country new forces are emerging. Simply by existing, without having to lift a finger in support of struggles elsewhere, the Nicaraguan revolution has changed the atmosphere – just as the collapse of Portuguese rule in Angola and Mozambique gave hope to the blacks of Soweto and Zimbabwe.

All over Central America the old battles between peasants and landlords, between guerrillas, bandits and regular soldiers, are being joined again. The ancient alliance between Church and State has been broken. Even the old ruling class is at odds with itself. The local armed forces, corrupt and divided, turn increasingly to the most barbaric forms of repression to sustain their crumbling position. The grisly work of the officially-inspired death squads continues unabated and unchecked. Priests and nuns, journalists and academics, trade unionists and politicians – no one is entirely safe. But the great bulk of the assassinations take place in the countryside, involving anonymous peasants – a largely unreported and unsung struggle.

Yet the great mass of the people, denied a voice for decades, are now finding new leaders and fresh ways of expressing their grievances. Honduras is still quiescent, but in El Salvador, units of the recently-united Farabundo Marti Liberation Front are trying to spark off a country-wide insurrectionary struggle. In Guatemala the Ejercito Guerrillero de los Pobres – the Guerrilla Army of the Poor – has embarked on the same project.

And all this is taking place just down the road from California and Texas, in the vulnerable backyard of the United States. If historical precedent is anything to go by, the area will provide the backdrop to the first great crisis of the Reagan presidency. For when has the United States allowed red volcanoes to erupt in its sphere of influence without trying to suffocate them? Guatemala in 1954, Cuba in 1961, Santo

Domingo in 1965, Chile in 1973. Against this record, how much longer will Nicaragua be allowed to survive? And can Reagan's America stand idly by while El Salvador and Guatemala explode?

El Salvador is the latest flashpoint in the growing crisis, a foreseen and inevitable development. You don't have to be a Pentagon general to have predicted the toppling of the Central American dominoes. The late General Anastasio Somoza maintained an intricate weave of relationships, both economic and military, with all the countries of the isthmus. Without their Nicaraguan godfather, and his easy access to the advice and expertise of the American military in the Canal Zone, the purposeful march of the Central American dictators has been faltering. Confronted with a new and changing situation, even the officers in their armies are divided as to what to do and how to meet the challenge. Some, a minority, demand reform. Others advocate sterner methods of repression.

On the left there is a new mood of optimism. After years of political opportunism and heroic failure, there is a feeling that change is now possible. People are sharpening their pens and dusting down their old handbooks on guerrilla war. The Sandinistas have a slogan, posted on the hoardings around Managua, '*El amanecer dejo de ser una tentacion.*' It means, roughly translated, 'the dawn of the revolution is no longer a dream.'

For the Americans – for the State Department, the Pentagon, the press and the business community – Central America has for long remained a conundrum. For more than a quarter of a century, ever since the CIA helped overthrow the left-wing government in Guatemala of Jacobo Arbenz in 1954, it was *terra incognita*. State Department policy towards the area was conspicuous by its absence. Propaganda in favour of the reformist slogans of the Alliance for Progress in the Sixties fell on deaf ears.

Oligarchic and military governments were put together and patched up by the Pentagon and American business interests on a purely pragmatic basis. General Somoza was a model for the area. The American press dutifully reported coups and earthquakes but otherwise took no interest.

Now all that has changed. Reporters from the *New York Times* and the *Washington Post* travel up and down the isthmus. Think tanks in Washington feed Central America into their computers. Ambassadors on special mission and assistant secretaries of state jet into the capital cities for emergency consultations. Meanwhile, businessmen and military advisers wring their hands.

The Republicans tend to blame Carter for handing Nicaragua to the Sandinistas on a plate – though that was never the State Department's aim, and the guerrillas had to fight for what they eventually won. Old Southerners argue, more convincingly, that the man who began the destabilisation of Central America was Henry Kissinger – 'the faceless wonder in striped pants' as they used to call him – who embarked on the process of 'giving away' the Canal Zone. More important than either was the earthquake of Christmas 1972 which destroyed the city of Managua and eventually, in the aftermath of intensified corruption and misrule, helped to destroy Somoza himself.

Whatever the origins of the crisis which has now spread from Nicaragua to the rest of Central America, it is one peculiarly of the Americans' own making, and one for which they alone bear responsibility. Unlike other trouble spots in the world – the Middle East, Africa, South-East Asia, Europe itself – Central America is an area where the Europeans have few interests in play. The United States is alone with its backyard, without allies. The fact that Britain owns Belize and once held the Atlantic coast of Nicaragua is largely irrelevant.

More significant are the recommendations of Venezuela and Mexico, now more than ever important as the suppliers of America's oil. They are both firm supporters of the Sandinista government and would deprecate any American move to overthrow it. But they need the American market at least as much as America needs them, and in the past they have never been powerful arbiters of hemispheric policies. And their attitude towards the unfolding crisis in El Salvador, which demands the most immediate attention, is profoundly ambiguous.

In their campaign rhetoric, the Reagan Republicans convinced themselves, misguidedly, that what was going on in Central America was Moscow-inspired. 'Must we,' said Reagan, 'let Nicaragua, El Salvador all become additional "Cubas", new outposts for Soviet combat brigades? Will the next push of the Moscow-Havana axis be northward to Guatemala and thence to Mexico, and south to Costa Rica and Panama?'

Seeing the world in such simple terms, the campaign rhetoric went on to demand simple solutions. 'If we are confronted with the choice,' said Jeane Kirkpatrick, now selected to be Reagan's ambassador at the United Nations, 'between offering assistance to a moderately repressive autocratic government which is also friendly to the United States, and permitting it to be overrun by a Cuban-trained, Cuban-armed, Cuban-sponsored insurgency, we would assist the moderate autocracy.'

This was perhaps meant as nothing more than the reiteration of an old Republican tradition. But in the Eighties the United States would be hard-pressed to find 'a moderately repressive autocrat' to run their Central American fiefdoms. Both in El Salvador and in Guatemala the old conservative interests that the United States has backed for decades are now fighting with every weapon they can find. There is no 'moderation' in their policies. Thousands of people have been assassinated in both countries as the dying order struggles to survive. So in practice the new United States administration (which, in General Haig, has a Secretary of State typically unversed in the detail of Central America) will be forced either to follow the Carter line (with a different rhetoric), or to embark on a programme of military intervention, however disguised. If it cannot patch up governments in El Salvador and Guatemala that try to find political outlets for the explosions from below, as Carter's ambassadors have tried to do, it will have to back up the dictators with more than words and money. That is certainly what the campaign rhetoric has led those dictators to expect. And it is exactly what Somoza's son asked for – and was denied – in the weeks before the Sandinista victory.

Would it not be possible, Tachito Somoza asked the

American ambassador in Managua, to send in several hundred American military advisers, officers familiar with Nicaragua, to move into the National Guard at command level and stiffen morale?

That is the kind of request that President Reagan's ambassadors in San Salvador and Guatemala City will shortly be receiving. It is a question to which Che Guevara always hoped the Americans would answer yes. 'Little by little,' he wrote, 'the obsolete weapons which are sufficient for the repression of small armed bands will be exchanged for modern armaments, and the United States military "advisers" will be substituted by United States soldiers, until at a given moment they will be forced to draft increasingly greater numbers of regular troops to ensure the relative stability of a government whose national puppet army is disintegrating before the attacks of the guerrillas. It is the road of Vietnam; it is the road that will be followed in our America . . .' It is the road that successive American administrations for the past 15 years have tried to avoid.

3 January 1981   **Richard Gott**

Thanks to Britain

I recall a dinner in Paris a few years ago. Our perversely playful host had invited the widows of a British wartime leader and of a French collaborationist of some renown. He sat the British lady on his right and the French *dame* on his left and while he spoke to them, they did not speak to each other.

I am sure our host enjoyed his small business. He knew the two distinguished women would leave as early as possible. When they had gone and he had duly registered the astonishment on our faces, as well as some tentative criticism about the presence of the notoriously pro-Nazi lady, he launched the postprandial debate he had been nursing all the way with these words: 'You know, if the other side had won the war, the English woman would be the villainess and the

Frenchwoman the heroine. All wars are the same: Victors heroes, losers villains.'

It was not a question of re-living the Hundred Years War in one night. The truth imposed itself, at least in my mind, in a searing flash: No, if the Nazis and their collaborators in Europe had won, they would not be heroes, nor the defeated villains; even in defeat, the heroes would have been heroes because in the Second World War no one was more heroic than the innocent victims. Oh, yes, what a lovely war, when everyone was sure of what side he was on, of where good and evil, respectively, resided.

But the war was not lost thanks to Britain. This is the simple and clear message I repeated to myself that night in Paris. No matter how awesomely heroical the massive resistance of the Soviets, how inevitable the triumph once the inexhaustible Americans had waded in, the war, for me, was won in the dark days of the Blitz. Or rather: *we* were not lost thanks to Britain. Without the gut courage of the English, we would all have fallen prey to the only demonic evil our·century of neon-lighted gloom has known. I will deem, as Origin deemed the Devil, even Stalin redeemable: he was the great perverter of a dream of justice. Nazism was programmed evil, a public policy and an avowed desire for evil. Somehow, Britain was there and because she was there they did not cross the Atlantic, they did not catch the Americans totally unprepared, they did not totally penetrate (though they tried mightily) Latin America.

So Britain appeared to my ten-year-old eyes as a shield. In one stroke, all the terrible crimes one could saddle on the back of British imperialism became *peccata minuta* next to its courageous stand against the diabolical and technological hatred nurtured by the Nazis. The problem of absolute evil is that it does not face absolute good because there is no such thing. The good of men and women is made up of certain values, many defeats, even more weaknesses, a sense of relativity, puzzled questions rather than dogmatic answers. The evil of Hitler did not limit itself to organising evil as a war machine. This had been and shall be done many times. He organised evil to penetrate the intimacy of good, its tenderness, the very weakness that happens to be, finally, the strength of the good. Think of the face of that Polish boy being driven at gun point from the Warsaw ghetto. Think of one single face (not all of them, please) from the photographic graveyards of the *Nacht und Nebel* programme of extermination.

So we forgot India and Ireland, Rhodes and Morgan, greed and piracy, insular exclusivity and uptight snobbishness. All the sins of England seemed to have been purged by the cataclysm imposed by Hitler on that little island. The world was large, the red areas we studied on our schoolroom maps never saw the sun set, but the sceptred isle was tiny and after the war it lost everything and suddenly there was only one red spot, a beacon for some, still; a shrinking case of imperial measles for others. See how the mighty have fallen, etc. But for the men and women of my generation, Britain was for ever associated with our own salvation.

I had been to one of the great British schools of South America, The Grange, in Santiago de Chile, during the war years. This enclave was a mini Britannia, with strenuous cross-country races, caning from time to time, rugby, and Ruskin, porridge for breakfast, and stiff-upper-lipped reception of military defeats. But when Montgomery broke through at Alamein, the assembled school tossed caps in the air and hip-hip-hurrahed to death.

In South America, clubs were named after George Canning and football teams after Lord Cochrane; no matter that English help to win independence led to English economic imperialism from oil in Mexico to railways in Argentina. There was a secret thrill in our Latin hearts: our Spanish conquistadores had been beaten by the English. Cortez burnt his own ships in Veracruz, but Philip II's Armada proved eminently vincible in England; the exploits of Drake (especially as embellished in an Errol Flynn swashbuckler) were a compensation to our own colonisation by Spain. If Britain was an Empire, at least she was a democratic one.

My generation, furthermore, was nurtured by readings in English literature. Many of us became novelists because we had first roamed Heathcliff's moors and taken the coach with

Copperfield and Mr Micawber into London; suffered with Tess D'Urberville in Wessex and revolted with D. H. Lawrence in Nottinghamshire, poked fun at the world with Waugh, and tried to understand it with Orwell. There seemed to be such an exemplary, unbroken fidelity to great writing in England, from Chaucer to Auden that, once again, political sins were absolved. We had to compare this literary vitality, as Spanish language writers, with the paucity of our own tradition, interrupted since the seventeenth century: no great novelists after Cervantes, no great poets in the three centuries between Gongora and Lorca.

We gathered at the Libreria Britanica in Mexico City, at the corner of a leafy plaza and a thunderous avenue, and pored over the fresh new volumes of English poetry, English philosophy, English detective stories. This was the postwar era and we knew the English were eating, still, less than we were in the middle-class suburbs of Mexico or Buenos Aires. We loved those beautifully plotted, superbly characterised British films of the era; David Lean and Carol Reed became household presences, as did the voice of Joan Greenwood, the face of Margaret Rutherford, even the melodramatic fingers of Margaret Lockwood. And then there were Britten whose operas we would hear on records and Henry Moore who had been inspired by Yucatan and Bacon who knew the world wasn't pretty and where had Elizabeth Bennett and Darcy been the year of the Peterloo Massacre, and had Becky Sharp been playing croquet in Delhi with her military consort while the great revolt took place?

So the two Englands, the two Nations, the literary Arcadia and the military Styx, the artistic Paradise, and the economic Purgatory, battled within our young consciousness in the Latin America of the 1940s. Yet the scars of Britain's own suffering were always on our minds. We could debate about England's triumphs and terrors within our own imagination; we never forgot that there was no such debate possible in the Hades offered by Hitler.

I suppose my Anglophilia also had something to do with the incredibly stupid pro-German stance of most of my Mexican school chums. The traditional reflex of Mexicans has been against the United States and in favour of whoever opposes the United States. In 1914 and then in 1939, this meant sympathy for Germany. You could admire in the Germans what you envied in the Americans, efficiency, technical prowess, know-how, discipline and the lot. I looked at the faces of my very non-Aryan schoolmates and bid them understand that they would become lampshades and their parents soap under the Nazis. Fights ensued; I was called pro-Yankee; I answered that I was only pro-British and anti-lampshades.

Then a most generous English critic and Hispanist, J. M. Cohen, gave me and other writers of my generation in Latin America the first taste of European publication and readership. He included us in his anthologies, reviewed us for the TLS, and launched our European careers. Spain was Franco: some of our books were banned in *La Madre Patria*. From England, the news of a new Latin American literature spread to France, Germany, Italy. We could also forgive England for the increasing sterility, in those years, of her own literature, the frivolity of her reading habits, the mesmerising telly, the fading away of the Ealing Studios and their universal pleasures, the incorporation of much of the British culture, that had ranged so far and wide because of its own eccentric, inimitable *cachet*, into the synthetic plush and bosh of international film-making, international fashion, international tourism: were Brief Encounter and Doctor Zhivago made by the same man? Lean times!

Latin America has always seen itself as an eccentric culture. The New World is a Utopia invented and then discovered by the Old World: humanist dreams, economic plunder and religious justification masked Indian empires, grafted African slaves, and ennervated the white Creole transplanted planters and whipsnapping whippersnappers. When we broke from Spain with English help, we wanted to become English (and French, and American) by extralogical imitation: the laws changed, the bad old habits remained and the result was corruption, oppression, and a self-conscious psychosis of defeat and inadequacy to the modern world.

The effort of the Latin American culture of the past three or five decades has been to dissolve this conflict between law and reality, which is truly a conflict between an unattainable future and a forgotten past. This is our eccentricity. The poems of Neruda, Vallejo and Paz, the fiction of Borges (Jorge Luis, the Argentinian mythologist), Cortazar and Cabrera Infante, the paintings of Tamayo, Toledo and Borges (Jabobo, the Venezuelan painter), the films of Littin, Solanas, and Leduc all tell us that there is no eccentricity at all in being here, today, in this world; that we have all become eccentric and therefore that we are now all universal because everyone is eccentric.

We do not have a clear idea of the role Britain is going to play in this eccentric world where being eccentric is more than living in draughty houses, maintaining a monarchy with all its trappings or dressing for dinner with cannibals. There was a strange universal sense of recapturing a past and then thrusting it into the future in the Beatles' supertransformation of hostile, forgotten rhythms (veritable *madeleine* of music) drawn from India, Tennessee, or Elizabethan England: Purcell's Parcel seemed much more attractive than Kipling's Cargo and then there was decolonisation and Indians speak English but the Dutch refuse to speak German still, and the Jamaicans became Latin Americans and taught us a thing or two about parliamentary procedure learnt from the British, and the Lords Carrington and Soames solved the problem of Rhodesia with a diplomatic *finesse* the brutal and ignorant American diplomats could never apply to El Salvador and in English we read Derek Walcott and V. S. Naipaul and Salman Rushdie and Nadine Gordimer and Chinua Achebe filling in for the passing paucity of British letters (but Golding came back, and Tomlinson and Hughes never went away and Ian McEwan and D. M. Thomas appeared on the scene) but oh Margaret Rutherford where are you when we need you most? Shall we hear the voice of Joan Greenwood again?

I mean: the world is going multipolar not just because of political reasons, but because the plural cultures of mankind are reappearing with all their rags and jewels and scabs and scarabs and contradictions: from Quetzalcoatl to Pepsicoatl, from Manhattan to Mahatma, from the Baroque to the Baroque 'n' Roll, from Frederic Chopin to Den Xiao Ping, from Sha-Sha-Sha to Ayatollah My Pretty Little Poppy, the motley crew of the Third World, but also the restless world of Central Europe as it reaches out and beckons to Western Europe, are undergoing a sea change of identity, differentiation, and assertion vis-a-vis the resurrected bipolar hegemony of the frozen fifties.

We all wonder whether Britain will sing along with Ronnie or establish its own, its proper voice in this coming world of diversity. Western Europe is certainly not immune to the soul-searching, the wrenching revision of its past and its future, the re-ordering of priorities for the twenty-first century, that are taking place in Mexico and Poland, in China and Zimbabwe, in France and Iran, in Israel and Libya.

Yet, who can ask too much of a nation that has given us so much? I would like an independent Britain free from the shackles of colonial mastery in Northern Ireland, free from its own past troubles and recipient to the news of the world; perhaps, not necessarily, a Socialist Britain proving that freedom and solidarity are not antagonistic, a Britain participating in Europe's real drive towards unity and independence from both power blocks, a Britain more and more supportive, for our own and for its own good, of development in Africa, Asia, and Latin America.

I do not know if this will happen. Only the British people can make it happen. But Britain, I have made it plain here, is like an old mistress that has given much pleasure and raison d'etre to our lives and should be treated with love and respect even if she has faded a bit. The lady's not for frying.

Let me go back again, this time to the early sixties. The British Council in Mexico was superbly represented by Maurice and Leonora Cardiff and they brought over Vivien Leigh to do Twelfth Night and Camile. We went backstage to meet her. She was not exactly the brave new Viola of the Renaissance love of will and verve; nor was she the nineteenth-century heroine, the eternal myth of the wronged woman mixed with the romantic myth of La Belle Dame Sans Merci.

She was a transparent, frightened beauty; you could almost see through her pale skin and deep into her magnificently sad green eyes. It was as if Ophelia had come back to haunt us; as if

Catherine Earnshaw had achieved the dream of being for ever a child menacing the tyrannical world of the adults: it was as if Miss Havisham had gone abroad to seek the sun, forgetting her vow never to abandon the salon where her wedding cake mouldered. Yet she had the fire 'that severs day from night'.

Britain: a tender, loveable ghost. Or again, Britain: a complicated, active, questioning friend. In any case: welcome to the Third World, kind hearts and coronets.

20 July 1981   **Carlos Fuentes**

Guardian diary 1: Merton and The Bomb

As befits the oldest college in Oxford, the dons of Merton are making prudent arrangements to protect themselves and survive. A programme of diligent preparations has been put in hand against the possibility of nuclear war, before the wondering eyes of the rest of the university.

Cellars have been cleared of old theses and empty port bottles while each staircase on the various quads has been notified where to go if the Bomb explodes. A special telephone connected to the national early warning system has been ordered for the porters' lodge and a radiation meter has been added to the college's equipment.

The Junior Common Room, after checking wisely that undergraduates were involved in the plans, is in favour of the initiative, and food stocks have been arranged in case the worst happens. Not everyone is impressed, though; a cynical voice from the college confided yesterday that in the event of disaster its owner would head straight, and unstoppably, for the Senior Common Room wine cellar.

25 February 1981   **Martin Wainwright**

Lest we forget

In the late 1950s and early 1960s this newspaper and others devoted large amounts of space to the negotiations for a treaty banning nuclear tests in the atmosphere. At that time scarcely a month passed without a large atmospheric explosion by one of the nuclear Powers. Between August and December 1962, the Soviet Union carried out 35 tests, some of them in the atmosphere, one of them (at Novaya Zemlya in the Arctic) involving a weapon of 40 megatons, which is some 2000 times more destructive than the bombs which destroyed Hiroshima and Nagasaki. The Soviet Union was attempting to catch up with and possibly overtake the United States, so that American tests were by that time fewer. Nevertheless the US carried out five high-altitude tests over Johnston Island in the Pacific during late 1962, at least one of them in the megaton range. The British tests were by then underground, although Britain had contributed its proportional share to the poisoning of the atmosphere. When the treaty was eventually signed in Moscow on August 5, 1963, and came into effect on October 10, there was immense and palpable relief, and nothing said since then has bettered the words of President Kennedy in a broadcast to the American people:

> This treaty is not the millennium. It will not resolve all conflicts, or cause the Communists to forgo their ambitions, or eliminate the dangers of war. It will not reduce our need for arms or allies or programmes of assistance to others. But it is an important first step, a step towards peace, a step towards reason, a step away from war.
>
> A war today or tomorrow, if it led to nuclear war, would not be like any war in history. A full-scale nuclear exchange lasting less than sixty minutes could wipe out more than three hundred million Americans, Europeans, and Russians, as well as untold numbers elsewhere. And, as Chairman Khrushchev warned the Communist Chinese, "the survivors would envy the dead". For they would inherit a world so devastated by explosions, poisons, and fire that we cannot conceive of its horrors.
>
> If one thermo-nuclear bomb were to be dropped on any American, Russian, or other city . . . that one bomb could release more destructive power than all the bombs dropped in the Second World War. Neither the United States, nor the Soviet Union, nor the United Kingdom, nor France can look forward to that day with equanimity.

More than 100 nations promptly signed the treaty, and since then only a handful of maverick weapons have been exploded in the air. The world, in other words, appeared to have made itself safer and taken the step towards reason, the step away from war, for which President Kennedy and Chairman Khrushchev gave thanks. But there has been one unforeseen consequence of the Big Powers' restraint. That is that the frequent demonstrations of the thermo-nuclear nightmare, which made war inconceivable for most of two decades, are no longer to be seen. The result is that war is no longer inconceivable, in spite of almost 20 years' continued development of destructive skills. Indeed preparations are made for the dawn of that day when the survivors will envy the dead. Is it not time to remind the theoreticians of nuclear war of what it is they are talking about in practice?

In August last year, at a conference to review the workings of another treaty, designed to stop the spread of weapons to non-nuclear countries, the director-general of the International Atomic Energy Agency, Dr Sigvard Eklund, made just such a proposal. He called for a demonstration nuclear explosion to give the world an idea of the destructive power of such weapons and to arouse public reaction against them. Little attention was given to Dr Eklund's suggestion, and that attention is now overdue. President Brezhnev, in his speech to the Soviet Party Congress, fell only just short of endorsing it, though he did, in his aged wisdom, make one of the most strenuous appeals for nuclear sanity to have come from any statesman in recent years. (Another came from the younger wisdom of President Carter in his valedictory speech to the American people.) Dr Eklund estimates that there are now some 50,000 nuclear weapons in the stockpiles, with an explosive power of *one million Hiroshimas*. The spectacle of just one or two of these 50,000 massive weapons actually being fired would be enough to deter for a long time the seductive voices which play with the theory of limited nuclear war or with protection against it for the population of the British Isles, or anywhere else in the northern hemisphere.

Dr Eklund did not propose a site for his demonstration. Nor do we. But it would have to be at a place where the radius of total destruction, of fire, of blast, of initial radiation, and of later radioactive fallout can be witnessed on the television screen as easily as a Presidential assassination and then monitored over the months and years. Possibly one reason why Dr Eklund's suggestion has not been discussed is the belief that men and women are sufficiently sophisticated to learn from the theory alone about how destructive nuclear weapons are. We doubt whether that is the case, any more than the thought of a street accident is as frightening as being involved in one.

It is the truism of strategic thinking that nuclear weapons are for deterrence, not for use. But with every reinforcement of the NATO and Warsaw Pact armouries that truism shades a further fraction into doubt, so that what today is becoming just imaginable may in five years be distinctly possible and in ten years be overtaken by a full-scale shelter-building programme. That totally cynical progression has got to be stopped, and there is every reason to suppose that the Russians would join in stopping it. Dr Eklund's vaccine, with a booster every decade, may yet be the best emotional and therefore political defence against an all-consuming contagion.

2 April 1981   **Leader**

A country diary: Keswick

This could be called the history of a field, perhaps of many fields now, but this one is on a valley slope edged by trees on three sides. Fifty years ago it had a lodge at one corner and a well-kept drive to a fine house. It was only grazed periodically. The turf had moonwort and adders' tongues in spring; in summer there were orchids – tway blade, fragrant and butterfly ones – and, in autumn, betony and scabious, all good for moths and butterflies. There were mushrooms too. Then the estate was broken up and timber was felled in a wood and dragged out smashing many field drains so that springs broke out in the grass. Gorse and briars grew on the drive but still tree pipits sang and nested at its top. In latter years however it had too many sheep and horses with foals and the land grew poorer but the ultimate disaster was ponies. They churned the wet ground with their hooves, chewed the hedges and tore up even its coarse grass in winter. Then they were given hay balls which fetched sorrel and docks. But this spring they were banished and the land was fed. Today I was asked back to see it again and, suddenly, time was turned back. The adders' tongue and moonwort have gone, perhaps for ever, but there are orchids – twayblade, a few spotted and armies of butterfly ones, greeny-white and sweet to smell. Dusky chimney-sweep moths wavered over the tall grass and a fat orange underwing was in its roots. I am told that there may be cows one day soon but perhaps some at least of the flowers will stay.

6 July 1981   **Enid J Wilson**

Caring clowns

Every good clown seems to have his own nemesis lurking around some dark corner, his doppelganger Hamlet waiting to get him. Stephen Potter had always been subject to attacks of serious-mindedness (he started out with an uncomic novel and studies of Coleridge and D. H. Lawrence), but the self-inflicted knockout came after long years of lifemanship and gamesmanship, his true life study.

Already, some thought, this had been carried at least as far as it would go and left its mark on the language. Prince Philip had talked of taxmanship, Adlai Stevenson of brinkmanship. He had got into Fowler's Modern English Usage, under Facetious Formations. Anything more would surely be a gambit too many.

But then came a thesis from the Department of Anthropology and Sociology in the University of Victoria, entitled Strategic Rhetorics in Face-to-Face Interaction: the Sociology of Stephen Potter. This looked like the ultimate triumph and should have been received in poker-faced silence. Instead, Potter, badly slipping by now, confessed serious gratitude and said how proud he was about being 'the only non-scientist writer of this century to introduce at least four words into English and American dictionaries.' It was over: the deadly doppelganger had struck again.

He makes a substantial addition to the roll of English clowns and in *Stephen Potter* Alan Jenkins has given us a likeable book about a vulnerable, perverse and self-contradictory man. The devil-may-care bohemianism was only one side of the mask; the other could settle into a suburban decorum that cared like the devil. He was modestly boastful and subjected his amateur affectations to a stern professional drive. In private life people found him very funny but could seldom remember any funny thing he had actually said.

One thing he did for the gaiety of the nation was to discover Joyce Grenfell. He got Herbert Farjeon along to hear one of her dinner-table turns and the next step was straight on to the revue stage. *Joyce*, a collection of autobiographical pieces and tributes by her friends edited by Reggie Grenfell and Richard Garnett, will be valued as a memorial volume but undeviating adulation does make for a certain monotony. Had she no faults, if only for readability's sake?

A slight tendency to bossiness, a severe attitude towards unpunctuality and the rustling of chocolate-wrappings in the stalls – these seem to be the only human weaknesses rescuing her from queen-mummery. But her age is to blame, not she, if goodness has become a boring word.

9 October 1980 **Norman Shrapnell**

Baubles, bangles

Mr Tom Torney, Labour MP for Bradford South, is to ask the Home Secretary, Mr Whitelaw, to 'outline the bounds of commercialism connected with the Royal Wedding'. '*Si monumentum requiris, circumspice,*' as they say at St Paul's; already, with four pulsating months still to go, it is clear that there are no bounds, and therefore that they cannot be outlined, even by that master of the impenetrably hopeful response, Mr Whitelaw. The casual foreign visitor, inspecting some of the wares now congregating in the shop windows,

*'I've got the results of your
x-ray. You appear to have
pictures of Prince Charles and
Lady Diana Spencer on your
lungs.'*

2 July 1981

might be forgiven for supposing that we were preparing to
celebrate the wedding of Miss Bo Derek to the late Count
Dracula, so marvellously haphazard are the 'artist's impressions' which some 'artists' are providing.

Already, fulfilling the darkest forebodings of the
Cambridge School, our long failure to clamp down on
imported textiles is permitting a flood of defamatory
reproductions of the happy pair to inundate the country on T-
shirts from Pakistan and elsewhere. Though the Lord
Chamberlain issues grave warnings against the use of
photographs in such contexts, the ears of the sub-continent
are apparently closed to him. A 'ban' on such excesses has
already been announced for home-based manufacturers, but

it seems to have little legal force. 'Manufacturers have always complied before,' we are told; but their resistance has rarely been tested before by such cut-throat competitive conditions.

Elsewhere, Lady Diana's step-grandmother, the writer Barbara Cartland, author of *Money, Magic and Marriage* and some 215 other dewy novels, is discovered organising 'romantic tours' at £1,000 a time, the highlight of which, by a quite magical coincidence, is to be lunch with Lady Diana's father and stepmother at Althorp Hall. Mr Whitelaw could, if he chose, question this arrangement as a piece of commercial enterprise for which there is little precedent among royal step-grandmothers; but he will have to be careful what he says since it might also be seen as exactly the kind of dynamic British opportunism which the Prime Minister believes she is generating by her economic policies. In general, however, Mr Whitelaw has little choice but to tell the House of Commons that he is entirely powerless in these matters: a Cumbrian Canute, motionless on the shore as a great sea of tat sweeps irresistibly over him.

7 April 1981 **Leader**

Opening his letters

Only a lunatic would have attempted it, says Muriel St Clare Byrne in the exultant tones Columbus might have used as land appeared in the west. She refers to her own venture with The Lisle Letters,* an argosy in which she set sail nearly fifty years ago and which drops anchor, at last, next month.

Written between 1533 and 1540, some 3,000 separate missives have survived. Like the Paston letters or the Verney collection they make up a cache of records of daily life, and a repository of family values. Also, they involve many of the great names and mainsprings of action in the Tudor world.

Their preservation is originally due to an odd accident:

Published by Chicago University Press, in six volumes at £125 the set.

their confiscation by Henry VIII, when their hub, and his Deputy at Calais, Lord Lisle the bastard son of the Plantagenet Edward IV, was arraigned on a charge of treason.

He was acquitted – and soon after died – but the whole file remained impounded, the state papers indiscriminately bound in with the letters on household management, court preferment, the education and advancement of the children, income and debt, provisions and fashions, and the love between the Deputy and his dear bedfellow, Lady Honor Lisle.

She was a Grenville by birth, previously married to a Devon squire, Sir John Basset, by whom she'd had seven little Bassets – Lisle likewise had been widowed. So you get their education, the placing of the girls as waiting gentlewomen, the putting of the elder son to the inns of court, so he in turn would manage the estate, and so forth. It is, as she says, the fabric of Tudor life in absolutely readable form.

It was the familiar style of the early days of letter writing, before the convolutions of the next reigns, that appealed to Miss St Clare Byrne, previously an Elizabethan by trade. Not only the learned, and the lowering figures like Thomas Cromwell – the gentlefolk affecting a villainous hand diabolical to decipher – but the common people, wrote in the most extraordinary rhythms.

She is a wonderful reciter, I soon found, of ripe quotations from many sources. This from an uneducated girl writing to her stepmother: 'Grant me a lodging at Umberleigh, for there is no place that I would so fain be in it.' This from a common varlet: 'I thank you again and again, and I your own in deed.' A lot of this letter stuff, she comments frankly, can really be very boring, but the Lisle Letters are incredible stuff, very beautiful, and silly historians have just been negligent or dismissed it as domestic.

It was Lisle's position at Calais, managing his affairs at a distance, that makes their range so comprehensive, politically and domestically. There's no recognised portrait of Lisle, but Miss St Clare Byrne reckons to have identified one, and supposes him to have been a gentle giant in the Angevin mould, whom the King lent a suit of his own armour, while his dear Bedfellow emerges as a rather small, vigorous, pushy lady.

It's not the cloud of suspicion of heresy that gives a sad tinge to the story – that came only at the end. Its editor, who believes she has established Lisle's birth in 1460, conjures up the central poignancy:

'One middle-aged, one elderly, married beforehand, who have completely fallen in love with each other. They had no children in common – that is the tragedy that runs through the letters. Always they're expecting the birth of the young Plantagenet. And of course it doesn't happen.' (The pressure was so great that Lady Lisle had a hysterical pregnancy.)

The story of Miss St Clare Byrne's tenacity in completing a work which consists of 6 volumes of 600 pages each, comprising 1,687 letters, besides her narrative, comments, notes and a prodigious index – boiling up to over 50lbs in manuscript – is itself extraordinary. It's the story of a survivor of a vanished class of freelance scholars. The last day of this month will be her 86th birthday and in all that time of academic and theatrical connections she has never had – indeed, she resisted – a regular permanent post.

To visit her in her eighteenth-century house, a narrow slice of a St John's Wood terrace behind a small patch of unkempt garden, is to find a very positive little lady bustling among layer upon layer of papers and books in drunken heaps, and well-worn furniture that has to be cleared of debris before it can be used. It's all there, she says, but half the time the question arises, where exactly?

A friend of a younger generation recalls her at the outset of her great project, slim in tailor-mades with collar tie and Henry Heath hat, the uniform of the intellectuals of the twenties. The pupils she coached at Somerville – her own college, and whose history she wrote – apparently called her The British Lion, and the vibrancy and patriotism are still there.

She spoke of her student days at Oxford in World War One, of a university almost cleared of young men except the invalids and the shortsighted, like Aldous Huxley, 'sitting beside me looking like a young god, though his photographs give you no idea of him,' of giving tea to these few, the condition being that a woman friend plus a don must also be present.

Her principal was Dame Emily Penrose, who she believes to have done more for women's education and its status than any other. She was very shy, she recalls, but awfully kind to a scrubby youngster. Dame Emily only came out of her shell when she read Browning. 'I revolted instinctively against Browning, but Miss Penrose was absolutely a Browning creature. To hear her read 'The Bishop orders his tomb . . .' was a theatrical experience. When she came to the last lines it was genius. Awkward, shy, stiff woman, but put her on to read Browning, and my God, she could beat the band!' Miss St Clare Byrne imitates the Penrose style for me, and it is also a theatrical experience. All the same, she still prefers Tennyson.

At Somerville she was taken up into the coterie that called itself The Mutual Admiration Society – in later years Middle Aged Spread. Among others it numbered Dorothy Rowe, who called her own poems 'bits of mould', Clarice Barnett and, her most intimate friend until her death and of whose work she is now the executor, Dorothy L. Sayers. MAS did not care for Vera Brittain, seeing her as a sentimental, melancholy droop, and Miss St Clare Byrne is sorry for her, having been so unpopular.

First time at MAS, she met Sayers, who happened to be declaiming her own poem: 'Door to the fire, let us weave a web of sound and splendour intertwined/Warriors riding two by two . . .' She imitates stacks of this, and it is another theatrical experience.

Later on, it would be she who primed Sayers to write the plays, by getting her to collaborate on Busman's Honeymoon. Miss St Clare Byrne's first love, from childhood, was the theatre, and she wrote England's Elizabeth for RADA, Well, Gentlemen for Gwladys Wheeler and the Stage Society, and the centenary play for Bedford Ladies College.

Naturally, the wonderfully versatile Dorothy pitched in to help with props. Miss St Clare Byrne darts on to a stool to peer in the top drawer of a tallboy to fish out memorabilia:

'. . . what the hell's happened to them all? I had a flood, into the tallboy – whole batch somewhere – hope I haven't lent them – people are awful – they steal everything these devils – props that incredible woman made for my play have vanished – what about the spectacular photograph of my dear friend conducting the Bach Choir from a table – ah! here's that anyway – ah! and all the Elizabethan sonnets she forged for me – she and the local chemist prepared the paper – here it all is to the Memorial Service after she broke her neck falling downstairs – and that's that!'

All this theatre and much else besides was in the margin, as it were, of the Lisles – papers on Elizabethan life and language, editions of Granville Barker, etc., studies of stage make-up and lighting, lecturing in London and Oxford, anything to pay the rent, with occasional helps from scholarships and grants.

The hearth of her extra mural work had been the Bibliographical Society, and the generation of scholars before her that became her friends were her childhood heroes, A. W. Pollard the Chaucerian, and W. W. Greg the Shakespearian. They were also men who could be approached only through canyons between towers of books.

The train was fired by her readings of the nineteenth century volumes of Letters of Royal and Illustrious Ladies, which had a few samples of Lisle. After T. S. Eliot at Faber had contracted her to work on the eighteen volumes of State Papers III in the Records Office, she revoked all her other contracts. Finding that instead of going to the Welsh caves in the war with other treasures, or Maidstone Gaol, they had been in the basement all the time, she ran home crying with delight – the Lisles had seen the blitzes through! In the upshot, Faber pulled out unable to stand the expense, and Chicago took over.

At the time she began, she had been working on Anthony Munday's Journey to Rome. The book was in page proof when war put a block on it. The Lisles have prevented her, she says, from getting back to it. The whole lot has been waiting humbly for forty years in a basket in the garden shed.

19 May 1981   **Alex Hamilton**

Boys will be fathers

A 16-year-old schoolboy set a series of legal precedents yesterday when, despite his protests, he was ordered to pay 5p a week towards the maintenance of a baby girl, whom he was said to have fathered when he was 13. It is thought to be the first time that the law has recognised that a male of under 14 can have sexual intercourse as well as being the first occasion on which a 16-year-old has been ordered to pay maintenance. His relationship with the mother, now aged 18, is also rare in that each partner could technically have been charged with indecently assaulting the other: first the girl, when the boy was under 14, and then the boy, when he was over 14 but the girl was still under 16.

The case was brought by the Department of Health and Social Security. The girl had approached them after the birth of her daughter in July 1979. She asked for supplementary benefit for her child and named the boy as its father. The boy has consistently denied that the child is his. The boy and the girl appeared at Hartlepool Magistrates' Court in Cleveland yesterday when the department applied for an affiliation order, naming the boy as the father. The magistrates ruled that their identities should not be revealed.

The girl said that they had begun to sleep together at her home in 1977, when she would have been 13 and he 12. 'We had sex almost every night during the summer of 1977,' she told the court. 'We were alone in the house at night and no one disturbed us.'

They had stopped seeing each other during the winter, but in 1978 they had begun having sex again. 'I realised in November 1978 that I was pregnant and I told him about it. He called me a liar and stopped coming to the house. I know he is the father. I have never slept with anyone else. I am not like that.'

The court heard that the boy had asked for blood tests which had shown that there was a 99.62 per cent chance that he was the father but he had continued to insist that this was

*'I hope it's not twins, my pocket
money couldn't stand it.'*

11 December 1980

wrong. He told the court: 'I never knew her very well. I only
went into the house to play cards with the lads. I was never
alone with her and I never had sex. She says I was always in
the house with her but on most nights I was either fishing or
playing football at the youth club. I'm not the father.'

The magistrates granted the affiliation order, but they fixed
the weekly maintenance payments at 5p after Mr Richard
Ward, appearing for the DHSS, told them: 'He is still at
school and it would be inappropriate if there was any
substantial order made for the maintenance of the child.' The
department can apply to the court to have the maintenance
payment increased if the boy's income rises.

Yesterday's decision is consistent with November's report

on sexual offences by the Criminal Law Revision Committee. It suggested the abolition of the statutory presumption that a boy of under 14 cannot commit rape. Technically, there seems to have been a *prima facie* case against the girl at the beginning of the relationship since she was 'committing an indecent act with a child under 14 years of age', an offence under the 1960 Indecency with Children Act. The roles were reversed once the boy attained his fourteenth birthday. He was then technically having unlawful sexual intercourse with a girl under the age of 16.

11 December 1980   **Nick Davies**

Remember forking?

In the social columns of *The Times*, the independent schools discreetly parade their wares each year. It could hardly be called advertising, but these notices give out a strong flavour of the mysteries of private education.

Bedford School: 'RC Williams is Head of the School and Captain of Rugby . . . The appeal for the recreation centre closed on August 31. The appeal for the restoration of the main school building will begin in October . . .' Charterhouse: 'Oration quarter begins today. The Founders Day dinner will be . . .' St Lawrence College: 'Mr R. I. H. Gollop has taken up office as headmaster of the junior preparatory school.' Queenswood School: 'The Old Queenswoodian carol service will be . . .' Harrow School: 'A. J. C. Collet (Druries) continues as Head of School and R. N. P. Hadow (The Park) is Captain of Rugby Football. The Goose Match will be played . . .'

Kelly College: 'The OK dinner-dance will be at Quaglinos on January 17.' And much more of the inscrutable same.

I chose one school more or less at random, Cranleigh: 'The Old Cranleighan dinner is on . . . Long leave is from . . .' The headmaster, Mr Van Hasselt, kindly agreed to let me attend the Old Cranleighan dinner, to meet old boys and glimpse the life of a public school spanning the last fifty years.

Old boys who come back to reunions are, of course, a self-selected group who may not be representative. There was no one there with much criticism for the old *alma mater*.

The school, set in the Surrey countryside, has a fine Victorian red-brick, creeper-clad building, with chapel and clock tower, grand old hall; all the accoutrements for a turn-of-the-century boys' school story. Adjoining it is a large and ugly modern building, testifying to the school's increasing wealth with the years. The headmaster is keen to stress, as often as he can, how much the school has changed in academic standards, and in class composition. Several times he warned me that the sort of people I'd meet among the old boys simply don't represent the school as it is now. 'The older old boys are very lower middle class, I'm afraid, rather terrible in a way, but awfully loyal,' he said shortly after I arrived. Cranleigh was founded for the sons of local farmers, strong on rugger, weak on brains.

It is now the second most expensive school in the country, at £1200 a term, plus about £100 for extras, and books. Many old boys regretted bitterly that they couldn't afford to send their children there now. In fact the divide between the old and newer boys was profound, expressing itself strongly at the table behind me during the headmaster's speech. The oldest old boys were rowdiest, singing 'Why Are We Waiting?' as they demanded the toasts be drunk quickly so that they could smoke. The younger ones looked somewhat disapproving.

The headmaster regretted that the OC dinner was held in the middle of university term, preventing the attendance of recent leavers. He said, emphatically, 'The modern Cranleighan *does* go to university,' and the old brigade behind me actually booed and hissed its disapproval, none of them having gone to university. Our English class system subdivides itself into smaller and smaller slivers, given half a chance. As the school clambers up-market, it wrenches out its roots, like a lower-middle-class boy made good.

'Schools cannot stand still. Changes there must be and changes there have been,' the headmaster went on. (One or two sighs and groans from the next table.) 'We stand for friendliness and humanity and high academic standards. We are a happy, well-balanced school, and rugby football still flourishes!' (Loud cheers and Hear Hears.)

'You will find a prodigious improvement in our academic standards, with a ninety per cent pass rate at A level, and six Oxbridge scholarships a year.' (A boo or two, muffled.)

'Despite the recession, falling birth rate, and rising fees, parental demand is as buoyant as ever. The number of prospective parents coming to my study is greater than ever.'

He went on to assess the political future. 'Criticisms of public schools are more strident than ever. It's such a shame. But the United Nations Charter, Article 13, asserts the liberty of parents to choose schools other than those run by the Government. This was ratified by the UK in 1976, ratified by the Labour Government.' (Triumphant hurrahs, and boos at the very name of Labour.)

He spoke then of the new house recently founded at the school, named after David Loveday, a former headmaster who later became a bishop. Now in his eighties, Loveday had been released from a home for the evening, to grace the top table in his flowing purple. 'Loveday House is a symbol of our confidence in the future and our ability to meet the challenge of the Labour party' (hiss). 'David Loveday loved God and Cranleigh, in that order, but only just. We are surrounded by that history and tradition of which we are all part, and not unproud.' (Loud cheers.)

At my table reminiscences were in full swing. There, in the great dimly-lit baronial dining-hall, walls embossed with mottoes and coats of arms, old boys rattled off their memories. 'Meal times, when you first arrived,' said one who had left some ten years ago, 'they were the most frightening. So many traditions to remember. Bread was called Toque, Ketchup was Shog. Fatigues were appalling punishments, and it was wretched being a Stooge' (fag in other schools) 'though lovely when you had one yourself.'

'Remember forking?' another old boy asked. 'We sat in order of age and hierarchy, and the top boy took his fork, like this, and rammed it into the buttocks of the next boy on the bench. Then he took his fork and jabbed it into the next boy, and so on, forking all down the line, till the poor rotter at the end had no one to fork. Ha, ha! Bloody painful!'

They tried to explain the elaborate intricacies of who was allowed to wear which ties. But traditions are not all old. Prefects only just started wearing gowns two years ago. 'In my day,' said one boy, 'the Captain of Rugby was God, no, I'd say more than God. I remember he had to shave twice a day, and we little boys went weak at the knees if he ever even passed us by.'

That launched them into bawdier memories. 'Remember old so-and-so's arrival at the school? He announced to the whole school: "I will not have boys pulling each other's penises until they are blue in the face" – very outspoken. We weren't homosexuals, don't get us wrong, but everyone tossed each other off.'

There was a break halfway through the proceedings, and the old boys (plus a few recent old girls, since the school now has sixth-form girls) trooped out for a smoke in the high vaulted corridors. I found myself shivering outside the front door with a brave cluster of sixth-formers, for whom smoking can mean rustication. 'Actually, it's jolly unfair,' one girl said. 'Punishments depend on who you are. If you're a good Oxbridge bet, you won't get rusticated.'

There is no corporal punishment any longer. A group of boys were expelled last year though, for shoplifting on a big scale in Guildford, and selling their wares all round the school.

After the toasts – the Queen, and The School – and the speeches, came the long-awaited School Song. Bellowed out into the smoky air, each verse louder and more forceful than the last, a rallying cry for a lost youth, a great communal assertion of a set of values and standards to be found nowhere else once they'd left school:

> *Cranleienses gaudeamus*
> *Una voce concinamus*
> *Una corde extollamus*
> *Domus nostrae gloriam.*

Out there in the real world things didn't seem to be quite

like that. In the library for drinks, the 300 or so old boys assembled, bedecked in frilly and fancy dress shirts, velvet and satin bow ties, the loud and the discreet. I met an ice-maker salesman, a builder's engineer, several ex-RAF men, several old farmers, a manager in a ball-bearing plant, an insurance man, an ex-policeman, a monumental masonry manager, a doctor, a lawyer, several teachers, and others.

Some were rich and successful, others were not. All were out there dealing, day by day, with people who had never sniffed the inside of an institution like Cranleigh. Had school made it easier for them to do so effectively?

'Leadership qualities, certainly gives you that,' one old boy said. 'A solid base,' said another. 'A set of standards you refer back to all your life,' said another. But what standards? Forking, for instance, imagine a team of managers forking their way down the hierarchy to the lowest sweeper on the factory line.

'It's not so much the education,' said several of them, nodding their heads wisely. 'It's the spirit, the ideals.' But how has that peculiar spirit of the rugger match and Up The Old School actually helped them make any sense of society? They were not talking about, and nor did they mean, the simple old boy network. They had some higher notion. School stood for noble co-operation 'learning to live together,' 're-sponsibility', 'learning to live by the rules of the community'.

But when they were out there, confronting their work-force, had those same virtues been any use? 'Well,' said one, not quite so certainly, 'leadership qualities are the same wherever you are, whoever you're leading.' Which is what they thought when they sent eighteen-year-old public school boys out to officer regular soldiers of many years' experience during the First World War.

There is nothing surprising about people being prepared to scrimp and save to give their children private education, while private education can give them a far higher chance of straightforward academic success. What is odd is that independent schools still preach a spiritual theory of leadership and superiority, a *noblesse oblige*, that must further alienate them from the rest of society.

The sixth-formers I spoke to didn't seem aware of this. It certainly didn't worry them. As far as they and the recent school leavers were concerned, this little community with its quirks and traditions, cloistered and protected, was just the ordinary, usual sort of school to go to. When I asked a few if they had ever considered going to a comprehensive, or if they would like to have gone to one, one gulped a bit and said: 'No. To tell you the truth, it never occurred to me or my parents.' Did he know anyone at a comprehensive? 'Well one person did decide to go to a comprehensive for the sixth form from here, but I don't know any others.' Any regrets? 'No. I think this sort of school gives the best education there is.'

Another said, with his hands in his pockets, 'Look, do you honestly think if you can afford to send a boy here, you'd choose to send him to some comprehensive?' To them, the question made no sense. They were in an 'ordinary' school, and it was that other inexplicable 95 per cent of pupils in comprehensives who were odd. I doubt whether many of the old boys ever get over that feeling.

10 November 1980   **Polly Toynbee**

Fort Beswick and its prisoners

When Fort Beswick was being planned there was a construction model in Lego which was photographed and displayed as an example of the great strides public housing in Manchester was to take. It might have been marginally better to build the thing in Lego, as things have turned out.

Today the estate is falling around the ears of those who live in it. And although it is not the nastiest modern housing estate in the land, its bleak aspect, appalling structural problems, and the determined hatred with which council tenants view it, make it a brutal showpiece of housing theory and practice.

The Beswick estate – Fort Beswick to those who have to live in it and the Wellington Street estate to those who don't – was completed ten years ago. Its 1081 dwellings were built of concrete on the assembly line method. Like Lego, the various bits were manufactured elsewhere and then walls, roofs, stairs and verandas were manoeuvred into position by gangs of uncertainly skilled workmen. Architects now shudder both at the method and at the concrete, but the estate was built in that way, and it was intended to house the Beswick inhabitants of the old, turn-of-the-century, red-brick streets of the area.

The estate was to provide those people with better homes. Beyond that, it is hard now to get details from the Town Hall about the genesis of Beswick. 'A lot of those people know where the bodies are hid, but they won't tell you,' said a lugubrious voice in the Labour Club. And so it proved. People were dead, retired; everything had been done with good intentions, things were different now, had been since 1968. Why concentrate on what was past, an admitted mistake, when Manchester was now building low, in brick, homes that people liked?

But a lot of people live on this estate, and on four others built along similar lines in the city. And the City Council now simply does not know what to do with Fort Beswick, and its vast, incurable problems of damp, noise, and galloping disrepair. It cost £4,681,000 to build – 50 years to pay off. The latest estimate of necessary repairs to the structure and the insane heating system is £5 millions. To replace the estate would cost an unimaginable £20 millions.

Sir Robert Thomas, leader of the Labour council which planned the estate, now says: 'We were under pressure from officers to build multi-storey.' That excuse was a favourite with both Tory and Labour councillors of the time. People also refer to 'hindsight' a good deal, less to the fact that whenever anyone took the trouble to ask the people of Britain, at that time, what they would like to live in, the answer was always monotonously the same: houses.

People on the estate live in a combination of deck access – or walk-up – flats and maisonettes, with some houses, that are linked by miles of concrete corridor – the daft 'streets in the sky' idea – and some of the buildings go up nine floors, though most are lower. The flats were built by a company called Bison, and the council has effectively given up hope of trying to get damages for the way in which the estate was put up. The firm responsible is now in Saudi hands.

But in a real sense the lunatic building system that produced the estate is a bit of a distraction; it's one example of a plethora of weird ideas that lasted long enough in the 1960s to be put into practice and then dropped as the first tenants moved in. (Wellington Street was completed *three years* after the City had decided in 1968 that it was only going to build low rise houses in future.) All over Britain there are housing estates that people wouldn't build now, although they are less than 15 years old. And the questions that should be asked about them are – how are they managed? Are people putting down roots and pulling up their resentments? Will the community overcome the fabric?

Beswick Labour Club is a fine place, handsome, successful, and old. In 1964 the officers commissioned an aerial photographer to take pictures of Beswick and they hang large and framed in the club today. They show the heavy industry – largely decimated, including the colliery that circled the area – and inside the circle the herring-bone plan of streets. It was wonderful then, Councillor Jack Flanagan says, wonderful.

The church treasurer, Ernie Wright, starts talking about the debating clubs that used to be popular in Beswick. 'We'd take a room in a pub, and have a subject, and people would join in, and sometimes the arguments were fierce. And the woman from the Salvation Army would come in, and she'd say "Oh I'd love to stay, but I have to sell *War Cry!*"

It's a lovely picture; it goes with gas lamps and beer at threepence a pint until somebody asks what kind of things were debated. 'Oh, all sorts; was Christian Barnard taking over God's role, that kind of thing,' and you realise that these things were happening only 12 or 13 years ago.

There are five new pubs on the estate, two are very pretty, designed like beehives in brick, but none has cheap rooms for hire. There is very little on the estate that functions simply as an activity, but a lot is offered as a service. So there are mother and toddler groups, a university settlement, an adventure playground, a youth worker, a community worker, clubs for the elderly, luncheon clubs for pensioners, and so on.

In a coy little clue to planning theory, the social services office, the Church of the Resurrection, and the health centre sit in a line near the shopping precinct and Millicent Edwards, the Rector's wife, is cynically amused by that. 'All your needs, you see, in one place. And on the other side there is the human chess board and the quoits, that the planners thought Beswick people would entertain themselves with.'

People are given a lot of things on this estate but not allowed to do much. Dependence is fostered in odd ways. There is the heating system. It's underfloor (hideously expensive but contained within the rent). You cannot control it; your only choice is to have it off or on. If you have it off you still pay for it, if you have it on, you stifle in bed at night (where you may not be able to open the window for the noise or rain). The Council must like this dependence – a paper written in the late 1970s talked about 'analysing the advantages and disadvantages of those systems which do not give individual control to the tenant'.

Then there is the housing profits system. This was drawn up to make the housing system fairer and more easily understood. There is a maximum of 200 points – consisting of things like age, number of children, present condition of housing and so on – that will ensure the transfer of your choice. Manchester has a waiting list of 38,000 people, of whom 20,000 want to transfer from their present council homes.

The main trouble on the Wellington Street estate rising from the structure is wetness. Mary Morley is a domestic helper in a local Borstal and before she goes to work she listens to the weather forecast and if it is going to rain she pulls the three-piece suite into the middle of the sitting-room and puts down buckets near the window. She's lived like that for five years and is now accomplished at showing the press and television round her sodden flat in Wynne Close.

Every so often she gets letters from the housing office saying things like 'the problem of water penetration has been identified . . . consultants are at present undertaking an investigation of the rain penetration problem . . . envisaged they will be in a position to recommend remedial work . . . in the near future.'

It isn't that the Council is callous. On the contrary. It appears to care deeply. It has adopted a policy of getting families out of the higher floors. It has a huge and hustling housing office on the estate run by a young Liverpool Chinese manager called Philip Leong which has over the years forced councillors and the Town Hall to concentrate on the plight of those living in Bison-built homes. Jack Flanagan says: 'We have a system of intensive management on the estate, because we know that with one hiccup in maintenance – there would be your ghetto.'

You can see the direct labour force around on the estate – they board up, replace windows, strengthen joints and are highly visible. Cleaners whizz round on yellow trucks, policemen from the enormous station opposite the estate parade the shopping precinct. Half a million pounds have been spent on design improvements, a plan to scrap resident caretakers has itself been scrapped, the best future for the estate is pondered. And yet, like some satanic equation dreamt up by a misanthropic mathematician, each factor in the planning of the estate appears to bring about the reverse result from that intended.

The estate was intended to provide better homes for the community. It has failed to do that. People live more noisily, with cheapskate fittings and surroundings, which require the constant attention of a monolithic Council. Beware of nostalgia for the old slums – it's no fun to walk 200 yards to a lavatory, or sleep five in a bed, or watch cockroaches move beneath the wallpaper. But people on Fort Beswick are paying £18 a week for homes that they don't on the whole like, and from April that goes up to £24.

The second stage of the equation was to move families and anyone considered to be in need, away from the estate. This in turn introduces a savage volatility. People look to the day when they will be out; the sense of grievance of those left behind becomes more acute. Up in Brennock Close deck access a young pregnant woman was chatting excitedly to her black neighbour. 'I've got the letter, we'll be moving soon. But when I told my friend she just said it wasn't *fair*, she couldn't have children at all, and on top of that she would never be able to leave because she didn't have a family.'

Mary Morley only knows three of the flats on her deck; a thin diabetic on the fourth floor says he used to know everyone eight years ago but now knows only a young man next door and a Spaniard by sight at the end of the deck. Everyone else has moved away and he feels marooned by illness and strangeness.

The Council cannot leave the estate alone otherwise it would literally fall apart. It has put itself in charge of housing the citizens of the city and therefore has to respond to the demands of people who have been told they have no right to make demands anywhere else. 'Since the end of the war over three-quarters of Beswick has been rebuilt. Most of this rebuilding has taken place in the last decade. Three-quarters of the houses in Beswick are therefore rented from the City Council. No private dwellings have been built in Beswick since 1945.' (City Council area plan for Beswick Ward.)

So the city now has a new plan for the estate. It will fill the empty homes, left by the evacuating families, with students and – though no official says this – with people who are so powerless that they can go nowhere else. So the bus stops on the Ashton New Road on rainy winter mornings to pick up Iranian students, Chinese students, girls in dungarees, and Muslim students in black chadors.

That is the third component of the equation. Philip Leong says that it is necessary to work out the right proportion of students to resident population. But Steve Butters, a community worker employed by the Council, says that in his experience everything planned by the Authority on the estate has ended in disaster so there is little guarantee that such proportions can be worked out.

A local doctor says icily that he will take no more of the 'mad schizophrenics' sent into the estate. 'I assume we're being used as a dustbin. I recognise those people who lived in Beswick and have managed to stay, as the type of people I used to deal with when it was friendly and everyone helped each other, but I'm not motivated to deal with the Hulme rejects. It spreads, you see, you get quite decent families here whose children are corrupted by other children – I had a child the other day, he was thirteen, and he'd attempted suicide. That was unheard of.'

This month the City Council decided that it could not afford to go ahead with the local Shena Simon secondary school that had been promised for years. It was to have housed all the community facilities that you could wish for – but Government cuts have done for it, in the same way as they have done for Manchester's rebuilding and rehabilitation programme.

Mad logic has prevailed again: two good Beswick libraries were knocked down when the bulldozer reigned and were only replaced – after protest – by one small prefab library. Shena Simon, of course, was the reason for nothing better being provided. But, by accident, one thing has survived.

'There is a large amount of vacant space in Beswick,' says the Beswick Plan primly, without mentioning the bulldozers, and then, incomprehensibly, says later on: 'There is a lack of extensive areas of open space in Beswick.' In the middle of this area stands the Bradford Baths and Washhouse.

Built in 1909, glowering and magnificent, and the only point of contact with the past that is visible on the estate, for 25 pence an adult can swim in its cool waters, admire its brass and glazed brick, and remember – it almost goes without saying – that the City Council has been trying to knock it down for years. The washhouse is cheap, efficient and popular. You can see figures bent against the wind pushing prams filled with washing across the 'vacant land' that surrounds the estate. Jack Flanagan says he thinks the baths and washhouse are now safe from demolition because the council hasn't enough cash even to knock them down.

Where the estate works it seems to work by accident. There are people living on it who want to be there because it is in Beswick and Beswick was where they were brought up. If you have a good neighbour, life is better, with some good laughs, and people like the widow living next door to a house where there are seven dogs and twelve cats living in sparkling cleanliness, have an open and jolly social life, with neighbours visiting even at midnight.

There are bingo clubs where news travels very fast, pubs where people seem to have re-formed the groups they had in the old pubs, and a church that runs a morning café which is a great meeting place. There is a small amount of beating the system. High up on one deck access a young man said that he liked the estate. It suited him and he indicated why. His front room was a bed factory. In it the young man makes pine beds, with workbench, stores of wood, awls, chisels, saws and polishers. He has perfected quiet drilling techniques and says he finds the rents most reasonable.

'The Council doesn't know what goes on on this estate. They're too lazy to find out. Direct Works know, of course, but their level of responsibility is rather low.' Car main-tenance businesses were a common form of private enter-prise, the young man said, though council raids tried to stop them.

That room was secret, illegal. It also showed what the estate has lost, irrevocably, because of the idea of total planning. It has lost any sense of people doing things. Walk round the estate, save for the shopping precinct where 30 mediocre shops struggle for business, and there is an eerie silence and hardly any human movement.

The Rector, David Edwards, said an extraordinary thing. The bells on his church were removed when vandals went for them but, he says, the level of destruction has dropped a lot. 'The young, it's as if they were too apathetic to do anything. They were angry before.'

Listening to some of the unemployed teenagers in the area talk about doing nothing, 'going down to the Arndale', 'going for Everton supporters with the Stanley knives', makes the stomach turn. But brisk admonitions about there being more to life than these loutish pursuits die on the lips.

What would you suggest? They trail silent streets and squares from which the past has been eradicated; their fathers' jobs – less so, their mothers' – have gone; they are the children of people who themselves could only work in industries and not crafts. They look out from Viaduct Street, or Ranworth

Close or over the city from Wynne Close and what they see is a landscape that has as little to offer as the moon. They should be self-sufficient, no doubt, but they are not. And when they come to the age of Council tenancy on Fort Beswick they will not even have the memory of what went before to help them.

28 March 1981   **Lindsay Mackie**

Elves at the sharp end

The headman was already awake. He was squatting by the fire, quietly conversing with a shaman whose family shared the longhouse. Everyone loved the shaman: he made people laugh. They looked like a couple of box kites sitting there in sleeping sarongs, clasping their knees for extra warmth as they fed wood chips to the fire. Overhead dangled a cluster of dart quivers, always warm to ensure that their poison mingled quickly with the blood.

The headman glanced up and held out a cup of coffee. 'Good dream?' It was a standard greeting, but the Semai take their dreams seriously, so I hesitated before replying. It had been a disturbing dream, probably the result of disorientation. In the night gusts of rain had gently rocked the house on its stilts, creating an impression of being afloat. Cold seeping through the floor had induced a clammy chill which the mind associates with fear.

I mimed the act of being strangled. The shaman frowned. 'Nik-nik,' he tutted, and touched the headman's arm. 'His father,' he explained. 'Dead. Come to see you.'

The recent death of the headman's father was a sore point. The Semai Senoi do not acknowledge death by natural causes, and half the tribe had taken the precaution of moving down the valley. The headman had remained to plant new crops, but now he was having second thoughts. By invoking the dead man's spirit in my nightmare, perhaps the shaman was obliquely telling his friend that he should not delay much longer.

162

The house was stirring. A small boy walloped the dogs away from a plate of cold tapioca, the headman's wife began suckling her ten-month-old son, and the two elder girls were opening the shutters. Outside, mist clung to the jungle like opium fumes, obscuring the distant peaks of the Cameron Highlands. Along the valley a family of gibbons started up.

It rained throughout the day. Only the shaman and his younger wife ventured out, festooned with small bags containing seed and a midday meal. He carried a *beliong*, the light Semai axe whose whippy handle absorbs the impact of cutting hardwood, and the shorter blowpipe favoured by men with weak lungs. With no sons to help him, he had fallen behind with the planting. He plodded off through the puddles, a gaunt figure in a loincloth.

Listlessly, the family settled back against their bed rolls. They were bored. One of the boys produced a Sanyo radio-cassette and slotted in Donny and Marie Osmond's Greatest Hits. Drips followed the rafters to seek out the neatly-stashed blowpipes, snares, baskets, twine, fishing rods, spear guns, axes and knives. The battery was giving out and the headman substituted a tape of Semai music. Chanting and the thud of bamboo stampers drifted out across the river, fretting at a childhood dream . . .

An old man had started the dancing, I remembered. Women had been pounding out a casual rhythm when the old man had begun to circle to the music. His wife lay sweating on a mat, sick with fever. Others had joined him, the women with bright flowers in their hair, the men's faces patterned with red Kesumba juice. Soon more than 50 Semai were whirling like a rugby scrum on the sprung bamboo floor, some flying off against the walls, others collapsing in a coma. By the early hours of the morning, the old man's wife was sleeping peacefully. That had been in 1953.

In those days the British had called them aborigines, or sakai. By then, five years into the Malayan Emergency, the colonial authorities realised that these timid, elfin people were going to determine the outcome of the jungle war against Communist insurgents. They could carry heavy packs 30 miles in a day across impossible terrain, locate remote ladangs where there would be food and shelter, inform on the enemy.

The Orang Asli, as the peninsula's aboriginal groups are now known, have been sold down the river with monotonous regularity. The pattern was set by early invaders from Indonesia, whose hunting parties drove them up into the dense forests of the main range. The Semai, recalling those times, produce their own V-sign: two hands cupped to the mouth in the unmistakable action of firing a blowpipe.

They experienced perhaps their most unexpected betrayal at the hands of two English brothers entrusted with their welfare. Pat Noone, a Protector of Aborigines who chronicled the Temiar tribe's dream culture, disappeared into the jungle in 1941 when his unit was overtaken by the Japanese invasion, and teamed up with the Malayan Communist Party, whose guerrillas were to provide the only effective resistance of the Japanese occupation. Noone, murdered soon afterwards, unwittingly gave the MCP a piece of information which has helped to prolong Malaya's miserable conflict until the present day.

He told the Communists that they could survive indefinitely in the deep jungle if they made use of the Orang Asli, who would feed them and provide accurate reports on the movements of the Japanese. More important, Noone convinced them that the Orang Asli doctrine of shared liability was a natural breeding ground for Communism.

In 1948 the Malayan Communist Party launched a campaign of terror aimed at expelling the British once and for all. They re-established contact with the Orang Asli and took to the jungle again. The British began the slow task of wooing the aborigines and exploiting their skills in much the same way that the Communists had done. Squeezed from both sides, the Orang Asli became principal pawns in Malaya's little rehearsal for the Vietnam War.

Pat Noone's younger brother, Richard, gave the knife another twist when he took over the Department of Aborigines in 1953. Well aware that the Orang Asli have strict taboos against all forms of violence, he recruited an aborigine regiment known as the Senoi Pra'ak to clean up the mess his brother had unwittingly helped to create. 'Without a positive, aggressive role in the campaign,' he wrote shortly before his death, 'and aborigine heroes to whom they could look up . . . they would remain second-class citizens.'

Twenty-three years after independence, the Orang Asli remain second-class citizens, and the war against the Communists drags on. The Senoi Pra'ak is a paramilitary unit of the Police Field Force, operating with the Army on special assignments. 'They have the best kill rate in the Army,' said a major. 'Those chaps have feet like a gorilla's. You wouldn't believe the way they can run up a telegraph pole at forty-five degrees.'

There are believed to be about 1000 Orang Asli spread throughout Malaysia's security forces. Their high drop-out rate is sanctioned on the basis that they provide a constant 'civilising' influence on their tribal groups, where they are counted on as the eyes and ears of the government. While on active service they are encouraged – some say pressurised – to adopt the Muslim faith. Many return home with a set of values which is inimical to Orang Asli society.

That night two young men lurched into the longhouse streaming with water, and joined the circle around the dining mat. They had propped something beside the entrance. It was a loris, a member of the sloth family whose large eyes had reflected the boys' torchlight: they had blown it out of a tree with a 12-bore shotgun. Still alive, it was trussed between two staves. With each struggle a red bubble welled up on its fur.

This was a welcome if unsavoury distraction from a tricky conversation. The shaman, who wore a time-piece of his own, had expressed a keen interest in my digital watch. The word *toc* denotes the negative in Semai. '*Toc* tick,' I explained (it doesn't tick). 'Tick-tock,' he murmured dubiously, holding it to his ear. '*Toc* tick-tock,' I repeated. 'Tick-tock-tick-tock,' he said, giving it a shake. The women giggled. The shaman grinned. It was a put-up job.

Everyone loved the shaman. In the afternoon he had returned from his allotment looking like death. For five minutes he tickled the headman into a state of wild mirth, teased the girls, and played the fool. Then he crumpled on the floor and lay there with the dogs licking him until someone brought a glass of tea. He might have been 40, but looked 20 years older. He said that having two wives kept him young.

When he was a boy, an old shaman had blown spirits into his chest. He had felt sharp pains in his heart. Everyone was afraid of disturbing the old shaman's sleep in case he turned into a were-tiger. Now people came to him to be healed.

During the night the storm blew itself out and the loris died. In bright sunlight the family set off to the edge of their world, the youngest children leading the way so that the adults could regulate their pace to a rate at which none tired. The path must have been centuries old, but no effort had been made to iron out its kinks and sharp drops as it followed the river's downward plunge. The Semai seemed equally content with their precarious method of crossing rivers, balancing on submerged rocks and leaping to the next before the spirits of the rapids gripped their ankles.

After a couple of miles they paused to shoulder heavy bundles of petai, stored beside the track to await collection. Petai is a popular wild fruit, said to inhibit diabetes, which together with the durian fruit provides the Semai with a modest source of income for three months of the year. They climb high in the petai trees to hook them down: hence their reputation on telegraph poles.

A dozen Semai, similarly burdened, appeared through the trees. They had slogged 11 miles through the jungle to earn a few dollars. The Semai are a handsome people, but this lifestyle takes its toll among the more remote groups. At 30, the women's hair is streaked with grey; by the time both sexes reach 50 their teeth have gone and skin sags on bone.

Two men lagged behind, blowpipes raised to the trees in the hope of picking off squirrels. Hands outstretched, a small boy crept noiselessly towards a bright confusion of butterflies, the souls of the dead. Tourism has put a price on those, too.

The jungle-concrete interface came into view. It was only a shaded platform presided over by a Chinese harridan, but to the Semai it represents the cutting edge of materialism. This is where they get ripped off and their children first learn their place in the scheme of things. It's the small print that governments never mention when they talk about integrating their indigenous minorities. There's always a store like this run by people from the lowest strata of the dominant society. More often than not they sell alcohol: this one was doing a good trade in Guinness Stout.

A spotty Chinese youth counted the petai bundles and wordlessly handed each headman a grubby sheaf of notes. A van was already waiting. This was one of dozens of collection points in the area, and the vans' specific arrival times meant that anyone could pinpoint where and when the Semai could be located with money supposedly burning holes in their pockets.

A few scavengers had already arrived. The girls wandered over to inspect a pile of cheap dresses and T-shirts spread out on a newspaper beside the road. The Indian merchant looked on with disdain. At a careful distance from the Chinese, a Malay laughed loudly and slapped the headman on the back. He was attempting to secure future supplies of petai. An elderly Indian wobbled up on a moped bearing cakes and ice lollies. 'Why you want to stay with jungle people?' asked the Chinese youth. 'No entertainment up there.'

The headman was pensive as the family walked home carrying rice, tea, tobacco and fish. At one point he turned and muttered something about leeches. I began to examine my legs, but he was looking back in the direction of the store. These visits clearly depressed him. His dignity paled to deference before the tradesmen's bombastic assumption of superiority. He dreamed, he said, of having a van of his own.

In theory, the Orang Asli are classified with the ruling Malays under the preferential title of bumiputras, or 'sons of the soil'. With 300,000 indigenous jungle dwellers in Malaysia's Borneo states, the peninsula could not appear to be neglecting its 60,000 Orang Asli. United, the two factions could one day represent a significant voting block against the Malays and Chinese who have made them feel like strangers in their own land.

In practice, however, bumiputra status is a thinly disguised device to increase Malay participation in the nation's economy, and has assisted no more than a handful of Orang Asli to university places. Malaysia is strenuously implementing the kind of development programmes that have already devastated the natural world in South America, and the government has shown little hesitation in subordinating the interests of its original inhabitants to the imperatives of economic expansion.

The Department of Orang Asli, administered by Malays, provides school and welfare programmes, but makes no secret of the fact that its primary concern is the security of the deep jungle, where its wards are expected to act as a tripwire against insurgency. The headman is unlikely to get his van. He will be lucky if he doesn't end up in one of the wooden settlements which are being knocked together for displaced Orang Asli.

Glimpsed from the mountainside above, his land pricked the eyes. It was a few days later, and he had called a halt in a long climb to visit relatives in the hills. A necklace of rapids and clear pools glinted on the valley floor. Blue smudges of smoke on the far slopes marked new ladangs where a few acres of jungle had been cleared for planting. Here the Semai were actually increasing the jungle's diversity with small clumps of tapioca, maize, bananas, chillies, sweet potato and sugar cane, in contrast to the monoculture phalanxes of rubber and oil palm that are supplanting natural vegetation throughout Malaysia.

During the climb, the headman made several careful detours around shafts of bamboo which lay innocently beside the path. Closer inspection revealed a spring mechanism rigged by hair trigger to impale animals on the game trail. The children occupied their spare moments modelling traps like this, some with the power to spear a tiger, others so delicate that mouse deer walk straight into the fibre noose.

A trap is closing on the Semai. The assumptions about progress that filter through to them are insistent and beguiling. The technology represented in a match-head dwarfs their achievement in designing a complex support system that could run indefinitely. In the national climate of asset-stripping, who could blame them if they sold their library of knowledge as firewood?

Beyond the mountain's crest, the headman's cousin was waiting in front of his longhouse. Green bamboo flasks of cool water were quickly produced, followed by warm segments of tapioca. In the corner a boy was suckling a tree squirrel from a leaf funnel containing tinned milk.

Our host pulled a piece of paper from his shorts and pushed it across the floor. It was a competition form issued by a British tampon manufacturer, offering 20 colour TV sets as prizes. All the applicant had to do, according to the Malay instructions, was to collect four distinct emblems from the firm's packets and provide answers in a descending order of merit. The man's wife held out a pencil.

One of the world's oldest legends is told by the pygmies, who are probably related to Malaysia's aboriginal Negritos. The story concerns a cataclysm which devastated the Earth's excessive populations in bursts of lightning, causing their hair and nails to fall out and consuming their bodies with fire. The pygmies attribute this conflagration to their ancestors' inability to control technology, claiming that their return to a primitive lifestyle was a conscious attempt to avoid another disaster. From the safety of their underground caves they would emerge to sire mankind again.

Rubbish, of course. I took the pencil and began to fill in the application form.

11 April 1981   **Stuart Wavell**

86th Street: what's left and for how long?

This morning, as predicted by the WQXR weather bulletins, there was precipitation and the wind chill factor eased. In short, it has been wet and warm. With the last vestiges of yellow-stained snow and grime-crusted ice washed away from the sidewalks, the denizens of West 86th Street have emerged from hiding to greet their corner of the world.

In the Lido Bello Hair Salon, Alan from Brooklyn sits waiting for customers, drooping ash and distress over the latest copy of *Opera* magazine. Slight, fiftyish, with wispy hair and a scaly scalp, he lives for Saturday afternoons when the Texaco Metropolitan Opera radio broadcast fills the shop and he can talk of Luciano, Montserrat and Placido to his old ladies.

His survival is one of the street's miracles. His rent has gone up again and still he persists. It cannot be his hairdressing skills or his charm that keeps his $7 shampoo-and-sets loyal. He has the belligerency of the timid. At his command, whining and arthritic clients shuffle to answer the phone, take the chain off the front door or simply wait uncomplainingly while he tries to cope with the unaccustomed pressure of three heads at once.

To hear Alan at work over some backcombing, however, is to feel part of the glamorous world of the international opera stage – a world he knows intimately from his hours of listening and reading, alone in his salon. 'That must be Siegfried singing,' as an aria starts on his radio. 'How can you not have heard of Siegfried Jerusalem? He's a very promising boy, don't you agree, Mrs Blumenthal?' And a head reared in 1900 Vienna, now washed on 86th Street, nods obediently.

Most of Alan's old ladies live in rent-controlled apartments, trying to shut out the clamour of landlords lobbying for the removal of all such controls. Their homes, for which they now pay between $300 and $400 a month would, on the open market, command over $1,500. If they were for sale, a $200,000 price tag would not be fanciful. Those on fixed incomes, young and old, shudder at the thought of cash in flight from South America and Europe crowding into their corner of Manhattan.

In the months of hibernation, changes have crept over this Columbus Avenue corner of 86th Street. George the Greek has refurbished his florist shop so that the $1.89 specials (a handy $2 with tax) stand in buckets on a bright new plastic floor. Improved lighting glints on George's elegant silver hair and on his chunky gold jewellery. If Harvey the Dry Cleaner next door is the street's favourite psychiatrist, George the

Greek is its philosopher. 'So what do you want to get aggravated?' says Harvey. 'Life is short.' 'Go home, be good to your husband and look after your children,' says George presenting a pink rose with a flourish. 'That's all there is, for life is short.'

It has seemed a lot shorter since Olga the Newslady collapsed and died one cold day over Christmas. Olga was a tiny Puerto Rican of 48. She wore scarlet lipstick that had a blue tinge in winter when she was frozen to the bone. No one noticed then, of course. Her smile was quick and everyone assumed that she had some trick, some extra stamina with which to work from five every morning till seven at night without so much as a whimper. Perhaps she didn't get tired like ordinary people?

Sometimes, when it was not too cold or, in summer, too hot, her husband would come down to her news-stand to pass an hour with his pavement cronies. Sometimes, her five children looked after the stand over lunch when it was quiet so that she could have coffee or sit down for a moment. Olga was proud of her family – of her eldest daughter, a beauty, of her grown son, a handsome young man. When she closed up the green wooden stand she would go home to cook and wash for them.

One day she went home and died. Her children run the stand now, shivering in the cold, perched on newspapers to ease the ache. It must be a hard living. Those customers who never dreamed that she suffered from asthma, who saw only what they wanted to, feel ashamed. They remember that they never gave her a Christmas offering because, unlike everyone else, she never asked. And so, to avoid unpleasant memories and bad consciences, they buy their newspapers elsewhere. Who, now that Olga is gone, will fight for the children for whom she worked and died?

When she was alive, it was somehow understood that no one would try to steal her business, meagre as it was. Now Shim Si, the Korean grocer, stocks newspapers too. Her children open later and close earlier than Olga. Shim Si, who like her was not born into the American dream, is there before and after them. His business improves; Olga's once tidy wooden shed looks shabbier by the day.

Shim Si has his own problems, it must be acknowledged. Until this winter it was also understood that this formal and impeccable doyen of late-night shopping would stock groceries and leave fruit and veg to Hyun Ki Chin across the road. Trouble started last summer: mischievous Hyun Ki Chin thought of presenting Walden Farm all-natural, low-sodium salad dressings to enhance his array of mange-touts, bean shoots, hand-picked asparagus tips and five different types of lettuce. A venture into organic breads was inevitable and now, to Shim Si's dismay, he has a full wall of groceries.

Shim Si countered with a greengrocery department; Hyun Ki Chin with a freshly-squeezed orange juice machine. It is of this war that Olga the Newslady's children are the hapless victims. The *New York Sunday Times* was Shim Si's answer to Hyun Ki Chin's Haagen Daz ice-cream display. Currently, Hyun Ki Chin is a piece ahead: his nieces, giggling, smiling maidens, have been introduced to the cash register which certainly overshadows Shim Si's parents who look like wisdom-embodying ancients from *National Geographic* magazine.

That our corner is in disarray owes much to the creeping gentrification of Columbus Avenue. Dry-cleaning stores closed; hearth furniture shops opened. The watch repairer disappeared; Shinera, the Japanese bed shop, fluttered into being with its promise of athletic nights and Italian sheets. It is the tyranny of the rent; the seduction of the singles' scene.

The gay young men in their Calvins, the Preppies in their strawberry pink polo necks, the waitressing ballerinas in their pointed Western boots, drift by the windows of the old-timers. But on this warm, wet day, the singles stay home lest their perms frizz and the old-timers hazard their way down 86th Street wondering what's left, who's left – and for how long.

20 February 1981   **Linda Blandford**

Dogged by fate

Enthralled by a royal cameo from the Radio Times feature on Landseer: 'When Queen Victoria asked him about the diminutive terrier he carried in a coat pocket she was told it was a champion ratter. A rat was called for . . .'

A rat was called for! And, unlike a plumber say, appeared on cue and possibly on a plate. The full power and panoply of monarchy was never apparent to me till now.

This aspect of Landseer as a royal rat catcher is a novel one. Landseer: A Victorian Comedy (BBC-1) suggests that the upper classes and their damned dogs did for him. As *The Times* said, with unconscious irony, when he died, 'He was patronised by the very highest in the land.' Hence the Buckingham Palace-cum-Battersea Dogs' Home pictures where you cannot move without crushing some promising puppy underfoot.

He amused house parties with his ability to draw with both hands simultaneously; their dogs died waiting to be painted. Countess, a noble bitch, had been five days dead when Landseer arrived and got her on canvas in the nick of time as The Sleeping Bloodhound.

Images of death, like poor old Countess, pursued him. A pair of polar bears eating Sir John Franklin, hero of the North West Passage ('Why, oh why, will artists choose such gloomy themes?' Can this be the first known use of 'Why, oh why?'); eagles savaging swans ('The Queen does not care for it'). And, of course, the Trafalgar Square lions, couchant on grounds of economy and sculpted from decaying corpses ('Anything as fearful as the gases from the royal remains, it is difficult to communicate'). Something, I suppose, like Henry VIII who, before burial but luckily after death, exploded. Images of the pit. Like The Divine Comedy, A Victorian Comedy is short on chortles.

Landseer never could paint people. He is the only artist whose Godiva is remarkable for the horse. By some sort of sympathy, the people are the most ponderous part of A

Victorian Comedy. The best are the tormented storm-tossed shots of Scotland, which reminds me of George VI saying to Piper, 'You seem to have been unlucky with the weather.' By and large, princes are not good painters.

3 June 1981   **Nancy Banks-Smith**

The Master's voice

Genius can make nonsense of the usually clear distinction between extroverts and introverts. The more Shakespeare or Mozart or Henry James give themselves to the world and worldly activities the more treasure they lay up in the other world of their art: the harder they work at living the more independently and copiously functions their creative imagination.

James's letter-writing was the hardest of work, as exigent as the social life which it accompanied and commemorated. Even at this distance there is something awe-inspiring about his success in London society, the number of hostesses who took him up, the dinners and crushes he attended, the weekends of 'gilded bondage' at Mentmore or Waddesdon. The warmth and charm which shines out to every correspondent must also have won the heart – if there was any – behind the 'cold pleasant eyes' of the English upper classes at play.

James never spared himself. The frequent and jocular asides to the effect that his correspondence is killing him are kidding on the level. After sitting down at nine o'clock, 4.30 finds him still at work, having switched for a couple of hours or so to letters from the composition of novels and stories. Every day he kept at it, and it is not hard to imagine the pleasure and gratitude with which an old friend like Grace Norton back in Cambridge, Massachusetts, must have received the voluminous sheets filled with gossip about London and Paris and penetrating comment on innumerable mutual friends, distilled in an atmosphere of special intimacy, his own kind of love.

James was living by his pen. In this, the most eventful and

dramatic period of his busy life, he had many successes and disappointments, tried and failed at the theatre, lost his much-loved sister Alice and many young friends by premature death – Lizzie Duveneck, Wolcott Balestier, the brilliant young publishing entrepreneur whose sister Kipling was to marry, Robert Louis Stevenson in the South Seas, to whom he had been the most faithful and vivacious of correspondents.

Nothing in the political or social scene was lost on him at this time either, and no little literary job to be done for money – even a translation of a late novel of Daudet, done for Harper's for £350, an inducement too generous to be resisted. James in these years is more Zola than Balzac, cataloguing every impression of his society and time, speculating on Home Rule for Ireland and the possibilities of civil war, kicking himself for having been in Bournemouth on the day of the great London unemployment riots of 1886, which he says he would have given anything to have seen at first-hand.

One of his most faithful and devoted correspondents, Constance Fenimore Woolson, did see them, but being rather deaf, and disorientated in England, had not realised anything unusual was going on. She had lodgings near James's in Bolton Street, off Piccadilly, from which he might have had a grandstand view of the troubles (he noted that all the glass was broken on the Piccadilly side).

Fenimore, as James always referred to her, was a southern American maiden lady who also had gained a modest prosperity by her pen; she passionately admired James's work, and there seems no doubt that she also came to love him deeply, while cherishing no illusions that her love could be returned by an equal devotion or an offer of marriage. James was much attached to her, made use of her and patronised her, but also made every effort to make her happy. He succeeded up to a point – two touching letters from her, of great length, are reprinted as an appendix by Professor Edel.

After Fenimore fell from a window in Venice, where she was living alone and recovering from flu, James at least had no doubt about its being suicide. 'What a picture of lonely unassisted suffering! It is too horrible for thought . . . she had always been, to my sense, a woman so little formed for positive happiness that half one's affection for her was, in its essence, a kind of anxiety.'

Of James's own *affaires du coeur* we find no trace in these busy years: the tycoon of style has left no opening for consciousness to be surprised by sex, as it was not infrequently to be in his later years, when the Danish sculptor Andersen, Jocelyn Persse, and most of all Hugh Walpole were to agitate and inspire him with the devotional feelings that poor Fenimore had once entertained for the Master. In the meantime he can feel thoroughly at home in the pleasure he gives to his worldly, satisfied female correspondents. And the ghost of Fenimore is turned into Miss Tita of *The Aspern Papers*, the most touching and in a way the most intent portrait of a lady he was to draw.

The letters to brother William, always long and affectionate, have a perceptible and fascinating undercurrent of rivalry and self-justification running through them, and comments on the brother's ambitions and achievements are on occasion not so much feline as snide – a word Henry would have abominated. And yet the most moving of all is the detailed account of their sister Alice's last hours which Henry sent his brother, a truly astonishing piece of writing both in its feeling and its unflinching detail, as gripping yet as devoid of mere effect as an account by Tolstoy would be.

Critically, some of the most rewarding letters are to Vernon Lee, the Edwardian bluestocking whose admiration for James did not stop her caricaturing him in a novel. He not only forgave but proffered sound counsel.

> *LIFE* is less criminal, less obnoxious, less objectionable, less crude, more *bon enfant*, more mixed and casual, and even in its most offensive manifestations, more *pardonable*, than the unholy circle with which you have surrounded your heroine.

Many novelists writing today might profit from that observation.

The Letters of Henry James, vol. 3, 1883–1895, edited by Leon Edel (Macmillan, £17.50).

12 March 1981   **John Bayley**

A grand ol' soap oprey

He couldn't, or wouldn't, paint women in the manner to which they have become accustomed. The breast furthest away from him would invariably be enlarged as if to compensate for the cruel laws of perspective. Their clumsy legs would stop at the point where a body became a dress. It was on the dress rather than the body that Edward Hopper would lavish his attentions, lavish his rich colours, modelling the buttocks as fondly as a potter manhandling a lump of clay. He also painted lipstick rather than lips, eye-shadow rather than eyes.

Perhaps it's because his wife Jo insisted on posing for all the secretaries, all the usherettes, all the waitresses. She hated cooking, 'which is why one so often saw the Hoppers in Village coffee shops and cheap restaurants. The vaguely melancholy man preferred not to talk at all unless he absolutely had to; the little woman with the ponytail never stopped . . .'

Something of this typical, difficult marriage seems to stiffen the figures in every Hopper painting. The men never seem to be listening to what the lipstick's saying, never seem to notice that the eye-shadow is looking at them. A typical Hopper family is bound together by force of habit. The daughter sits in an armchair and reads, the father comes home from work, the mother has just been shopping. We've watched the television serial, read the book and now, at the Hayward Gallery, we see the pictures.

The Americans have been having a love-affair with Edward Hopper since the thirties. It is he rather than any of the strutting peacocks of Abstract Expressionism or Pop who is accepted as the greatest American painter. He is the closest they will ever get to a Hogarth, a painter with a finger firmly on the pulse. They love the way that he was prepared to look into the ashcans of their cities, they love the way that a Hopper painting seems to verify their official Hollywood biography. Even his Civil War paintings focus on the extras.

Why else would a dull picture like *Early Sunday Morning* become 'his most famous painting'? It consists of a row of seedy shops, placed full-frontally across the picture surface, a barber's pole and a fire hydrant. There is nothing else. This is Hopper's secret, he allowed his audience to fill in the missing bits, the missing figures, the missing neighbourhood, the missing America. It was someone else who changed Hopper's original title of *Seventh Avenue Shops* to the much less anonymous *Early Sunday Morning*.

Other American artists were too busy selling stories, supplying information, to realise that every-one of their audience had stories of their own to tell. Reading Alfred Kazin's long, entertaining introduction to the Hayward catalogue you soon realise that Kazin is writing about himself and using Hopper as an excuse. 'I did not know I loved New York, I did not know there was a New York to love . . . until I saw it in museums,' he begins, before launching into his own recollections of 'roof edges across which I had actually seen cops chase robbers,' and where 'undernourished Jewish featherweights sparred on the gravel before they got knocked out of the ring at Canarsie.'

You suspect that similar thoughts are going through the minds of Hopper's few protagonists, the boss and his secretary, the usherette and the ticket buyer, the waitress and the diner. 'The loneliness thing was overdone,' he once said, referring to the one word that became indispensable from a review of his work. His figures aren't lonely, they're just thinking. His compositions, as the drawings show, have been so carefully worked out that the figures, like the fire hydrants, daren't move for fear of upsetting the balance. Each one is posed separately and then carefully positioned in the room. No wonder they find it hard to communicate. They're too busy holding their breaths, waiting for the painter to finish.

The exhibition is divided into three sections dealing with his early, middle and late periods (since he lived to 85 each period spans decades rather than years. At each step he was ten years older than you think). The last two sections are almost indistinguishable. A slap-happiness finally enters his brushwork to compensate for the uniformity of style.

The early period work is interesting not only for its diversity but also for its light-heartedness. There are views of Paris twinkling in the spring sunshine and rocky coastlines bursting with weather. Hopper's mature work always seems to rely on artificial light. Even the sun behaves like a giant light-bulb.

A series of self-portraits show him adopting the traditional artist's squint. So intent is he on capturing a likeness that others will always mistake him for a very intense young man.

For it was art rather than life which taught Hopper how to brood. He copied Manet's *Olympia* and learned all about theatres and cafés from Degas. Almost all his solitary secretaries sitting in trains, mulling over their coffees or ignoring their bosses, are direct descendants of Degas's *Absinthe Drinker*.

A curious painting from 1914, *Soir Bleu*, points directly towards his glorious maturity. A group of figures have been plucked out of their rightful context and forced to visit the same Parisian bar. The pierrot belongs in a circus; the ritzy couple belong in the Ritz; the old sailor belongs in a dockside tavern; the admiral belongs in the ship's mess. No wonder they won't acknowledge each other's existence. In future, having been accused by critics of producing 'an ambitious fantasy', Hopper would make sure that all his cast came from New York.

But he never lost his love of artifice. He never really tried to pass it off as reality; that was his audience's doing. 'Notice how artificial trees look at night,' he said, before proceeding to paint them blue. If you look closely enough at anything it will seem artificial, which is why his paintings of other people's houses, with their pointed edges and strident shadows, always look so strange. There is nothing about these houses which suggests that they are also homes.

Much of his adult life was spent travelling. From high up above New York, on the subway, he could not only observe his fellow passengers but also peep into other people's windows, other people's lives. And so by always approaching a scene through a window he forces us to do the same. Others overheard snippets of conversation; Hopper oversaw snippets of daily life. The husband reads the paper and the wife tinkles with the piano. The office at night is a silent place no matter how hard you hit the keys of the typewriter.

It was during his nosy, middle years that Hopper produced the most memorable of the silent moody images with which this exhibition is so well endowed (even allowing for the cuts made since its American showing). You soon forget to question his occasional clumsiness, the liberties he takes with the female anatomy, and just enjoy the sight of America yawning.

This collective sigh of boredom is enlivened by his spectacular sense of colour. It's not only his women's lips which are coated in dazzling lipstick. Their dresses like their gas pumps come in glorious flamingo reds. Their wallpaper comes in refreshing lemon-yellows across which the sunlight fizzles like sherbet. Their artificial trees have never seen the sunlight in their lives, which is why they've turned a subterranean blue.

14 February 1981   **Waldemar Januszczak**

A country diary: Kent 2

I made the mistake of looking at the mansion set back in parkland too long and too intently. When I completed my stroll down the footpath to the moated site I wanted to see, I was quickly surrounded by an impressive band, like something out of a film about the Foreign Legion. I just had time to note that the moated farm now bore the device of a long-horned cow and a name that originated at least 2,000 miles from Kent. Why was I photographing their house? I had no camera, but my binoculars, which are unusually small and better suited to the front row of the stalls than distant landscapes, excited them. I was obviously up to no good. Somehow I felt that my explanation of medieval colonising patterns in the Low Weald and the significance of moated sites in the thirteenth century did not interest them. When I was accused of walking over their land, I was provoked into a short but pertinent lecture on rights-of-way in general and that particular right-of-way especially as an ancient drove road. I pointed to the long-horned cow to emphasise the point. Cattle drives, in Kent? They looked incredulous. The shotgun one of them waved about may have been pointing out the more notable features of the landscape but I doubted it and got even more British, talking about the Queen's Highway. After all, I was standing on the road at the time. Then came the unanswerable question. Why was I walking? I looked down at my boots, my grubby trousers, and the rest of my paraphernalia, felt the sweat on my brow from the exertions of a summer day, and knew there was no answer they would understand. The culture gap was too wide even for the delights of the Weald to bridge. I had to leave them to their misgivings.

7 August 1981   **John T White**

An ill wind in the dale

The snow began at midnight on Thursday and it was obviously going to be heavy. By morning, a depth of five inches was lying everywhere and a strong east wind was driving it against the walls. It was hard to see, let alone work, in the biting blizzard.

In the middle of the lambing season all the plans made by farmers in this dale, as in hill country throughout the North, had come to nothing and thousands of ewes and their lambs were suddenly in danger. This was an emergency almost without precedent.

Very often the weather for lambing can be bad but the worst snows are usually over. Floods and lack of grazing are the normal hazards. This year, lambing had begun a week before in warm and sunny weather. There was already a fair growth of grass on the hillsides and the farmers were beginning to think the season would be one of the most successful.

But the blizzard continued without a break all day on Friday. The lane up the dale was being continuously ploughed. The main road to Skipton, 20 miles away, was blocked, should anyone have wanted to go. By nightfall the level snow lay 15 inches deep and it didn't stop until it had reached nearly 18 inches by the small hours on Saturday. When the sky cleared moorland drifts of up to 20 feet could be seen from down below. The RAF cancelled an endurance test for commandos.

Throughout Friday night families slept in relays if at all, going out every hour to deliver lambs from the ewes brought down into crofts on the valley bottoms. Those that had already lambed were packed into barns with the last scraps of the dwindling hay. Weak lambs were brought into kitchens and fed by the bottle.

But that created problems too. At five past three on Friday afternoon the electricity had gone off and was not restored for more than 24 hours. Milking had to be done by hand, which the cows don't like unless used to it and which is a long process when sheep, freezing outside, are calling for attention. Milking finished at one farm at 1.30 a.m., by which time it was late to start making a fresh tally of how the lambs, indoors or out, were faring.

By daylight Saturday, it was possible to survey the wreckage. Bad, with scores of dead lambs, but not as bad as some had feared in the dale itself. For farmers higher up on the slopes of Pen-y-Ghent there was a miserable spectacle with hundreds of sheep and lambs unaccounted for under the snow. At the head of the dale, seven cattle from a herd turned out to graze only the day before had panicked, trampled each other into the snow and died.

Saturday gradually cleared but the work was not over. The hogs (last year's lambs) had all been sent on to high pasture between 1500 and 2000 feet up. This entailed a long tramp through deep snow to dig for those trapped in the drifts and pull them out, heavily weighted by ice, by their horns. Fourteen were rescued in one four-hour journey, every stride an effort. Their heads were just visible above the snow and there must still be many others lost to sight.

No one knows yet what has happened to the wildlife. Throughout Friday, birds which normally stay on the hills and in the woods were scrabbling for food on the roads. The curlews, which nest on the ground, had just started breeding, filling the air with their cries. There must be precious few nests left after this blizzard. The drifts up against the high moorland walls everywhere show the tracks of grouse searching for exposed clumps of heather.

At nightfall last night it was freezing. The outlook for the lambs not so far rescued was bleak. The sky was overcast and farmers were beginning to wonder whether the blizzard which, they had heard, had spread to the Midlands and North Wales, was going to return overnight. If so, there would have to be yet another set of calculations.

No one remembers quite such a sudden disaster. Heavy snow fell in mid-May in 1935 but it had gone by next day. The bad winter of 1978/79 had eased in time for lambing. By midday yesterday, there was still thick snow up the hillside, some of it being blown back into the valley.

An elderly farmer living by himself had sent his newborn lambs to high pasture on Thursday. By Saturday morning he had tramped up three times to try to rescue them. 'If we could live on our losses,' he said, 'at this rate we should soon be doing very well.'

27 April 1981   **Geoffrey Taylor**

Something nasty in the Limousin

When Pierre and Marie-Annik Bouvier gave up city living for a goat farm in Limousin, with another young couple and all the children, the one thing they never bargained for was uranium under the ground. So far all that has happened is that men from COGEMA, a subsidiary of the French Atomic Energy Commission, have appeared with geiger counters on the fringes of the hilly, well-wooded ten-acre field at the edge of the forest.

It was Mr Yves Puibaraud himself, manager of the Limousin Uranium Mines, who broke the news to Bouvier that radio-activity had been recorded showing exploitable

183

uranium under the farm. Nothing would happen for a year or so because the mine was too busy elsewhere, at least six miles away, and new seams were coming up all the time. But eventually a shaft would extend under the ground, with its air vents belching steam and the hum of its ventilators and drilling machines.

Bouvier is not waiting for that. A natural opponent of nuclear energy, he has helped mobilise a 'Ban the Mines' resistance movement which has blocked roads to COGEMA lorries, staged farmers' hunger strikes against mining that dries up age-old wells, and linked up with Greenpeace, Friends of the Earth and other movements to fight an expanding 'uranium network'.

The movement complains that for years COGEMA has been ruining the verdant Limousin with its gaping open-cast mines and its monstrous, more or less radioactive slag heaps. More ominously, the mines are said to allow radioactive waste water to trickle into rural streams and even reservoirs of drinking water for Limoges and Bellac.

Bouvier has acquired an ancient geiger counter which he applies to the steamy air vents of the mines and reports that radon gas, imprisoned for millennia under the uranium-bearing granite, poisons the atmosphere and settles on plants and streams. He says the gas poisons the milk and meat and vegetables as well as the water. And the relentless administrative punch behind the mines (the prefect has declared their work to be in the general interest) enables them to expropriate land and confiscate buildings.

The ecologists are mounting a special uranium campaign for the presidential election, calling the mines 'the dirtiest and most murderous link in the nuclear chain'. At Limoges a leading ecologist explained: 'With Giscard and Mitterrand neck and neck, they will have to woo us.'

All this is painful and bewildering to Mr Yves Puibaraud, the studious and affable geologist in charge of the mines. If Bouvier is the anti-uranium hero of the Limousin Hills, Puibaraud is the long-suffering anti-hero. Bouvier was 25 when he came to his farm seven years ago. Puibaraud was not much older in 1948 when he arrived in the region with a task of most urgent national priority, ordered by de Gaulle himself: provide France with the means of its own nuclear deterrent.

The Americans had been trying with British and Canadian help to monopolise uranium sources in the Western world. The key to French independence was to mine the ore at home and Puibaraud's geiger counters mapped out the fractured seams of granite where the 'yellow cake' containing the ore could be mined.

Today the main customer is not the army but EDE – the Electricity Generating Board, the world's biggest consumer of uranium, committed to the only nuclear expansion programme unhindered by doubts and protest.

Lately, uranium prices have been falling as other nuclear programmes slow down. And to add to the glut, France is operating much richer mines in Niger, Gabon and Canada. But that old haunting fear of penury remains. Niger and Gabon could go the way of Chad, and France could be left naked. So Puibaraud goes on producing a thousand tons a year, for which he has to shift millions of tons of granite rubble. He has acquired nearly two thousand acres of land, mines ore at 40 sites, employs 1,100 miners – and goes on exploring with results that encourage him.

He feels badly maligned. 'A good geologist cannot operate without goodwill. We work under great stress. In the end we have to come up for air.' He has spent much of the last 30 years negotiating for land, fending off lawsuits over dried-up wells, allocating funds for alternative water supplies and, in cases of last-ditch resistance, resorting to expropriation. Sometimes he goes to law, as he now proposes to do against Pierre Bouvier and three other militants who barricaded roads against his lorries.

'Most of the time I've been dealing with peasants who you can talk to. They want compensation and we're talking about money: we're talking the same language. Now we're dealing with anti-nuclears: that's a different language.'

With the breakdown of language, the high-handed secrecy, which is the bane of French bureaucracy, spoils attempts at understanding.

At Auriat village, south-west of Limoges, a few alert inhabitants recently went through a nightmare worthy of a science-fiction fantasy by John Wyndham. One night they saw unknown men digging a deep shaft in a village field. The mayor, who by French law and custom is supposed to know, knew nothing. The men just shrugged and said they were sinking a 1000-metre shaft in the granite to see if it could store highly radioactive nuclear waste. After inquiries through the prefect and the member of parliament to the Minister for Industries, this turned out to be true. But the minister added reassuringly that for the moment it was only a scientific inquiry.

The worst fears of all – that city drinking water is lethally radioactive – has for the moment been laid at rest. A leading consumers' organisation conducted tests showing only 1.5 pico-curies per litre coming out of taps in Limoges and twice that amount in Bellac and concluded the inhabitants 'can be reassured'. The reading was well below accepted safety margins and indeed below the known radioactivity of Vichy water.

But the survey warned that alpha radiation in rural springs and streams was up to fifteen times the rate, already high, recovered upstream of the mines. It said radon gas was being spread around the countryside.

Puibaraud's first observation is that the Limousin has been radioactive for millennia. 'If it wasn't we'd never find the uranium.' Charts have been produced showing most famous brands of French mineral water many times more radioactive than any measured here. But ecologists retort that nobody cooks his soup or vegetables in mineral water, nor do entire families drink it throughout their lives.

Sceptical about alternative energy, Puibaraud points out that experimental production of bio-energy in Italy and France has produced considerable quantities of radon.

Protests in the region finally induced the Ministry of Health to publish its water readings, hitherto kept secret. But the dissidents remain sceptical. 'Why don't they publish figures for previous years? Maybe we've all been fatally irradiated years ago,' said Mrs Lucette Pratbernon, of the Limoges

Anti-nuclear Liaison Group. 'And why do they publish readings for only three radioactive elements and not the other nine released from the mines?'

Puibaraud replies wearily that the other elements released are so minute as to be unmeasurable. 'And if we made public our own internal readings nobody would believe us, so what's the point?'

What is the safe norm? For drinking water it varies from 3 pico-curies a litre to 120 according to which standard you take. And how do you measure it? Bouvier's ancient geiger counter measures pulses per second, officials use units measuring pico-curies or sometimes milirems. Nobody seems sure about how to correlate the figures.

It is this vagueness which frightens people like Mrs Pratbernon. She envies the militant sheep farmers of the nearby Larzac Hills, who have been fighting the army for 10 years to prevent their fields being used as an artillery range. 'Their enemy is tangible. Ours is invisible: something sinister nobody can really measure.'

To convince us the mines are safe after all, the Atomic Energy Commission sent its chief safety engineer, Mr Jacques Pradel, head of nuclear protection services, from Paris specially to brief us. He showed us round the Limousin laboratory which takes 83 readings a day of the atmosphere in the mines. We saw the readings being fed into a computer which checks the doses for every miner.

'Admittedly, with 1000 miners working for 30 years, we cannot reach a scientific conclusion. But so far we've had no more lung cancer than any other group,' said Mr Pradel. The company's doctor, Dr Chameau, has made a name for himself in his field with the discovery that rats subjected to 300,000 pico-curies a litre of radiation from radon invariably get lung cancer. Now he is working on smaller doses.

Pradel is confident that the radium miners who, before the First World War, died of lung cancer in large numbers in Yugoslavia and the United States, were 'simply not getting enough ventilation'. So we went down to the rock face in a mine near the company's headquarters at Razes. We felt a continuous blast of compressed air, designed to dilute and

187

disperse the radon, pumped in through plastic tubes. And waste water was being drained off through special channels to purification points, where chemical catalysts precipitate radioactive elements as mud, which is evacuated.

When Mr Pradel said over lunch that radiation from air vents was no higher than in any hole in the ground in this region, we challenged him to demonstrate. Sure enough, his geiger counter measured 350 pico-curies at the shaft exit, just 300 in a hole in the ground, and almost 300 in the God-given radioactivity of the air.

The real argument is not about radioactivity but about society. Mrs Pratbernon conceded that miners are well paid for their work. 'But I cannot accept that for a few extra kilowatts of electricity some poor wretch will die of cancer.'

Less sophisticated scepticism is expressed by some of the older farmers. Mr Louis Lachaud at St Sylvester, whose well was dried up four years before the company laid on a new pipe for him, expressed the time-honoured pessimism of his profession. 'Okay, but what's to ensure this one won't dry up, too? They're still digging away, aren't they? They'll end up by drying out the whole area.'

Still deeper scepticism from his neighbour Rene Dessaignes, who claims he lost his best two acres to the mine. 'As I see it, people who swear by this nuclear energy today are the same sort of people who swore by the Maginot Line. And how long did it take the Germans to knock that down?'

14 March 1981   **Walter Schwarz**

Bananas

Will farmer John Burner of Salcombe, Devon, win a new swimming pool for the Dolphins Club of Grimsby by beating the National Trust in the battle of the Art Deco gateway bearing the name 'Overbecks' in illuminated red glass?

The question, as one amused participant observed, sounds like something out of *Clochemerle* – particularly when you learn that it also involves the only place in mainland England where bananas grow, and an electric shock machine designed to halt the loss of hair and virility.

The story starts with the eccentric German bachelor of Grimsby, Mr Otto Overbeck, who invented a so-called rejuvenator. He also invented alcohol-free beer in the 1930s and was a great sponsor of youth sports, particularly through the Grimsby Dolphins. Mr Overbeck made enough money with the rejuvenator – gadgets like that were popular then – to retire to a Victorian house near Salcombe with one of the best sea views in England and a sub-tropical garden, which is where the bananas come in. He put his seal on the place by building an elaborate gateway with teak and bronze embellishments and flamboyant ironwork in Art Deco style, topped with an ingenious electrical system which lights up the word 'Overbecks' in a blaze of red.

When he bequeathed it all to the National Trust in 1937, his will said it must retain the name Overbecks or be sold to finance a new pool for Grimsby. Recently, however, the Trust has begun dismantling the gateway to restore it, and given that the surrounding Trust property has always been called Sharpitor after the local hill, the name of the house is nowhere visible until you get inside it and start poking about among the relics of Salcombe which it contains, along with a youth hostel.

Enter Mr Burner, owner of adjoining land and, by common local consent, an unconventional entrepreneur and something of a character. There's a running battle between him and the Trust – and the local council – over his various notions of building on his beautiful land or, failing that, cutting down all the trees on it and starting a pig farm. The latest round is that the Trust is taking him to court for allowing his fences to fall down and his stock to enter and chew on the bananas – so Mr Burner, who has investigated the will, isn't going to let pass the chance of a legal counter-coup. He says the Trust has broken Mr Overbeck's will by taking down the name on the gateway and surrounding the house with new signs calling the place Sharpitor, and the 600 adults and children of the Dolphins should have the £1 million a sale would probably raise.

'It certainly got the dovecote fluttering among our legal people,' said Warren Davis, the local National Trust officer. 'But we feel quite confident it can't happen. It's just another salvo in this running battle we've got. Quite amusing, I suppose.'

16 February 1981   **Stephen Cook**

Forever Ambler

Around the time he was reshaping our expectations of the spy novel, Eric Ambler stayed in Tangier for a while and daily took his anis in a small beach cafe called L'Onde Bleue. The bar girl was a plump Rumanian who watched for approaching warships, and whenever one appeared, declaimed in Dietrich tones: 'Ah, My boyce are coming home.' It was a couple of years before the war.

She knew, Ambler says, just what the boyce of each nationality liked, and the British matelots liked egg'n cheeps. She was every sailor's friend, minding their cash when they went off to the whorehouse, or obliging selected clients in the back room.

All she asked in return was that her sailor friends should send her a postcard from their next ports of call, which she could then – as they all appeared to know – take to the German consul.

It was not the most efficient way of discovering the deployment of allied warships, it has a distinctly First World Warish, Somerset Maugham feel about it. But at that time, she was the only real spy Ambler had met. She was, at least, far removed from the world of Buchan and Sapper.

Ambler specially disliked Sapper, for his latent, sometimes patent fascist leanings. Ambler was well to the Left, his books at once gritty and prophetic. His first, written in 1935, deals with a device which is recognisably a hydrogen bomb. His twentieth, *The Care of Time*, published this week by Weidenfeld and Nicolson, deals with current and future pains like TV, oil sheikhs, and nuclear shelters, and the hope must be it is not as clairvoyant as the last.

Send No More Roses came out four years ago, and described ways the rich use to avoid enormous tax bills, and milk the Common Market. Since when, we have had the Vestey scandal, and Irish farmers driving cattle to and fro over the border to collect the Euroloot. Ambler waved that away – too crude. In his system, the butter train scooping up endless subsidies moved only on paper.

'I've nothing against the rich,' Ambler said, 'but really some of the things they do are monstrous.'

His parents were not rich, they were stage people, living marionettes, who discouraged him from following them. Though the grammar school career was intended to lead him into the ways of respectability, it almost ended in expulsion, for selling copies of an obscene poem attributed to Byron; Ambler's first profits from literature.

An irate mother of one of the boys, finding a copy in her son's blazer, took it to the headmaster. 'The boy fingered me at once,' said Ambler, 'though several of us were circulating the poem.'

At this remove the choice of the word 'fingered' still suggests the shock of that craven betrayal. Public school mores were nowhere more religiously honoured than in grammar schools.

Later there was a London University degree in engineering, a spell in the advertising department of an electrical firm, then a £6 a week job in an advertising agency, before he sold his first book. It brought £30, and more important, a six-book contract with Hodder and Stoughton, carrying a £100 advance on each novel. By writing two a year, he reckoned he would earn £4 a week, and be able to live in Paris. A hotel room cost 14 francs a night, and the franc weighed in at 80 to the pound.

The third of the six books was *Cause for Alarm*, and the Americans bought the film rights for $3,000. It was 1938, he was 29, and awash with money. He was about to write *The Mask of Dimitrios*, which a lot of critics still think is his best book.

Cause for Alarm also brought an invitation to tea with a man from what used, jokingly, to be called 'a department of the Foreign Office'. He wanted to know all about the unmarked paths by which Ambler's engineer hero escaped through the mountains from Italy to Yugoslavia.

Very miffed, he was, when Ambler told him they were invented after a close study of contour lines on a large-scale map. Ambler maintains this was his only contact with the secret service. Yet the topic, and Ambler's gentle voice and manner, produced the recurrent illusion that I was talking to Alec Guinness's Smiley.

Ambler does not recycle his characters, as Le Carré and Fleming, and others have done. His stories are usually about skilled technicians embroiled in sinister events by accident or their special knowledge.

It might be a writer/journalist (*Dimitrios, Intercom Conspiracy, Care of Time*). It might, more rarely, be a businessman (*Passage of Arms*) or a doctor (*Dr Frigo*, in his and many other eyes, his best post-war book). When a professional spy is there, he is not the central character.

If we are to take Ambler's word, he has never been involved in espionage. (During the war, he commanded a Bofors gun on Churchill's lawn at Chequers; later, wrote training films with Peter Ustinov). So what he knows about the secrets trade he knows by imagination, by gossip, and by reading. 'There's a book about spying by Baden Powell, you know, which has chapters on things like How to Avoid Being Recognised.

'You would walk very quickly until you turned a corner, then put your hat on a different way, and come back round the corner walking very slowly. That was supposed to put anyone following you off the scent. If you were making a drawing of an enemy fortress, you were supposed to disguise it as a drawing of a butterfly.'

After the war, Ambler spent most of his time writing film scripts, including twelve years in Hollywood until he returned in 1970 to settle with his second wife, in Montreux. He is seventy-two now, and his books are inevitably the subject of a clutch of American theses. Over there, his novels are usually coupled with the name of Graham Greene, 'which must be very annoying for Graham'.

It was Greene who devised a plan to sabotage the Tillings bid to take over Heinemann, who published both of them. Greene proposed that he and Ambler, plus two other best selling Heinemann authors, Priestley and Georgette Heyer, should simultaneously announce their intention to publish books with another house.

Ambler objected that he had an exclusive contract for his fiction with Heinemann, but Greene persuaded him to collect his travel articles and any other non-fiction stuff he could, and publish that. So one day, the trade press was full of the announcement that these four famous authors would publish their next books with Bodley Head (where Greene was a director).

'But it didn't have the slightest effect . . . Then I had to write the goddam book. There just wasn't enough material, so I had to write more.'

In desperation to fill, he included a piece he had written about the trial of John Bodkin Adams, a south coast doctor acquitted of murdering some of his patients.

'It was entirely sympathetic to Bodkin Adams. But the title of the collection was *The Ability to Kill*, and when W. H. Smith saw a copy they took counsel's opinion, and refused to handle it. The counsel's view was based on the case of a man who had sued Madame Tussaud's successfully, because an effigy of him had been placed too near the entrance to the Chamber of Horrors.' He had to write another piece, exactly the same length, to fill, and the whole first impression was pulped.

For his seventieth birthday, a couple of years ago, his German publishers put out a lavish celebratory volume, and he was interviewed endlessly on TV and radio. He found they kept on asking the same questions and as the interviews were all due for transmission around the same time, he tried to give them different answers. One question that always came up was, Where do you get your ideas? About the ninth time he was asked that, he was a bit stumped for something new to say, and hesitated.

'Ah!' said the TV interviewer, 'You can't answer that?' 'I said, "It's not that I can't answer, it's just that I'm often asked that and I'm trying to think of something fresh to say".'

The interviewer clearly smelt triumph. 'You mean you give different answers each time you are asked?'

Ambler said, yes, well, he didn't want to give a stale answer.

The interviewer leaned in, a card player who knows he is laying down the winning trick. 'Why,' he demanded, 'why do you not simply tell the truth?' That was the question Ambler really couldn't answer. He is taken very seriously in Germany.

30 May 1981   **Hugh Hebert**

Still standing

Max Wall is not only a great comic. He has now become a national institution. As such, one doesn't so much review him as revisit him, inspecting the fabric for signs of wear and tear. All I can say is that on the evidence of his current show at the Garrick, he looks pretty well indestructible, since he shows the true comic's ability to keep us entertained for a couple of hours with the minimum of resources.

He gives us all the well-loved rituals: the Birth of the Blues sung in frantic competition with the pianist; the attempt to play Liszt's *Hungarian Rhapsody* while cracking a flea and coping with the fact that one arm is mysteriously longer than the other; the famous grotesque walk with hunched shoulders and lunar-shaped bum.

But on top of the act we now get a constant running commentary on it: not only the despairing, heavenwards glances at the dreadfulness of some of the jokes and the finger clicks betokening success, but even attribution of sources. Max has now become a walking variorum edition giving us footnotes ('there's a lovely bit of Gillie Potter for you') as well as the authentic text.

But what is his real secret? It's partly that like Jack Benny, he seems to have all the time in the world: he has the confidence to pause in mid-gag, stroll upstage to get his cornet and then saunter back to give us the punchline. It's partly the feeling that he would be unfazed if the Garrick roof fell in: as a restless patron bolts for the exit in the midst of a routine he wanly remarks, 'He's gone to tell a friend to come in.'

Another Max, one Beerbohm, said of another comic: 'But, above all, our delight was in Dan Leno himself. In every art personality is the paramount thing and without it artistry goes for little.' What we respond to in Max Wall, I submit, is not merely the grotesque clowning, the demonic gurning, the savour of innuendo, but the sensation of going in to see a comedian and emerging having met an original and eccentric man.

18 February 1981   **Michael Billington**

The Queen and Gandhi's loin-cloth

Lord Mountbatten Remembers (BBC-1) in which we encounter The Mysterious Business of Gandhi's Loin-cloth.

After winning the war and outwitting assorted 'slimy politicians', our hero is advising Gandhi on a suitable present for Princess Elizabeth and Prince Philip: 'I know what. Why don't you spin a thread on your spinning wheel and get some of your honorary granddaughters to crochet a little table mat?' Contrary to the fate of most crocheted table mats, Princess Elizabeth was very taken with it and kept it in her own drawers.

But somewhere between India and England, Gandhi's tablecloth seems to have suffered a sea-change. Queen Mary, for one, was convinced it was a loin-cloth. I am a dedicated reader of royal memoirs, finding them so irresistibly funny that I have to clutch some passing commoner for support. *Mountbatten Remembers*, or How I Was Always Right, is rollicking knockabout fun and a case in point. On the matter of Gandhi's kilt he differs with Lady Airlie, lady-in-waiting to Queen Mary for 50 years. In *Thatched with Gold*, Lady Airlie describes how Queen Mary was 'deeply shocked at the sight of Gandhi's loin-cloth, publicly displayed'.

'What a horrible thing,' she explained. 'Such an indelicate gift.' Prince Philip spoke up for the loin-cloth, but Princess Margaret 'scenting danger, darted ahead, pounced on the offending garment and hid it quickly'.

It is all very extraordinary. Did Gandhi send a table mat, as Mountbatten believed, or a loin-cloth, or do old ladies suspect, with some justification, the worst? It is a mystery fit for the files of Arthur C. Clarke as he ponders the mysteries of this and other worlds under his golf umbrella, or, possibly, his penis gourd.

There are two more Mountbatten programmes to go and two more Clarke's . . . Cherish them.

This week the Sage of Sri Lanka was pondering Dragons, Dinosaurs and Great Snakes. In deepest New Zealand a bunch of Japanese in topees and binoculars were searching for the moa, a sort of 12ft blue turkey with a bad temper, and you'd have a bad temper if you'd been wiped out. The ingenious Japanese had calculated – by computer, how else? – the probable call of the moa and invaded likely locales, making mating-type cries. Somewhat to their relief, I feel, there was no reply. There are few things more disconcerting than meeting a 12ft turkey which thinks it has found a mate after 200 years' enforced chastity.

I shall remember with deep and abiding joy the look on the face of a Congolese, snappily dressed in a floral shirt and tropical-weight trousers, when asked by Professor Mackall of Chicago if he had seen any dinosaurs lately. Messrs Mackall and Powell, well equipped with mosquito hats and machetes, were seeking the fleeting diplodocus and, indeed, heard of one which had been trapped locally and cut up by the pygmies. 'They said it took forever.' Well, it would, wouldn't it? They were, however, forced to leave the Congo before locating another as 'their visas ran out'. The Sage, as downy a bird as the moa, evidently found this entertaining too.

12 November 1980   **Nancy Banks-Smith**

A short fuse from Babylon

There isn't much doubt, Franco Rosso says, that *Babylon*, his film about young West Indians in South London, will receive as many brickbats as compliments. He is on dangerous territory and knows it, like most of those who make a movie in Britain which tries to attract a wide audience and say something serious at the same time. All he hopes is that it will encourage a few others to be similarly daring. The British film industry, he believes, is dying from sheer inertia.

Babylon is the first feature of this Italian-born Englishman, and if he is nervous it is largely because everyone seems to expect so much from his film. 'People within the industry mostly want to be loved and to be successful so they don't make this kind of film. And some of them think it is asking for trouble even to broach the subject of racial tension. On the other hand, there are those who think that we haven't gone far enough, that we've tried to make an entertainment film out of something much too important to fiddle about with.

'All I can say is that we have made a start, and that you can't do everything in one film. It was an intensely difficult film to make, and a lot runs on it. We made the conscious decision to try for as wide an audience as possible without diluting our argument, and if we have even partly succeeded, that's an enormous plus,' Rosso says.

The film, which opened last week to good reviews, was made last autumn in South London with support from the National Film Finance Corporation and the Chrysalis Group. It was written by Rosso and Martin Stellman, and produced by Gavrik Losey, the son of Joseph Losey. And its cast mostly live within the area in which it was filmed, as does *Babylon*'s director.

'What we were trying to do,' says Rosso, 'was to tell a good story that was also a warning. That was a year ago. But now that warning seems even more necessary. We are sitting on a powder keg where racial trouble is concerned. Bristol proved that. It also proved that we were totally unprepared for what

*'Pretty boring and predictable
questions really: Marital
status, job, how do we get to
work, have we ever tried to
stage a coup or been members of
the KGB ...?'*

31 March 1981

happened there, and what could occur again and again as
unemployment rises and the economic squeeze tightens.

'What was happening to young blacks when we made the
film is now happening to young whites too. Yet we are doing
nothing coherent about it. We're just hoping it will all go
away. The thrust of our film is that it won't.

'But I don't think we've made a film that suggests there's no
hope either. If *Babylon* angers some blacks of the older
generation because it suggests that their children are trying to
organise themselves politically, then it has done its job. They

are indeed trying to organise because they know that, if they don't, no change will be forthcoming. They should be encouraged not discouraged. It isn't just a matter of "black is beautiful" but of "black is powerful". People must begin to listen before it is too late. They are part of society like everyone else. And power and influence is their right.'

Rosso, who was born in Turin 37 years ago but arrived in England at the age of six, personally identifies with some of the blacks' problems. He himself had a hard time at school ('It's the blacks now, but it was the Italians and others then') and ended up at Camberwell Art School more or less as a way out.

Later, and for the same basic reason, he applied for the Royal College of Art, choosing set design because it was the only course available. He made a film there called *Dream Weaver* which Tony Garnett, and many others, admired. And Garnett eventually offered him the job as assistant editor on Ken Loach's *Kes*.

His other films include *House On The Hill*, the story of a black Borstal boy which caused a storm of controversy when it was banned by ATV, and *Dread, Beat and Blood*, a highly praised Omnibus film about the reggae poet Lynton Kwesi Johnson. Apart from writing and direction, Rosso also works consistently as a film editor. Now he wants to make another feature with, he hopes, the rock star Ian Dury in the leading role.

This, he says, will be a thriller that's set in London about a small-time conman who dreams of just one big hit. But when the opportunity comes, he doesn't take it. 'He's trapped in his own body and in the role he has made for himself. And he wants to get out.' Dury is keen to make the film and Rosso says he is the kind of star performer a film director dreams about. But there is the question of raising the money.

If *Babylon*, which cost £372,000, earns a profit, the job of funding a second Rosso film will be easier. But one thing is certain: he won't go abroad to make it. Nor will he make it with American money and American constraints.

'I'm keen on continuing, but not at any cost. And the cost to me of deserting this country would be too great. Perhaps, of course, I won't get any offers. If so, I might try producing. Or I might go back to making my living as an editor. It's a job I love and I think I'm good at it. I'm quite pleased with myself with *Babylon* too, but I couldn't have made it without Chris Menges, the cinematographer, or my marvellous cast. I don't regard it as my film. It's everybody's, and that goes for the Film Finance Corporation too.

'If we win through, in spite of all our difficulties and uncertainties, it will really have proved something – that you can make films for the cinema that are British and about British life. They all say you can't but I think that's nonsense. There's never been a better chance than now. There's so much to say. *Babylon*'s just part of a new beginning.'
11 November 1980   **Derek Malcolm**

Who's sari now?

If anything over the last days was more preposterous than the picture of Mrs Thatcher wearing an Indian chunni on her head it was the luckless Denis grinning madly under a selection of funny tea-cosies. This was most certainly Mrs Indira Gandhi's revenge for the British Nationality Bill. Though that, as we shall shortly see, is no joke.

The tendency of self-regarding public figures to let themselves be made to look like asses in ethnic garments of grotesque unsuitability is one that the older civilisations encourage, especially at times of tension. This is rarely necessary in the case of the Royals whose own gear is usually peculiar enough anyway. Nor is it wholly a Western aberration; even the late Mahatma Gandhi felt compelled in his London days at the Bar to wear a bowler hat, though not to be sure with a loin-cloth. But he did it out of humility, not pride.

I would fain have been a fly on the wall at the confrontation of the two daunting lady Prime Ministers. If a case can be made out for women party leaders, of which I am not yet at all persuaded, the two Premieresses do not advance it. They are both what the Irish call Hard Men. In a straight fight I would certainly have put my money on them, because in the issue, which inevitably was Mrs Thatcher's Keep Britain White Bill, Mrs Gandhi was for once on firm ground both tactically and morally. Mrs Gandhi is also an unyielding polemicist and would, I imagine, have had little trouble with a lady whose idea of debate is making didactic pronouncements in her jolly-hockey-sticks voice and complaining in India, of all places on earth, about British overcrowding.

It must have been like Queen Boadicea taking on Joyce Grenfell. In the matter of the proposed new British nationality law Mrs Thatcher is manifestly and clumsily in the wrong and, I suspect, is beginning to realise it, hence the defensive shrillness in her broadcast on Indian radio.

The *Guardian* at the weekend quoted a bitter editorial in the *Hindustan Times*, which I happened to have already read. 'Perhaps without an Empire and far-flung outposts to lord it over the British have reverted to what they basically are – a small little people with small little minds, inhabiting a small little island . . .' This is a characteristically Indian over-statement (to be both small and little is diminishment indeed) but Mrs Thatcher is doing her best to make it true. She could not have chosen a worse ground on which to challenge Indira Gandhi. Mrs Gandhi, as I well know, is a bitter opponent. She is far from always right, but this time she is. If Mrs Thatcher bulldozes this Immigration Bill into law, possibly by the guillotine, she will make Britain the one nation in the world with a three-decker classification of citizenship, with three varieties of passport and legal status. It is openly and uniquely racist. Mrs Thatcher denies this. And then with all the delicate tact of a Sherman tank she says on Indian television that, really, there is a limit to the numbers of coloureds her country can put up with.

Perhaps there is. Is Mrs Thatcher the one to define it? Does Mrs Thatcher have much acquaintanceship among the coloured community? There cannot be all that many coloured inhabitants of Downing Street, or for that matter of Flood Street, Chelsea.

Meanwhile Mrs Margaret Thatcher is off to fresh fields,

among the sheikhs and emirs of the Gulf States. They will be more to her taste, and possibly she to theirs.

But stay, what will she find there? Indians. Indians in great numbers, doing everything from administering the oilfields to mending the roads, profiting both themselves and the states in which they work, offering, it would seem, neither economic challenge nor social disorder. Can it be that the Arabs know something that Mrs Thatcher does not? Like, for example, both sense and sensibility?

21 April 1981   **James Cameron**

Catching up with an old flyer

Lunch-hour at the Talipot Café in the quieter, smarter quarter of teeming tooting Port of Spain. You come across the spick little place by accident. It's in a residential lane and enclosed in gleaming, high, corrugated iron on which some palm trees are hand-painted in greens and yellows and purples. A talipot is a rare palm which thrives in Sri Lanka: there is only one in Trinidad.

There is a set menu, local Trinidad dishes to go with dainty pots of chutney. A couple of civil servants whisper over a business lunch. Two middle-class Indian lovers stare each other out over a tiny table.

The ashtrays are non-existent, and anyway I don't like to smoke because I am placed next to an earnest young vicar in a clerical collar, black suit and waistcoat, with fluorescent green socks showing above his shined black shoes. He sips his soup soundlessly and with meticulous care.

The cool matches the silence except for the elderly waiter whom you would not hear coming, so delicate, soft and fast is he on his feet. But he never stops whistling. Very saintly but real tunes. Music while he works. A happy man. He looks as slim as a stick and as fit as a flea. He is also the owner of the restaurant and his name turns out to be E. McDonald Bailey.

It's probably a generation thing. In our English village,

whenever anyone went mad on the old drop handlebars you said, ''Oo d'you think you are, Reg 'Arris?' If he fancied himself on the wing in the rec, it was ''Oo d'you think you are, Stanley bloody Matthews?' And if I sprinted past a pal to be first at the bus stop he'd say, ''Oo d'you think you are, McDonald Bailey?'

Now here he was, serving my lunch at his Talipot Café in Trinidad. His 10.2 seconds broke the world 100-metre record for Britain at Belgrade in 1951 and it stood for five years. Between 1946 and 1953 he held sixteen sprint titles, a record unlikely to be broken.

He is a charming cultured man, now grey but still very handsome with a rare and lovely smile. His wife Doris is out the back in the kitchen. She is a cheery Cockney – as she must have been when they met first in the Paramount dance hall in Tottenham Court Road in wartime London. He was in the RAF, she was a WRAC. They have five children, who also all love music and two of them are professionals.

E. McDonald Bailey (E. for Emanuel) first left Trinidad for England at eighteen in 1939 to run in the AAA Championships against the likes of Holmes and Sweeney. The boy took nearly two weeks to get to Plymouth in a German banana boat. In 1942 he was coached by Wint and McKenley in Jamaica. In 1944 he joined the RAF and settled in England.

The first athletics newspaper picture that whammed into my consciousness was the 100-metre final in the 1948 Wembley Olympics. Remember? When every picture told a story, not gave you a close-up of a panting nostril or whirling ankle. Ewell la Beach, Dillard, McQuorquodale, Patton . . . our McDonald Bailey was last and although the Scottish Mac was fourth, the nation sighed.

'Getting into that final was a triumph, looking back on it. But with three weeks to go I went as flat as a pancake. We sorted that out, then with ten days left I got an abscess under my arm, and then, would you believe, laryngitis. Yes, I suppose it might all have been psychological.'

Four years later in the Helsinki Games he was hot favourite. He took the bronze. 'I must admit it, I found there was enormous pressure in being favourite. It was wet and I was upset at the lane draw for the final. When the gun went I tensed. I ran half the race tense. Ridiculous! If it had been 105 metres, do you know I might have made it!' Ramingo and McKenley beat him.

To a rousing Fleet Street hoo-ha he joined the Rugby League. He did not play many matches. 'Eddie Waring signed me. He was a journalist and a bit of a wheeler-dealer and I joined Leigh. I wanted to have a bit of time to learn the fundamentals. But they threw me straight in.

'One thing I do remember is the guts and natural ability of all those young guys in the North. But there were no training programmes for us in those days. They played to get fit but did not get fit to play, if you see what I mean.

'Yes, I was nearly killed a couple of times in practice. They would run straight at me and this guy's knee was hitting me in the chest and winding me every time. Then an Australian told me to let a man overtake, then catch him up and bring him down from the rear. I enjoyed tackling after that.

'I was trained as a sprinter but then my groin kept going when I tried to sidestep. Still, I very much enjoyed the experience.' He still loves the game of Rugby League.

The myth that he couldn't catch was buried during his time in the North where he played some cricket and proved himself an outstanding ball player. Then in the Fifties he left England to become sports organiser for Guyana. Ten years later he returned to Trinidad and worked as promotion manager for Shell. After long spells in London and Dublin he is now back in Trinidad – doing what I dare say he has always wanted. At least his smile and that music while you work very much suggests so.

'Waiter, a little more mango in my chutney, please.'

'Certainly, Sir, right away, Sir.'

''Oo does he think he is, McDonald Bailey?'

7 *April 1981*   **Frank Keating**

The players' man

He had been so hale and full of beans. So dynamite-chuffed at the end of the West Indians' innings in the morning. His nose crowded out the already jammed pavilion Long Room bar. His smile illuminated it. If, batting first, a side did not make at least 300, in this place they could consider themselves well and truly stuffed – and he was beaming because his boys had just bowled out the unbeatables for 265.

Across the change-of-innings pavilion barge and bustle, I caught his eye. You could only grin back as he gave a thumbs-up. The last time I saw him was a little later on the players' balcony during England's afternoon collapse – choked he was, but always first up with a great big consoling arm round the incoming batsman and some perky get-stuck-in encouragement for the outgoing.

Then, late in the evening, somebody whispered me off the dance floor and told me the numbing news. It just could not be true. Why, he was so very happy that his wife had come out for a holiday only last week. No, you could not take it in – nor could the players after the team manager Smith had summoned them before breakfast to his room at the end of the pier that juts from the hotel into the Caribbean. The young men tiptoed back across the boards almost in single file, the tan drained from their faces and looking shellshocked as if they'd heard their very bestest friend had died in the night. For many of them he had.

Only since knowing him these past two months did I realise how heartfelt, even desperate, had been the demand from the players and the press that he be added to this touring party. When it was named in the autumn he was missing from the list for the first time in England's last five tours. Lord's were cutting costs – but the genuine outcry was relentless enough to make them admit their mistake and change their minds.

He was the players' man, both spiritual and temporal. Each morning he gave them all their individual alarm calls. In the nets he bowled at them and followed through to cajole or advise with tiny hints on technique; always a smile; always relishing the day like mustard. Perhaps he knew there wasn't all that much time. On match days he was ever lifting spirits and humping kits. In the evenings his boys would gather themselves and a few beers around him and listen to the tales of long ago when cricket tours might have been to other planets for all these new jet-aged players knew.

Ken Barrington had done it all. The first of his 20 foreign centuries for England had been here at Bridgetown. For a dozen years till a first warning heart attack in 1968 when the doctors ordered him to take off his pads, he had squared his shoulders, jutted his jaw and come back for more; he was England's rock-solid, often unconsidered trellis around which the public's favourite fancy-Dans and flash Harrys entwined their colourful summer blooms.

He was invariably up the other end, grim and determined as he conscientiously swept the stage for the entrance of the Mays and Cowdreys and Dexters and Graveneys, the last great quartet of the golden line of legend. They would not have done even half as much without Barrington.

I will never forget that mid-summer Monday in 1963 during that second Test match of unremitting tension at Lord's when in the last innings, England, needing 233 to win, lost Stewart, Edrich and Dexter to the blazing fires of Griffith and Hall with only 31 scored.

Barrington and Cowdrey dug in and ducked and battled it out on into the afternoon. They were on the point of swinging the match with an epic stand when a withering delivery from Hall broke Cowdrey's forearm. Crack! At once Barrington, in answering fury and in spontaneous hate, struck Hall for venomous one-bounce fours over mid-on.

The rage was on him in manic defence of his wounded officer – but then just as suddenly he took a deep breath, calmed his soul to concentrate, and turned to stand again to see out the day in England's cause. They always called him the Colonel, as befitted a soldier's son. But he was more of a kindly sergeant-major without any bark or bite. Mind you, just a large beak and larger beam.

He first signed for Surrey as a leg-break bowler, but they

soon realised that he had too much grit and guts to stay long messing about with the twiddly stuff.

In the end, it was a grim business he had worried and worked himself into. But after his ticker first complained at the unrelenting life at the top, he emerged to everybody's astonishment and joy from behind the ropes with one of the loveliest, hale-fellow natures that could be imagined. He bought up a successful Surrey motor business, then asked if he could be of any more help to cricket.

Now he was in his element, talking about the old days. When one of his youngsters complained a fortnight ago about some aspects of the hotel service in Guyana he said: 'I dunno. When I first came here in the Fifties with Peter May we stayed down the road at that wooden place and the cock-roaches were so big that you'd tread on them as hard as you could and you'd lift your foot and they'd wave up at you, say "good morning", and potter off into the woodwork without a care in the world.'

When his boys moaned about tedious waiting in VIP airport lounges he'd grin, 'Blimey, we had twenty-seven hours in a Pakistan train once with only a bucket as a latrine.' Or: 'You should have come out here with us, mates, in our banana boat. First six days through the Bay and all that time you wouldn't see another player except the dying geezer in the next bunk. We were all simply seasick.' Or a complaint that a Trinidad steak was a bit small: 'Crikey, I had five months in India and Pakistan once when my total diet, honest to God, was eggs and chips. Closey, my room-mate, was so ill for days that all he could do was crawl from his bed to the loo on all fours every five minutes. He'd had a curry. I stuck to egg and chips. You can't muck around with eggs and you can't muck around with chips, can you?'

We would log his malapropisms; some pinched-lip types thought we were sending him up. He loved it, and laughed back at himself. 'Well, Frank, you all know what I bloody mean, don't you?' Sometimes they were quite ingeniously perfect. A batsman got out because he was 'caught in two-man's-land'. When that minor riot occurred last month in Port of Spain, it might have been worse than one he had encountered in Bangalore. Because there, to mingle with the crowd, the police had sent in 'two hundred plain clothes protectives'.

Between their sobs yesterday his boys could only have faith that now he will 'sleep like a lark' in eternal peace.

16 March 1981   **Frank Keating**

'We're British television. Who are you?'

The third most exhilarating thing on earth is watching wholly unpredictable news coming through live on television in the dead hours of the morning.

It takes much the same sort of nerve and luck on the part of the commentator and crew as diving off a highboard on to a wet flannel. When ITN picked up the link with Algeria just after midnight, they were on their own. The BBC appeared to have gone to bed. Jon Snow was stumbling with excitement as he spoke. There is something unusually human and off-guard about TV commentators in the small hours of the morning. It is almost as though they thought no one was looking.

At this precise point the Algerian landline that linked Snow and a chap called Sam Hall, just like the song, snapped, leaving them both in the dark in every sense. 'Sam,' cried Snow, 'what can you see?' Just so must Columbus, down to his last ship's biscuit, have yelled to the man in the crow's nest, who replied that he thought he had sighted the West Indies.

From the crow's nest, Sam sighted the West Indies: 'The plane, we think it's the plane, is sitting on the tarmac. The hostages, if they are on the plane, have not come off it.' It was not the plane and for an hour ITN, with no official information whatever available, flew by guess and by God.

At irregular intervals, the landline failed, then fired again. (It was typical of the night's confusion that Snow thought they were on satellite.) Sam Hall gave a fascinating glimpse of how foreign correspondents work, swinging from intuition to inspiration. His first hint of the hostages' release had been three days before when à gang of cleaners with pointed sticks had picked up every single piece of paper on Algiers Airport. 'And that was when we knew agreement was near.' Waiting for the hostages, he had exceptional scope for this sort of extra-sensory perception.

The picture went again. 'Whoopsy,' said Snow, who was now way past worrying. It returned with RTA printed crudely but clearly on a scrap of paper. 'Radio and Television Algiers, or whatever they call it,' said Snow (actually they call it Radiodiffusion Television Algerienne), 'who have lashed up this little operation are very anxious to get their name on the air.'

So were Air Algerienne. We looked at a lot of planes for a long time. The doctors' little executive jet pulsated with red lights like peculiarly painful boils. Strange lights flared to and fro like little fish in this big black pond while one huge fish, its size only to be deduced from its lights, swam forward slowly and stopped.

It offered infinite opportunities for precarious deductions. The crew stood by the door: 'They are not standing in the way airline personnel stand when they have finished the day's work,' said Snow. 'Someone's just come out of the loo.'

In terms of television, spending that penny must have cost around £100. Umbrellas were observed on the tarmac. 'A man is holding an umbrella over someone important. You don't hold an umbrella over someone unimportant.' I never knew that.

It had the feel of airports everywhere: endless delays, a growing conviction you are in the wrong place on the wrong day, and then suddenly the face you came to see. 'There they are!'

And there they were. 'A shamble of hostages' in anoraks and combat jackets and eagle-printed T-shirts. Women in yellow ribbons. A Marine wonderfully overgrown with hair. 'What an enormous number fifty-two suddenly seems.' How wonderful.

Later at Frankfurt ITN's John Suchet took another of those brave dives into damp sponges. 'Hi, we're British television. Who are you?' It was Lt-Col. David Roeder, the air attaché from the embassy, who said: 'This is absolutely super. I've never been so proud to be an American in my life.' And Thomas Shaefer, the military attaché, added: 'There's not words in the American language to say how happy we are and how grateful we are. Thank you, America.'

'Nobody,' said the BBC, reporting the same arrival, 'got near the hostages.' Well, thank you, ITN. It was super in any language.

22 January 1981   **Nancy Banks-Smith**

Tip-toe through the tappings

For months now, anxiety has grown about the use of telephone tapping and other forms of surveillance by the police and intelligence agencies. Reports from the Post Office Engineering Union have suggested that telephone tapping is used far more widely than the Government has revealed and that the procedure is not properly accountable to Parliament. The union has expressed alarm about the possibilities for abuse created by advanced telephone technology. Sir Robert Megarry, one of our most senior judges, has said that phone tapping cries out for legislation since the safeguards that exist are merely administrative devices. Even the Canadian High Commissioner has weighed in with suggestions that Britain was tapping transatlantic phones to monitor the Canadian constitutional crisis. Last April the Home Secretary sought to allay public concern by appointing Lord Diplock, chairman of the Security Commission, to monitor the practice of intercepting phone calls and the post. Yesterday, Lord Diplock conveyed to a perturbed nation the message that all was well.

The system, his White Paper informed us, was working satisfactorily and with minimum interference with individual privacy. Applications for warrants to intercept phone calls or the post were backed up by accurate and candid information. Procedures were appropriate to correct any mistakes. Above all, interception was performed in the public interest.

Lord Diplock is, without doubt, an honourable man. The police and intelligence services are also, doubtless, packed with individuals of the highest probity. The Home Secretary is unquestionably diligent to a fault when it comes to the signing of warrants. But one or two niggling questions do persist. What is the extent of this surveillance? We still don't know. What kind of people are considered legitimate targets? Lord Diplock does not tell us. His definition of 'activities which are capable of constituting a threat to the peace or safety of the realm' is deeply enigmatic. In short, the way Lord Diplock proposes to reassure us that our interests are in safe hands is simply by being Lord Diplock. The Home Secretary is probably much reassured; so too must be the security services. But without legislative safeguards, there doesn't seem much prospect of peace of mind for the world outside.

4 March 1981   **Leader**

Part-time glory boys

The boys in the gym dance round Tom Daly. Short explosions of breath and unrequited punches bring them into his focus: 'In Stepney and Hackney, in the little clubs, you'd have featherweights at nine stone six wanting to fight middleweights at eleven stone just because they wanted a few shillings. It was six rounds for ten shillings, then. I find it very difficult to see that it's as hard for them today.

'Fighters came from Wales. Fifteen rounds for five pounds; they were supposed to get their fares out of that, but they all cadged lifts down on lorries.' Daly's bald head pokes out of an overcoat. He is entirely in black. You could take him for a parish priest in Ireland. Old, pink, sleek. Yet vigorous.

The clerical garb is appropriate. Daly has just been to a Requiem Mass for Jim Wicks, Henry Cooper's former trainer. Outside the church they all came up to him, the fighters and the sports writers, to shake hands with a survivor of part of a generation whom the Depression turned into Hungry Fighters in the 1920s and 30s.

Among the income group most affected by the then collapsing economy there was a boom in boxing – the sport which remains close and true to its roots still. Now, half a century on, with a milder recession, there is another resurgence in boxing. In the last 12 months, a record number of young men – 206 – have turned professional. And the number of licences granted by the British Board of Boxing Control – 630 – is the highest for 20 years.

Board Secretary Ray Clark is convinced this is due in part to hard economic times. But the difference this time is that – so far – fights provide additional income, rather than the only income. Very few boxers can afford to rely solely on the ring. 'They can do roadwork in the morning, gym-work in the evening, and keep a full-time job as well,' says Clark.

They are training, the hopefuls, in the locations long known to boxing and with the men who have outlived grimmer days. Daly, veteran of 300 contests, has, at 75, two lads he is training. He is in a tall-windowed room above the Thomas à Becket pub in the Old Kent Road. The people, at least the types, and the fittings, have been there for decades.

There are current fightbills and old photographs on the walls, but the real picture of success, which every boxer holds, is beyond the ring: the point where brutality breaks into glamour – John Conteh modelling French underpants, or Henry Cooper baptising himself in the sweat-free world of Brut. The ad-men hold the strings to the best purses.

The gym is like a Turkish bath: old radiators wheeze; punchbags maddeningly absorb energy. There are puddles of sweat. It is like a torture chamber in which the pain is self-inflicted: a big, big guy is grinding his chin on a sort of chopping block with his butt high in the air and his arms pressed into the small of his back.

The butt belongs to Andy Palmer, who turned professional and came to London from Liverpool 15 months ago, together with Jimmy Brown, a flyweight. 'We came on spec. We'd no accommodation, no job.' Now both are porters at the BBC. 'I had four years as an amateur. What do you get for it? A little fuckin' medal and a pissy little watch.' Now that he's a pro 'if you have eight fights in a season and win all eight, you might get £1600 or £1800.'

Palmer, who is part West Indian, is a heavyweight. *Boxing News* ranks him 21st in a list of 46 in that class. How long can he go on? 'Heavyweights don't mature till they're thirty' – so he's got five years to prove something. 'Seriously, I could go all the way. I'm no fuckin' worse than the next man.' Has he been bashed up yet? 'Look, I'm still pretty, aren't I?' He is, apart from a cheekful of acne. But, whether it's dumb or visionary, he has the confidence of his trade: 'I think everyone in boxing fancies himself. There's very few that think they're not going to land the big haymaker.'

Joey Singleton already has. He has a labouring job and comes from Liverpool as well. He is the leading contender for the British and European welterweight title, the most crowded class, for which *Boxing News* ranks 89 fighters. He turned pro six years ago. 'You don't do it for any one thing. It's money, it's a better standard of living.' How much is he getting? 'You never ask a boxer how much he is getting. You just say "are you happy with what you're getting?"' Singleton must be; he's putting it in a building society, and now he's looking for that traditional investment beloved of boxers – a pub.

Singleton is a crop-haired babyface with pixie ears which probably retract when he's in the ring. Boxers are concerned about their appearance: the mirrors round the walls, at knee-level and shoulder height, are as much for vanity as for strategy. Boxers also are superstitious; when they say 'touch wood', they touch it. What they never admit to is the fear of being physically mashed . . . But then Tom Daly and Frank Duffet have both survived without damage and they both insist that boxing now is a safer sport.

'In the old days, they fought today, tomorrow and Tuesday,' says Duffet. 'Now if you've got an injury, it's twenty-one days before you can get medical clearance. They didn't used to give a wound time to heal.'

'You can't find a fighter now with a cauliflower ear,' says Daly, fingering his own unscathed ears instinctively.

'Winston,' says Duffet.

'Winston?'

'Howard Winston,' says Duffet and goes back to his lads and their footwork.

There is something agreeably dandyish about the old trainers, scheming to outwit their rivals while living vicariously through boxers young enough to be their grandsons. Duffet has three blacks, one a sprayer, one a kitchen porter and one out of work. They pay 60 pence a session at the gym, with tea and a shower included and ten per cent of winnings to the trainer.

Many of the lads who do not make the big time will probably quit after three or five years in the ring, the trainers agree. It is easier to balance the risk if they have full-time jobs – Duffet points to a fightbill, 'Seventy per cent of those are working' – but for minorities, hopes are massively invested. Boxing has always been a way up for minorities, the Irish, the Jews and now the Blacks. 'The Coloureds now,' says Daly, 'they're getting the spiky end, the jobs the Whites don't want. But they're revolting against that. Those with a bit of pride, a bit of ability, they turn to boxing.'

Even for a professional, the purses can be few and far between. There is an alternative. It is to thumb your nose at the BBBC and sign up with an independent promoter. That same night, in a huge hall attached to the Downham Tavern in south-east London, 1,500 punters were in their seats and men were going round with plastic sacks to collect the empties long before the first bout staged by the self-styled Independent Boxing Authority started.

Backstage, Sonny Hooper, a shrewd trainer with a shock of white hair, helps one lad with his gloves and the MC with his black tie and explains the scene: you could be a fair professional, licensed by the Board, yet get only two fights a year. 'If you're not a classy boy, how can you get a fight?' Jo Carrington, a florid-faced, expansive promoter, talks derisively of professionals being offered £60 to £80 a fight by big promoters.

The answer for some is to go independent, which assorted mavericks do from time to time. The star of the evening arrives in the large person of Harry Starbuck, a heavyweight's heavyweight, 42, and harder than Dempsey, the word is. His billed opponent, one H. H. Glenville, fails to appear for medical reasons, and the substitute is Johnny Clark who has a big smile and a big gut and is floored by Starbuck three times in the third, at which point the ref stops the contest.

As the previous four bouts have all ended early and abruptly, the punters are getting restless. The promoter, Tom Lenahan, who has been signalling like a subdued tic-tac man, now makes the sign of the cross. And makes for the exit to bring on the next pair of contenders. There is a Libyan lorry-driver, Olympic material he says of himself; and a motorway worker with fists like reinforced concrete. All getting, I guess, £200 or £250 a night for their share of the glory.

27 December 1980   **John Cunningham**

Getting on like a House on fire

One's sympathy for Mr Nicholas Fairbairn, the Government Minister who was jostled by Labour MPs during Thursday night's riotous scenes in the Commons, is limited. Mr Fairbairn, one of the toughest criminal lawyers in Scotland, can look after himself.

He usually carries a large and hefty stick. When the knob at the top is unscrewed, the stick can be up-ended and comforting quantities of scotch whisky can be dispensed into a convenient receptacle. His anxious constituents may rest assured: Mr Fairbairn will recover from his Night of Terror.

The fact is that Thursday's rowdy scenes were a miserable skirmish, a mere child's pillow fight, compared to the open warfare which has been carried on in the Commons in previous years. Even the red lines woven into the carpet a few feet before each front bench recall those days. MPs on their feet are not allowed to walk beyond the lines, which are drawn two swords' lengths from each other. They reflected the real danger that an angry MP might attempt to run an opponent through.

There is an engraving of the fist fight in the Commons over

215

the Home Rule Bill in 1893. There are at least two dozen members actively engaged in the punch-up, smashing each other in the face, grabbing each other's clothing, shoving opponents over the benches and generally behaving in a manner which would be thought lacking in etiquette in Glasgow at closing time:

This was an extreme example of a common occurrence. In 1661, Pepys thought the young men who sat in Parliament were 'the most profane swearing fellows that I ever heard in my life, which makes me think they will spoil all, and bring things into a warr if they can'. Dickens, probably the most distinguished parliamentary correspondent the place has ever seen, said it offered more noise and confusion than anywhere else he knew, 'not excepting Smithfield on a market day, or a cockpit in all its glory'.

Mr Fairbairn's remarks about 'mob rule' were foreshadowed 150 years ago by Hazlitt, who remarked that few people who had distinguished themselves in the Commons had ever done anything else.

Such riots have their own traditions, as rigid in their way as those surrounding other parliamentary customs such as the State Opening and the ancient cry of 'Who goes home?' For instance, at some point the Speaker generally says something along these lines: 'I want to tell the House we are endangering our parliamentary principles. What has happened tonight is quite unprecedented.' Those words were used by Speaker Thomas this week. He was quite wrong. Such scenes are no more unprecedented than Halley's Comet, and a great deal more frequent.

In 1931, when Mr John McGovern, the Labour MP for Glasgow Shettleston, refused to sit down when told to do so by the Speaker, the Serjeant at Arms approached him and tried to change his mind. Mr McGovern swore at him. Then six of the Serjeant's aides came to carry him off. He took them all on. One was cracked on the head, another winded and a third had his shin bruised.

Then the real fight began. Four other Red Clydesiders plunged into the fray, and attacked the attendants as in a rugby scrum. The attendants managed to get hold of Mr

McGovern and carried him horizontally from the Chamber. Then Labour MP John Beckett attempted another tackle on one of the attendants, missed and crashed to the floor.

Nor are these simply memories of a bygone age when people were more hot-tempered than the calm professional legislators of today. On average, I'd guess, the sitting has to be suspended by the Speaker once a year because MPs are making too much noise to carry on. Furthermore they quite often hit each other, sometimes in public. The late Tom Swain, a mining MP, thumped a Tory who had displeased him in full view of the Speaker. A Labour MP once bopped Mr Neil Kinnock in the face because of something he thought he had said.

In 1976, in a celebrated incident still relished by Westminster watchers, Mr Michael Heseltine, incensed by a narrow vote the Labour Government had won and by the subsequent chorus of *The Red Flag*, which arose from the government benches, seized the Commons mace and swung it around his head, so earning himself the sobriquet Tarzan and a lifetime reputation for being rather silly.

In 1972 Bernadette Devlin slapped the Home Secretary, Mr Maudling, and pulled his hair, in protest against the death of 13 innocent people in Londonderry on Bloody Sunday. There was the CS gas incident when a young Ulsterman called Bowes Egan hurled a canister on to the floor of the House. In 1978, Dom Mintoff's daughter, Yana, flung animal dung at MPs in the Chamber – again a protest over Ireland.

People are always saying that standards of behaviour in the Commons are declining. They are, perhaps sadly, wrong. Incidents like Thursday night's may be aggravating for the government trying to get its legislation through, and particularly distressing for the poor wretched Speaker who has to control events. But they have a pedigree as long as the old place itself.

15 November 1980   **Simon Hoggart**

Orange lemons

Most journalists know that it is either very difficult or very easy to write about matters of which one knows little. I know a bit about one or two things, and repeat myself immoderately, and hardly anything about a great many other things, about which I shut up. It may just have been noticed that one area into which I never venture is Northern Ireland.

It must be about 10 years or so ago that I was asked by an American newspaper to go and look for a while at some sort of minor unrest that seemed to be developing in Ulster. It was not especially grave or important, but there was the notion that possibly – just possibly – there might be something in it, and nobody reported anything from that dreary part of the world.

I do not go in much for premonitions, but I had an oddly vivid one then. I knew hardly anything about Ulster. Years and years before I had been briefly to Belfast to have a ride round the TT Ards Circuit in the Guinness Bentley, and it struck me as a place of meagre attraction. For some reason I had a powerful feeling that Ulster had the makings of more than a little local difficulty.

I had had about 20 years of little local difficulties that grew up – like Korea and Vietnam. I was fed up and tired, and I felt that anyone who got mixed up in Northern Ireland might well be in for a long ride. I think it was the first assignment I ever turned down.

This surely entitles me now to sound off about the place at least as much as those who opine about Bonnie Prince Charlie's phone-calls without having heard them, or analyse the motives of the late Bobby Sands, when they would not know a martyr from a maverick.

Apparently there are more international reporters in Ulster now than ever before, waiting, as Bernadette McAliskey is reported as saying, 'for the starter's orders for the civil war'.

It is an accepted and fairly reasonable comment that, as always, their presence will be self-fulfilling, encouraging the tensions they demand. This is marginally unfair to the trade. Nobody has yet suggested that the pop press is paying Ulstermen to murder each other, though in the current climate, after the Sutcliffe business, it may not be long before somebody tries.

The spectacle of Belfast children – who in their lives have known no other fun than throwing stones, capering, and showing off to the TV cameras – is deeply depressing: how will they ever come to terms with a dull situation like peace? The Brit soldiers, only just older than the kids, play cowboys and strike attitudes with their guns, accepting the morbid melodrama. Stocking masks and hoods are standard make-up for the baddies, riot-shields for the goodies; the thing is a sickening charade.

It sometimes seems to me that my generation of correspondents spent its time covering successive chapters of imperial disintegration, as it were watching a newsreel endlessly and obstinately replayed. The sequence varied hardly a jot: India, Malaya, Kenya, Cyprus, the scenario was the same.

Whitehall replied to the independence demands by insisting that it could *never* – a famous word – surrender its responsibilities, imposing emergency laws; gaoling the Gandhis and Nkrumahs and Kenyattas and Makarioses and Mugabes; calling in the army; failing in the end to prevent the result that had been inevitable from the start; and sending over some unfortunate minor royal to pretend we had meant it all along.

Ireland has taken a few centuries longer than the rest; there is no other difference. Except one: the people of Ulster do not want independence: it is one side or the other. But the white rednecks of Rhodesia did not really want it either; they got it just the same. And Ian Paisley will be at one with the dreary Ian Smith, sulking in his tent.

To find oneself vigorously on the side of Mr Enoch Powell is a most eerie feeling. What can have gone wrong? Nothing has gone wrong; Mr Powell has gone right, if that be possible. Enoch calls Paisley 'a bully and a coward'. His reasons, however, are not quite what they seem. To Enoch Powell's oblique and ingenious reasoning, Paisley is a fifth columnist.

'Is he not the secret weapon of those who want to send Ulster the way of white Rhodesia?'

Well, blow me down. And to think we never guessed.

Mr Paisley is just about the meanest and coarsest public figure in the land, not to speak of being a truly outstandingly unattractive boor. It has been worked out that Mr Paisley has never publicly uttered a word of generosity about anyone except himself, and an occasional favourable reference to Jesus Christ, whom he refers to as his Maker, which I should have thought was a pretty poor testimonial. Can it be, as Mr Powell suggests, that all this is an act to discredit the Loyalists and make the pro-Brits look fools?

Yes and no, says Mr Powell. 'He is afraid for his own skin, afraid of the fringe men of violence on whose backs he would fain ride, provided he can distance himself from them when serious trouble looms.'

You could have fooled me. But I am more easily fooled than Enoch Powell. Or could this just be the double-double-cross of all time?

That, to nobody's surprise, is the Irish Question.

12 May 1981   **James Cameron**

Playing soldiers

Colditz was never like this. They had windows there, were allowed to sleep sometimes and weren't allowed out to the pub on Saturday nights.

The replica on Salisbury Plain this weekend had one other major difference – the 24 'prisoners' paid £30 for the privilege of being treated worse than the prisoners of war they were emulating. Inevitably, the combination holiday camp/Stalag was named Butlitz by its mastermind, Bob Acraman, once a parachute regiment sergeant, who ran it in the former army isolation hospital he normally uses for teaching sport parachuting.

The place was stiff with Nazis who spoke in British

accents. The only genuine Germans were two reporters from *Stern* magazine in Hamburg, who were wearing khaki battledress. They had difficulty understanding this strange British enthusiasm to relive the dark days of war.

Most of those dressed in the uniforms of the Second World War were members of the Battle Re-enactment Association, who like to spend their weekends dressing up as Tommies, GIs or members of the Wehrmacht.

It was a little difficult to establish precisely how many POWs had actually paid to come to the camp on the outskirts of Weyhill, near Andover, Hampshire. Mr Acraman said 19 had handed over money for the humiliation of it all but most of the improbable assortment of RAF officers, army other ranks and the occasional Pfc from the US Army, claimed to be from the BRA. 'I think we can proudly claim that we gave everyone absolute hell,' said 41-year-old Mr Acraman, resplendent in his Commandant's uniform and with an alluring replica of Lili Marlene simpering at his side. 'I am sure most of those here learnt a great deal about themselves and their abilities to endure this sort of deprivation. They'll know now whether they would have been able to face up to actual war,' he said.

There were parades through the nights, punishment drills and the chance of being locked in the 'cooler', a large metal cylinder that was formerly the hospital's steriliser. And unlike most genuine POWs they all had to try to get over the barbed wire, not only to get free but to simulate sabotage of an aircraft factory. There was also, it seems, something of a mass break-out on Saturday night, to the pub.

Gary Howard of Ilford, a dealer in militaria, played the part of the senior British Officer and claimed to have covered 45 miles along the escape route. 'At one stage we went past the Boscombe Down RAF station and they must have thought they were seeing ghosts from the past,' said Mr Howard, dressed in an RAF Flight-Lieut's uniform complete with pilot's wings. The pursuers, though, had to wear mufti. 'The police said they could not allow us to roam the country carrying weapons and dressed like Nazis,' said Mr Acraman.

'Of course, some people will say we have been glorifying

war but that is really not so. There are a great number of people who have a genuine desire to know a little of what it must have been like. Not getting shot or blown up, of course, but being afraid, exhausted, with a lack of food and constantly having to keep going through dreadful weather. This drill we have had all weekend has been absolutely marvellous for us.'

The stalwarts of Sturmgruppe Adler, as the German branch of the BRA calls itself, said they had had a pretty tough time too. 'I only got my first sleep this morning and had to spend three and a half hours up in the watch tower in the blinding rain at one stage,' said 18-year-old Tony Dudman. He was holding a genuine Mauser K 98 rifle, although it had been bored clean to fire .410 shot and this qualified it to be classed as a shotgun. 'It's really just like joining the TA,' said his comrade in field green, Graham Lancaster. 'We take the authenticity very seriously and put a lot of work in it.' Mr Lancaster, aged 31, is not married but says his mother is glad to get him out of the house, when he goes off to play soldiers. He used to be in the genuine British Army, the 3rd Queen's Regt, and said: 'The lads here this weekend have had it lighter than the sort of battle training we were given as recruits.'

Nazi music and selected speeches by Adolf Hitler blared out from the loudspeaker on the parade ground, and after it was all over some of the German group, who had gone to have cups of tea in the canteen, gave an authentic rendering of the *Panzerlied*, the marching song of German tank crews.

One of them, suddenly noticing a stranger in their midst, said to me: 'Don't get us wrong, we're not Nazi sympathisers, we just like to live the part to make it as real as possible.'

24 November 1980   **Malcolm Stuart**

Upper class fascist

Sir Oswald Mosley was the only credible dictator the British Right has ever produced. He was certainly the only politician who could have led either the Tory or the Labour parties. He was a brilliant orator, a political thinker of some stature, a man of genuine courage and inspiring leadership. But in the end, it is by his flaws that he will be remembered. The best epitaph came years ago from his son Nicholas: 'I see clearly that while the right hand dealt with grandiose ideas and glory, the left hand let the rat out of the sewer.'

His main flaw was an arrogant impatience; his second was that ultimate sin for a politician, an abominable sense of timing. He founded his British Union of Fascists just in time to win them the reflected brutalities of Hitler's Nazism, rather than the reflected glories of Mussolini's early achievements.

It was a decent man's distaste for the repression in Ireland that led him out of the Conservative Party in 1922, while MP for Harrow. He sat as an independent for two years before joining the Labour Party. But it was impatience that led him to resign from the Labour Government in 1930.

He was born into the wealthy squirearchy. His alcoholic and eccentric baronet father later recalled that the medical fees alone (in 1896) to bring young Oswald into the world had been £100. 'Born with a golden spoon in his mouth,' father commented. During the 1920s, the young Sir Oswald had a private income of £20,000 a year.

Educated at Winchester and Sandhurst, he fought in the First World War with the fashionable 16th Lancers and the Royal Flying Corps (his famous limp came from a training accident while flying). His first wedding, to the daughter of Lord Curzon, the Viceroy of India, was attended by the King and Queen. His second, in Berlin, was followed by lunch with Hitler and Frau Goebbels.

In the 1920s he campaigned politically on behalf of the men he had fought with in the trenches, for decent housing and jobs for the demobbed heroes. He began as a radical Tory in the style of the young Harold Macmillan. By the late 1920s, he was a Labour Left-winger, progressive enough in his ideas to advocate dramatic reflation and Keynesian techniques to get out of the slump. Elected to Labour's NEC, he almost carried the 1930 party conference at Blackpool, and in pure frustration, he resigned his Ministership and was expelled from the Party in 1931. Had he stayed with Labour, most observers reckon he would have led it.

He was always convinced that he was right, that he and he alone could save and lead the nation. Frustration with Labour and Conservatives ('the old gangs', he called them) led him to found the New Party, with considerable support from allies in the ILP, the left Labour party. It sank miserably at an ill-timed and ill-chosen by-election at Ashton, and as Mosley looked at the angry Labour crowd denouncing him on election night he murmured to John Strachey, standing beside him: 'That is the mob who has prevented anything being done in this country since the war.' Strachey later recalled his conviction that 'it was at that moment that Mosley became a Fascist.'

He travelled to Rome with Harold Nicolson to talk to Mussolini, and in Il Duce's vision of Fascism as 'a movement of action', Mosley found his inspiration: an ideology that could do without 'the talking shop' of Parliament; with the patriotic determination to make policy irrespective of alien control of finance capital; a force of youth to drive out 'the old gang'; a party with a discipline that would echo that of the trenches, and with a dash that would echo the RFC.

What he got, in fact, was thuggery. It was the appalling brutality of his stewards at the Olympia meeting of 1934 that lost him the support of key sections of the Conservative Party, and particularly the support of Lord Rothermere and the *Daily Mail*, which had until then devoted full pages to a 'Hurrah for the Blackshirts' campaign.

He cast around for various forms of electoral support. He tried a campaign to win over the slump-hit middle classes and workers in the northern cotton towns, and dropped it as it began to achieve some success. He shifted direction to London's East End, trying to whip up support among a white slum population disoriented by the social impact of im-migration – in this instance Jewish. It led to the famous Cable Street riots of 1936 – and the Public Order Act which still bans the wearing of political uniforms.

In recent years Mosley tried to deny that he was ever anti-semitic. His defence verged on casuistry. His BUF election posters read 'We will not compromise with Jewry,' and his Blackshirts regularly chanted 'Let's get the yids.' He defended Hitler, organised his party on a para-military basis and yet had the gall to say that his Blackshirt guards were guarantors of free speech. The fact of the matter was that Mosley was too ready to permit the use of foul methods to try and promote his aims.

His Fascism was finished by the public relations disaster of Olympia, and his subsequent isolation from that upper class which had backed both Hitler and Mussolini as bulwarks against Red revolution. There was no such threat from the Left in Britain in the 1930s.

After the war, there were increasingly pathetic attempted comebacks. In 1948, at Venice he tried with other ignored and discredited men to propose a united Europe. There were more scuffles in the East End in the late 1940s, and an anti-immigrant by-election in Notting Hill in 1959. There were discreet negotiations with the neo-Nazi Colin Jordan in the 1960s as immigration seemed to promise a comeback for the Right. But the last half of Mosley's life was spent in a small French château, waiting in faithful impatience for a call from Britain that would never come.

4 December 1980   **Martin Walker**

The all-round view

The soldiers must have envied Dürer his panoramic vision. From where they stood all they could see was the neck in front; from where Dürer stood – or rather from where Dürer hovered – you could see the whole of the battle and half of Germany. An entire army became small enough to play snakes and ladders with across a landscape which measured its miles in centimetres.

Produced in 1527, Dürer's Siege of a Fortress is the earliest example in an exhibition at the John Hansard Gallery of Southampton University devoted to panoramic vision. We were not born with eyes encircling our heads but that has never stopped us trying to see everything at once. Looking sideways has long been an essential part of looking forwards.

It is typical of man that this first God's-eye-view should be of what the general saw. It is also typical that what began as an artistic dream, a new way of looking at the world, should eventually become a mechanical reality with the invention of the camera. And it did not take the photographer long to realise that his panoramas were infinitely more plausible than those produced by an artist's hand.

But it is obvious from the first print that, whereas those panoramas produced by hand seem genuinely concerned with expanding our vision, the photographic ones are mainly concerned with reducing it, with packing as much information as possible into one frame. It's as if the photographer is always asking whatever is on the far left or right – be it a mountain, a skyscraper or a bathing beauty – to move in a little, please.

And so the best photographs in the show are not the ones which are content to do their panoramic duty and fit what looks like the whole 2nd Division, with General Pershing at its head, into the other half of Germany. Right from the start, in the sequences of multiple exposures, it becomes evident that the panorama could concern itself with time as well as geography, that several events could be memorised in one image, that the sun could rise and set in the same picture.

There were also those photographers who used the charm of the format itself, the long, low horizontal, to achieve some striking effects. F. J. Schlueter's view of Goose Creek Oil Fields, Texas 1919, looks like a scene from War Of The Worlds, an endless, stagnant horizon bristling with more oil pumps than old London had church spires.

But surely the most extraordinary image in the show is the one in which your eye appears to travel across the whole of an Arizona desert before it reaches two old men who've got out of their car to survey the land. Almost against your will your eye has to travel all that way back to the start with them. Most of the photographic panoramas come from America; it needed a new type of vision to stretch as far in any direction as these landscapes.

In the same way, the first hand-drawn panoramas had coincided with the opening out of the world, with the proof that it too could turn through 360 degrees, with the birth of the modern city which had begun to sprawl sideways and out of the traditional artist's frame. Wenceslaus Hollar shows London before and after the Great Fire. Dürer's cosmic vision, the impression he gave of seeing everything at once, has been replaced by a narrative, a London which unfolds from left to right, a London which follows the river bank from Westminster, past all the spiky city churches, past the giant Tuscan portico which Inigo Jones grafted on to old St Paul's, right along to the old London Bridge.

Most of the sights collected in the first section of the exhibition adopt the Hollar approach and allow you to follow a city, a coastline, a battlefield or a beauty spot from left to right. Water was popular because, as in Hollar's London, it provided a natural edge along which the artist could unravel his vision. Where there was no river to look across, it is interesting to watch how they tried to cope with the difficult front edge of a picture, the one edge which could never be melted into the distance.

Much of this engrossing show is spent making difficult ends meet, attempting invisible seams, pretending that you really can see through 360 degrees, pretending that you really can be everywhere at once: in San Francisco before, during and after the fire that followed the 1906 earthquake, in Galveston to witness the Third Annual Bathing Girl Revue of 1922, at the beginning and the end of Manhattan Bridge.

Magic was involved from the start: an eighteenth-century advertisement for Eidophusikon, one of Philip de Loutherbourg's lantern shows, promises a 'view of the Mediterranean by moonlight, in the course of which will be introduced a Total Eclipse of the Moon' (it somehow seems fitting that this new gallery, a much needed venue in a notoriously artless region, was originally built to house a huge tidal-flow model of the Solent for use by Southampton University and oil companies. It is thus the only Solent-shaped building in the world).

The modern section of this exhibition is distinctly self-conscious, with the panorama finally reduced to chasing its own tail. Yet there is a view of New York worthy of Dürer

227

himself. By apparently suspending himself between two skyscrapers Howard Sochurek has emerged with a terrifyingly vertiginous city, a New York which falls away so abruptly at its sides that it looks to be flowing over the edge of the world.

1 June 1981   **Waldemar Januszczak**

Stalking Chalkie along the prom

Along the grey windswept seafront at Lowestoft yesterday walked a lone nervous figure in a green anorak. From time to time he doubled back on his tracks, or – glancing behind him – sat down to read a newspaper.

Who was this uneasy man and what was he doing on such a rain-drenched day in such a place? The answer came shortly after 3 p.m., when a young man in jeans walked shyly up to him and uttered the phrase 'Tonight's the night, Chalkie White.'

For Chalkie, the game was up. Another nerve-wracking day of deception and subterfuge was over and he could look forward to a nice cup of tea before setting off to his next job at Newquay.

Chalkie White comes from a distinguished tradition of mystery men, a British summer institution that began between the wars with the *News Chronicle*'s Lobby Lud and was celebrated after a fashion in Graham Greene's *Brighton Rock*. Each day a picture of Chalkie's eyes appears in the *Daily Mirror* and each day the Great British holidaymaker memorises them, together with the line he must say to claim the £50 prize. It is usually some such sentence as 'To my delight, it's Chalkie White.'

The *Guardian* has agreed not to identify him, but it can be revealed that he is a 31-year-old Bedford man whose brother stands in for him in places such as Margate, where he is too well known. Even during such a summer as this the British holidaymaker takes Chalkie very seriously. Women and children have fought over him. Holiday plans have been

228

altered at the last minute in an attempt to catch him. 'Last time I was in Lowestoft three weeks ago,' he said, 'a woman and her husband followed me down to Ramsgate and slept overnight in the car to make sure they were up early enough to catch me next day.'

Chalkie takes his job correspondingly seriously, and does his best not to be caught, though he rarely succeeds. 'I start by staying in a hotel two or three miles out of the resort, otherwise you get collared at breakfast by a waitress. After that you try to look exactly like the rest of the people on the beach – miserable and aggressive. It's a good plan to have a little sleep in a deckchair, because people are usually too timid to wake you up. One little boy today came up and then ran away. He told me later he thought I was a pervert. It's a problem in this job.'

While Chalkie keeps on the move, often changing his clothes as he goes, his brother starts promotion stunts on the beach until by lunchtime there is hardly anyone left in Lowestoft who has not been asked the dreaded question.

Chalkie's life is fraught. He has often been punched by people who thought they should have won the prize and was once hit over the head with a handbag by a woman who thought it was misleading of him to wear a beard. He has been swept into the sea by a giant wave at Hastings, was arrested for making too much noise at Bognor, reported to the Press Council for allegedly giving the money to the wrong person, and thrown out of a pub in Bridlington when, at 3 p.m., he tried to give away the £25 consolation prize and was presumed by the landlord to be drunk.

'People think it's a cushy job but sometimes I hate it,' he said. 'You get this terrible sense of paranoia. Everywhere you go you think everyone's looking at you and talking about you.'

Chalkie has tried not to let his annual six-week shift change his life. But he has been doing the job for nine years now and it becomes a little harder every year. Last December he realised just how hard when a nine-year-old boy stopped him in the Brent Cross shopping centre and duly accosted him for £50.

16 August 1980   **Alan Rusbridger**

Preparing for the space war

The Soviet Union launched an earth satellite, No. 1241 in the Cosmos series, on 21 January. Moving in a nearly circular orbit about 1,000 kilometres above the Earth, Cosmos 1241 has a life expectancy of 1,200 years. Unfortunately this satellite is unlikely to exist for 1,200 years or to collect any scientific or other information of benefit to mankind because it is merely the target vehicle of an anti-satellite system. On 2 February, Cosmos 1243 was launched – the interceptor satellite, designed to use radar guidance for an approach to Cosmos 1241 with a view to its destruction.

During 1980 the Soviet Union made eighty-nine space launches. The United States made only twelve – a disparity that led one NASA official to comment that the 'Soviet Union launches more flights in a week than NASA does all year.' Since three of the Soviet launchings each placed eight satellites in orbit for military communication purposes the disparity is even greater. Eighty-one of the Soviet payloads were for military purposes. Ten of the United States satellites were placed in orbit for the Defence Department and only one (for the study of solar flares) was launched for scientific purposes. The pattern has been similar for many years with the same concentration on the payloads for military purposes.

Is this what Neil Armstrong had in mind when he stepped on to the moon? On the contrary, he had the vision of Jules Verne that 'it was only such an age that could have given birth to explorers so daring, engineers so accomplished, lovers of abstract science so singularly pure and unselfish.' What then has gone wrong? Why have the major efforts in space become inward-looking, and dominated by military and commercial interests instead of proceeding to the magnificent exploits made possible by Apollo?

The answer is buried in the history of the last quarter century. In the attempts to re-establish the international basis of scientific research after the Second World War there were many informal talks amongst the scientists. One of these which was to have a dramatic impact on the world occurred in April 1950, between the British geophysicist Sydney Chapman and the American scientist Lloyd Berkner. They developed the idea of a worldwide observational and experimental programme as a means for stimulating research in geophysics. During the next few years Berkner and Chapman presented this proposal whenever a relevant international gathering occurred. Enthusiasm soon developed and the International Council of Scientific Unions was persuaded to designate the period of sunspot maximum in 1957–8 as the International Geophysical Year (IGY). Expeditions were planned to Antarctica as part of the global observations of meteorological, geophysical and ionospheric studies.

In October 1954, a Special Committee of the International Council met in Rome to consider proposals from the forty nations which had agreed to participate. One of the problems was to explore the upper atmosphere and ionosphere and the possibility of using sounding rockets was envisaged as an outstanding technical advance. The drawback was that rockets would collect data for only a few minutes and this consideration led the Special Committee to adopt, on 4 October 1954, the following resolution: 'that thought be given to the launching of small satellite vehicles, to their scientific instrumentation, and to the new problems associated with satellite experiments, such as power supply, telemetering and orientation of the vehicle.'

This recommendation in support of a relatively small scientific enterprise was soon followed by one of the major errors of judgement in world history. On 29 July 1955, President Eisenhower announced that the United States would launch a satellite during the IGY. One day later a similar announcement was made by the Soviet Union. Many will remember the general reaction of excitement to these announcements coupled with the disbelief in Soviet capability. In fact, these reactions bore no relation to the state of the projects in the two countries at that time.

Eisenhower disregarded the advice of a group of scientists and engineers led by Wernher von Braun who had proposed in the summer of 1954 that an army Redstone missile together with a cluster of three solid fuel rockets (a Jupiter C vehicle) should be used to place an American satellite in orbit. Eisenhower rejected this advice in favour of a proposal that the Naval Research Laboratory should develop a satellite launcher based on sounding rocket technology. This decision coupled with his ruling that there should be no interaction or diversion of effort from the US Ballistic weapon development led to the disaster of Project Vanguard.

With no such inhibitions about the civil-military interface the Soviet Union never wavered in the plan to use the rocket of a military inter-continental ballistic missile to launch an earth satellite. When Khrushchev announced on 26 August 1957 that the Soviet tests of a 'super long-distance intercontinental multistage ballistic missile' had been successful it was clear that the launching of a Soviet satellite was imminent. The rocket which launched Sputnik 1 on 4 October 1957 was the world's first successful ICBM – a missile developed to launch a heavy atomic bomb and not a harmless scientific satellite. The impact on the Eisenhower policy was dramatic. The Secretary of the Army again pressed that von Braun should be allowed to launch a satellite using the Jupiter ballistic missile. He asked for thirteen million dollars with which he said the Army would launch six satellites. Three weeks after Sputnik he was given three-and-a-half million dollars with a target date of 30 January 1958. One day beyond the target, Explorer 1, the first American satellite, was launched by an army ballistic rocket.

The fulfilment of one of the IGY scientific plans was of far less consequence and importance than the revelation of the military domination over the techniques. In any event the financial considerations were overriding. The ill-fated Project Vanguard was originally budgeted at eleven million dollars. Wernher von Braun was given three-and-a-half million dollars to convert a military rocket on which a very large sum of money had already been spent. At that time billions of dollars were being spent simultaneously by the army, navy and air force on the development of ballistic rockets. The billions of dollars necessary to develop the rockets which launched the Sputnik and the Explorer satellites were available only within the context of defence requirements.

The decision of President Eisenhower had been governed by two factors. First, a judgement that the IGY proposal to launch a satellite was an entirely peaceful concept and that the use of a military rocket would place security and other constraints on the project that would be harmful to the scientific community. Second, a desire to avoid interfering with the military ballistic rocket development. The fallacy in the judgement was the failure to realise the advanced state of Soviet ballistic rocket technology and that no such scruples would be exhibited by the Soviet Union, coupled with a remarkable innocence of the costs.

The Eisenhower administration reacted to the challenge by establishing NASA in 1958 to direct the scientific exploration of space, both manned and unmanned, and von Braun's army group was absorbed into this new organisation. NASA was created, and has served for more than twenty years, as a strong civilian-orientated agency, but it has not been able to achieve a civilian domination over American space activities. In the Soviet Union there has never been any question of civilian control. The rocket group of the Soviet armed forces always has had complete control of launching Soviet space vehicles and the tie with the Soviet Academy of Sciences has been indivisible. Nearly all the launching rockets (ninety-five per cent in the Soviet Union and eighty-six per cent in the US) have been developed and funded as military missiles.

Although the early dominance of military interest was established through the launching rocket, another important factor quickly emerged – the use of space vehicles for defence activities. The eighty-one military payloads placed in orbit by the Soviet Union in 1980, were for reconnaissance, surveillance, naval communications, navigation, early warning, ocean reconnaissance, electronic intelligence or for tests of space interception. These payloads like the American equivalents are the products of the most advanced electronic and engineering industries.

These defence interests soon reacted on civilian aspects of the space programmes – particularly in the navigation and communications sphere. Seaborne or submarine missile launchers required to know their location with extreme accuracy and the application of the techniques for commercial shipping developed quickly. The global network of Intelsat satellites in stationary orbit now carry two-thirds of the world's international telecommunications. In December 1980 the launching of Intelsat V, providing capacity for 12,000 calls and two television circuits, inaugurated a new series that includes facilities for communication with ships at sea. These, and the many other applications to human benefit, are entirely admirable. They are also routine, intellectually dull and consuming most of the space effort left over from the defence interests.

Meanwhile members of the scientific community who provided the incentive and the vision twenty-five years ago are begging the small amount of capacity and effort remaining. Even without the military burden of the Soviet and American space budgets, the European Space Agency (ESA) will spend not much more than ten per cent of its budget on satellites for scientific research in this decade.

In a message circulated last summer, the new Director General, E. Quistgaard, urged the European scientific community to campaign for an increase in the science programme budget which, because of restrictive decisions made ten years ago, is fixed (about £48 million at present exchange rates). Beyond present contracts this leaves room for only one significant scientific satellite for the remainder of the 1980s. Quistgaard wrote that 'from whatever angle one looks, this is an extremely low figure'. Indeed, it is a disaster for European space science – even a decision on the next scientific project has been postponed until the end of 1982. With this enforced subjugation of science to the political and commercial interests of the European partners the decision of the scientific community in ESA to proceed with Giotto – the probe to intercept Halley's comet in 1985–6 – appears all the more courageous. It is one of the few visionary and exciting space projects of this decade.

President Reagan's speech on 18 February left little hope for the future of United States exploration in this century.

The implied cuts of the only planetary explorations (the Venus radar orbiter and the probe to Jupiter) stand in stark contrast to President Kennedy's speech to Congress on 25 May 1961, '. . . this Nation should commit itself to achieving the goal, before this decade is out, of landing a man on the moon and returning him safely to Earth . . . ' The immense resources of America were harnessed to the Apollo project, requiring revolutionary scientific and technical concepts coupled with developments in organisation and logistics of entirely new dimensions. A third of the world's population followed the culmination of the lunar journey in 1969, but the culmination of the scientific programme required the large-scale extension of the concept. Instead, Apollo was abandoned and the NASA budget cut so that today, even numerically, it is only three-quarters of that which made Apollo possible.

Wernher von Braun, the genius behind Explorer and the Saturn rockets, was in his fifty-eighth year when Apollo II reached the moon. Now his plans for modifying the Saturn rockets to get man to the planet Mars by 1980 were rejected. The Apollo facilities were dismantled and the men who made Saturn a reality were dispersed. The American space program became ruled by the argument that by spending a few billion dollars to develop the space shuttle, the cost of placing satellites in orbit could be reduced. The strategic argument, both commercial and military, for a large earth orbiting space platform triumphed over the scientific argument for the exploration of the planetary system and deep space.

There have been major scientific advances from the meagre share of the space effort granted to the scientists. The study of X-rays and gamma-rays from space (the discovery of gamma-ray bursts was made accidentally by a military satellite), the landing of instruments on Mars, the Pioneer and Voyager photographs of Jupiter and Saturn, and the Soviet television pictures from the surface of Venus are a mere sample of the rich discoveries that would be possible by a re-direction of the space effort away from terrestrial interests. If the space shuttle succeeds in the plans to launch the large space telescope in 1985, some at least of the astronomers' interest in deep space will be rewarded. Meanwhile the Soviet Union, less conscious of the need to save roubles by developing re-usable launching vehicles, has forged ahead with Soyuz-Salyut. Their strategic earth orbiting space platform already exists. Whether they too will continue to concentrate solely on the terrestrial issues remains an enigma. As von Braun reached his zenith of achievement with the Saturn rockets, the Soviets sadly lost the genius behind their space programmes – Sergey Korolev. No doubt space lacks a von Braun and a Korolev as much as it lacks money.

The problem with the space enterprises today is not so much the lack of finance but the failure to distribute the available money with any degree of vision. In 1981 Britain will contribute the equivalent of 80p per head of the population to the European Space Agency but the Department of Industry will direct 66p per head of this to space telecommunications and other terrestrial applications.

We have, indeed, followed faithfully the advice, given in 1959, of the distinguished members of the Advisory Council on Scientific Policy that it would be the 'grossest folly' for the country to engage in a programme of space exploration.

19 March 1981   **Bernard Lovell**

The city of oil slickers

The best way of gauging the grotesque and good fortune of North Sea oil is to look up some old pals in the Aberdeen area.

In home A you are confronted by one of those fantastic vertical record players that Raymond Baxter used to demonstrate on *Tomorrow's World*. In home B you discover that the householder is now part owner of 15 oil wells in America. In home C you hear that Charlie, fat Charlie, is earning around £70,000 a year out in Africa somewhere. Knowing Charlie, was that really likely? 'Golly yes. He's on a bonus of one per cent of turnover and that's around £6 million these days.' Fat Charlie is a friend you last saw stacking cornflakes in a Spar supermarket. Your informant is a friend who years ago was inching towards a career in laundry management. Now, as he rattles off the prospects for his worldwide offshore machine tool franchise, you realise that you and he exist on entirely different planets.

On his planet there seem to be fairly inexhaustible lakes of lolly waiting to be sucked up by anyone with his head screwed on and half-decent contacts. Cash-flow problems, lay-offs and closures are merely entertaining meteorite shows thrown up by a scatty firmament somewhere in The South, essentially a divine warning to slackers in the Chamber of Commerce. Indeed, the extent to which The South is perceived as a civilisation tottering on its last legs might come as a surprise to those Englishmen who think of the Scots as pitched somewhere between Macbeth and Dr Finlay. 'Don't you need a lot of policemen down there,' asked an elderly veterinary surgeon, 'to keep control of all those coloured people?'

Most of this sort of talk can be heard along Deeside. An interesting feature of the oil bonanza is the way in which its social infrastructure has neatly distributed itself by caste. All the riff-raff – helicopter pilots, divers, roust-abouts, junior geologists, hydrographers – have settled in the boring, windswept townships – Inverurie, Ellon, Portlethen, Stonehaven – that lie north and south of Aberdeen. All the big wheels live up Deeside, a string of 'smairt' sheltered riverbank communities that runs south-west into the Grampians and reaches its spiritual climax 50 heathery miles upstream at Balmoral. Here the homes are granite haciendas, the lawns longer, the Audis larger, the Reaganite fundamentalism more fundamental. Spread over a couch at one point in the perpetual party round, the beefy boss of a colossal American offshore exploration company was elaborating on the British economy. 'Hell, Thatcher's doing a great job. The States needs someone like her. I don't believe those unemployment statistics. I mean, two-and-a-half million! Where are they? You don't see them in the bars or in the streets, do you? Retired army officers make up most of the numbers, I'll bet.'

But this is what oil does to you. Any source of unimaginable wealth can cloud perspectives, but oil's especial charm is that it leaps out ready-made, independent of any manufacturing class who might want to foul things up by demanding a slice of the action. The action appears never-ending. It was profitable to set up production platforms when oil was 6 dollars a barrel. By next summer, I am informed, it will have risen to 60 dollars. A month or so of working in this sort of climate and you quickly start believing that anyone incapable of getting even a third-class ticket for the gravy train must be (and you hear the word a lot around Aberdeen) 'unemployable'.

Examples of this hallucinatory potency abound. Total flew hundreds of employees, and their spouses, and their children, to North Africa for a picnic. Chevron are settling into one of the most extraordinary buildings to have been built in Britain this century, a black glass, slate, and stone château that is half Disney, half Dracula. Down the road is J. Ray McDermott, who started life with a crew boat in the Gulf of Mexico and whose construction company is now one of the world's top 500 businesses. Here and there you see the site cabins of Bob Farquhar, the Aberdonian who made a fortune by the simple tactic of staking out Aberdeen airport and shaking the hand of any incoming passenger who looked remotely American.

Of course, in the scramble for the lolly, some of the other blokes will cut a few corners. 'It's not just a question of buying a few drinks for the right man,' I was told by the head of an Aberdeen engineering firm. 'It is hi-fis and weekends in the south of France.' One enterprising individual on the payroll of a major oil corporation is said to have distributed contracts on the understanding that the sub-contracting was carried out by the firms he ran on the side. Under pressure from the increasingly embarrassed Institute of Purchasing and Supply, Chevron, BNOC, and several other big spenders send out stiff notes each Christmas to selected firms, advising them that the Buying Department will accept no sweeteners whatsoever.

Not every Aberdonian has his hand in the jam pot. An unemployment rate of 4.8 per cent still means that there are 6293 on the dole. There are 8000 on the council's housing waiting list. Almost as sad are the ones who just missed out, the bright boys of the early Seventies who got themselves good steady jobs in banking, merchandising, the Civil Service, only to see their less talented successors swept to extraordinary affluence. A young ordnance surveyor in a pub was especially aggrieved. 'I'm being asked to move to Falkirk. To FALKIRK. I love my work. It's a fine life, and healthy, but I know now it'll never make me rich, at least not as rich as them. And now to be sent to Falkirk . . .'

Some businesses deliberately sidestepped oil when it started. 'Ach weel, it'll only last five years an' then far'll we be?' It's in the blood. Aberdonians have always measured themselves against fairly enduring things like the sea and the land, so the eyes narrow at the approach of anything new-fangled and charismatic. When Covenanting superstar Montrose appeared on the scene they took him on twice and lost twice. They had nothing to do with the '45. After 30 years of rock and roll the city has only thrown up one half-decent singer, and a girl at that: Annie Lennox of The Tourists.

Burns dismissed it as 'a lazy town', which was a bit hard, but there's always been a streak of refined stoicism that a decade of high technology has failed to break down. The dresses in the Union Street windows look like leftovers from the Coronation. The shoe shops smell like overburdened tanneries, and unceremoniously pile their shoe boxes out front.

Culturally, Aberdeen is all but moribund. It must have the highest ratio of capital plus intellect to population anywhere in the world, yet dance, drama, and music depend utterly on intermittent transfusions from Edinburgh and Glasgow. The unmusical tradition runs particularly deep. 'Pride of Aberdeen', written and recorded last year by Paul Ames in the wake of the football team's unexpected success, includes the remarkable couplet:

> At the final whistle
> Drew with Partick Thistle.

The inevitable boredom takes its toll. A sleek French geophysicist complained that much of his salary now goes on monthly Air Anglia flips to Paris. His wife had taken the children and fled back over the Channel. 'She was going crazee with the nothing to do.' Others seek their diversion closer to hand. Licensed squash courts have sprouted, where bearded young air traffic controllers, transplanted north from

Heathrow, thrash each other to death and then swop horror stories over lager and limes. (Avoid French helicopter pilots like the plague.) For the less energetic there are some exceedingly gauche country clubs, expensive cars (the Mercedes agency must be the biggest in the country), and drugs. Detective Superintendent William Archibald and assistants are fighting an uphill battle against an inclination introduced by the American labour force and hardened by the 'no alcohol' ruling that applies offshore. Cocaine is generally much easier to conceal than whisky and, as a scientific observer put it, 'the only tell-tale signs are increased activity and an undue amount of nose-scratching.' Desperadoes have recently taken to plundering the lifeboats for their sachets of morphine.

Of course little of this concerns the Aberdeen planet's chiefs, who are too busy working on the very latest wheeze for making money. (You heard about the Aberdeen chemist who banged on the window with a sponge when someone left a fiver on his counter? Sometimes you think it could be true.) This involves investing in American oil wells. I had always thought the Great American Oil Boom went out with John D. Rockefeller. Not a bit of it. All over the States, widows, taxi drivers, hamburger salesmen are pouring their life savings into Drilling Funds in the confident expectation – the science of geological investigation now being what it is – of making a killing.

Intercourse with Houston brought this to the attention of the planet chiefs, a great many of whom are now subsidising assaults on promising portions of the US land mass. In his office just off the city centre a crisp young speculator explained the congenial system. The Government lifted the dollar premium so it's easy to put money in there. A fair proportion of it is tax deductible. You invest in a near-certainty that's offering 3 to 1; that is, a return of three times your investment. You take your profits from that and invest in a wildcat at 8 to 1. Put in £100,000 and you're almost a millionaire.

'It's easy. It's so safe you could put your granny into it.'
6 February 1981   **Erlend Clouston**

Messages from my father

My life has been dishevelled and irregular, a grief to my father. He would gladly have taken the words that so often flew over us on the Brazilian flag, Order and Progress, as a family motto – if I'd been like him and his father. Perhaps because of this, perhaps because we spent so much time apart, perhaps because I look for clues that he loved me in spite of sending me away so much, I try to reckon what sort of man he was. I have a mosaic of anecdote, and now my mother has turned out the photograph albums of his hobby, as further pointers.

In the last years of his life, when he appeared to have shrugged off his disappointment at my being a writer, and I visited him in retirement from his career in South America, we sometimes went to a football match together. They were always Fourth Division games.

Father never played football after leaving school at fourteen, when he became a messenger boy in the telegraph service, working Saturdays. But he liked to watch, so long as there was no possible chance of excitement, on or off the pitch. He detested anything unruly, in or out of football. An uncle once recalled Father's only visit to the Cup Final, and the courteous tones in which he implored several thousand people on the terraces to allow him space to breathe: 'Gentlemen, please don't push! The pitch is wanted for the players.'

In Brazil he attended three matches. Each was more sensational than the last. In the first, a needle match in Rio, the referee was shot. During the course of the second a knife fight began in one corner of the stand, which attracted a mêlée from all over, like a poultice drawing noxious elements, whose combined weight caused the supporting pillar to give way, and 300 people plunged to injury and death.

He declined to see the Brazilian game any more, much as he believed in respecting excellence in local culture. Unfortunately in Florianopolis, as senior businessman in charge of the most solid British commercial enterprise, he was also appointed Vice-Consul, an honour that embarrassed him and caused him to heave a sigh of relief when he found his name garbled by the printer in the diplomatic yearbook. On sundry official occasions he suffered at being guest of honour – one of these being an invitation to sit in the box at an interstate match. A severe riot interrupted the game.

All about him his hosts were being punched, kicked and felled, and some were beginning to choke on the tear-gas. Summing up the situation with his usual sang-froid, he left the protection of the police, and clambered down on to the field. The only safe, neglected place in the stadium, he noticed, was the goal, so he stood between the posts with his arms folded, brilliant in white ducks until peace returned, to find him still immaculate.

So we watched Aldershot, never very successful, along with some 1500 other people and he praised their sportsmanship for turning out at all, particularly when we found a pathetic comment in the programme note advising patrons that but for the bounty of a local fishmonger, who had presented the ball that day, the match could not in fact have been held at all.

Sometimes recently Aldershot have been on the verge of promotion. I don't think he would have relished such a consummation. He liked to spread a blanket on the bench, with hamper and Thermos, and during a particularly painful December, when it seemed that the end of the season would see them applying for readmission to the League, asked if I thought they would prefer that he should send them a turkey, or a ball, for Christmas?

His quiet manner belied him. He had energy and drive. From being the last in the telegram chain, the lad who took them to the door, he switched to being the first, one of those who tapped them out. He took this chance, and his skill and productivity led to his being told that some knowledge of electricity would help him further.

He readily consented to night school and homework in the small hours: his own father was a baker from Yorkshire who rose every morning at three to light his ovens. My grandmother made the cakes and looked after the confectionery. They were very thrifty. At a great age they would still get off a bus a fare stage early to save a ha'penny, and grandfather, for instance, kept a razor blade going six months by sharpening it on the inside of a tumbler. Father was imbued with habits of order, and hygiene, and the concept that a pound was no more than a heap of pence.

Those habits persisted through and beyond more than 40 years overseas as a Cable Engineer, mostly in South America and finally as Manager in Brazil. When the yellow flag hung at our gate to show the yellow fever inspectors were about, every water surface was always coated by disinfectant Father himself had laid. When as host he served a strong cheese at dinner, he always sent a powerful magnifying glass round with it, so his guests could calculate the risk attached to ingesting such a lively *bonne bouche*. Ironically it was from a salad that he made himself, having supposed the water that he washed the lettuce in had been previously boiled, that he contracted the typhoid that nearly killed him.

My grandmother had trained him always to have a daily change of underwear, and in the heat of Brazil he doubled the prescription. This led one day to a problem in the company, when he was transferred to Maranao, on the Equator, and by all accounts a hell-hole. He raised only one objection, and it concerned his wardrobe. The only access to Maranao was by a small two-seater monoplane which, according to Mother, flapped its wings when it took off and landed. When other priority goods were loaded, there was no room for all Father's luggage.

He was adamant that he would not go unless his complete range of underwear went simultaneously, where he could keep them in plain view. After a spate of urgent telegrams – no doubt he handled the transmission himself – a solution was agreed. When Father took over the Cable station at Maranao, he arrived with an extra plane on the same flight, its cargo made up exclusively of vests and pants and shirts and socks.

I quizzed him once about another story from Maranao that had puzzled me. The community of Europeans there had been very small, and the problem of satisfying my mother with a Bridge four was always acute, and yet he had repatriated his assistant, a social gem in the sense of being a very accomplished player – why? 'He was having an affair with a Brazilian woman,' Father replied.

Was there anyone else he could have had an affair with? 'Not very well. Not at close quarters, anyway. I liked him, as a matter of fact, but his activities didn't redound to the credit of the Company.' But wasn't it a terrible blow to the Bridge evenings? 'We missed him, of course. He was companionable. To a fault, one must say. But one had to trim a bit in these emergencies. There is such a thing as Dummy in Bridge – and I never knew Dummy take a mistress.'

Women figure at only one period – but in that time intensively – in the pictorial record of Father's chronicle as carefully set out in his albums. Until that high-density epoch, the summer that he turned 27, no woman interested him. Not enough to be photographed anyway, and he had photographed a very large number of far duller subjects.

He had been stationed in Chile, Bolivia, Capetown, and the islands of St Helena and Ascension, where the telegraphists, being the cynosure of cables from every continent, are said to have the greatest fund of off-colour stories in the world. And he had, apparently, given all his leisure time to golf, motorcycles, climbing, spotting wild-life and studying technology, without a thought more tender than for his chiefs in Electra House. Then suddenly, as if he'd acquired a more curious and enlightened viewfinder for his camera, there is this concentration of women.

My belief is that when he went home on leave for three months that summer, a broad hint was dropped by the management to the effect that in raising his grade, they'd like to send him to Brazil, but that the Company felt easier when its agents in the tropics were married. So that if by any chance he had a lady in mind . . . He obviously hadn't, but with his usual thoroughness he set about making a survey of candidates.

Mounted on a giant Harley-Davidson, with a sidecar to be filled as and when the opportunity arose, he buzzed about the Home Counties, picking up girls, whisking them off to idyllic country spots, buttering them scones and serving tea, and then returning them, well photographed, to base. They all look very sweet and demure in their sylvan settings. Looking at the sequence of my potential mothers, I wonder what they all made of him, and whether he was less reserved than usual, under the pressure of finding a wife in three months. And how different would I be now, if he'd come to an agreement with Number Four, for example, a tall, elegant Nordic blonde?

In the event, my genetic inheritance was determined at no great distance from Grandfather's bakery in Amersham. He set out one morning on the hunt with a full tank in the usual way, first obliging my grandparents by dropping off some loaves and cakes locally, for their regular customers. In this way he met a small, dark Celt – he can't be accused of restricting himself to a blueprint – who was the receptionist in a nearby hotel. The beginning was not auspicious, since her opening remark was to tick him off for not making his delivery at the tradesmen's entrance.

She says that he made the impression on her of being 'a poodlefaker', which is understandable in the context of that summer's efforts, but that, I think, taking the long view of history, is not really accurate. Because, having married her, he never looked at another woman. I write this with conviction because, with Father, to look at something or somebody, was to photograph them. The albums are as barren of further feminine images, as the women were of any conception of me.

It's odd that a man who took such pride and care in his hobby, and was immersed for several decades in riveting exotica, should have such outstandingly bad results. Yet he was courageous enough, even foolhardy, in exposing himself to danger to get an unusual picture. In Chile when a German warship hove to, and began shelling the port, he shouldered his way against the tide of fleeing natives en route to the hills, and stood on the dock with a steady hand to work his camera, pointing straight into the blazing cannon's mouth. They should have been unique, historic frames, but alas they resemble not so much a fearsome ironclad spitting venom but rather a spent matchstick wallowing in a smudgy waste of wax.

I'm not sure how many homes he and Mother made

together. Twenty-five? Thirty? They were like hermit crabs repeatedly moving into alien shells vacated by others. They collected neither books nor pictures, but only suitcases. In my childhood I was allowed to travel with one favourite toy, the smaller the better. Tricycles, scooters, and bicycles were in turn left behind. I came to feel that all property is on loan, and I still have only a half-hearted interest in possessions. Mother became a dab hand at packing essentials. She had the knack of the Perfectly Balanced Suitcase, and could have packed a dozen eggs to go over the falls of Jararaguassu and survive intact at the bottom.

They went again to those Atlantic islands, and St Vincent – I have my own memories of turtles on the shore at Ascension, and of riding in a basket on a donkey on St Vincent, to balance the bottles riding in a basket on the other side. Then there was a whole succession of cable stations up and down the Brazilian coast. Sometimes I went along too as a satellite, but often I was despatched on a far orbit, to another state, for schooling in various peculiar establishments – sometimes for years without a reunion, so that when we met again it was almost as strangers.

We lived in bungalows and towers, in flats and hotels, a *pensao*, a beach-house and a barrack, besides other places more conventional. Sometimes we had curtains, sometimes blinds, sometimes shutters. The furniture might be bamboo, or teak, or walnut; backed with straw, canvas or studded leather. The common feature was that Father had every chair, table and bed stand in cans of disinfectant, to frustrate the termites. Sometimes they'd beaten him to it; a hollowed-out leg would snap and he'd abruptly vanish beneath the table. He'd rise, dust himself off and repeat his favourite saying, '*Paciencia no Brasil.*' He was the perfect example of patience sitting on a crumbling monument.

I occasionally recognise vague similarities to their lifestyle in accounts of the Raj, but there was one almighty difference. In Brazil they lived the neo-colonial attitudes in a country where we had never been the colonists. Father never stopped longing for Britain. His whole career was a dogged effort to earn a title to respect when he would eventually go back to buy a house he wouldn't have to leave. But there was no cultural back-up for it; the umbilical cord withered.

Law, language, religion, customs were all foreign, and only partly European. They affected his working life, but they didn't enter his bloodstream, as they did mine. During his long absence, Father was unaware of the vast social changes in his homeland: he came back like a time traveller, with his puritan conscience, speaking an archaic slang, to a country he no longer recognised. It was a huge disenchantment, and I was another.

Each time we moved to yet another port, my first actions were, invariably, to make myself a new catapult, and to examine the book stock in the cable station. Faces and places changed, but as I roamed along the shelves, the names of familiar authors appeared in increasing numbers. They were my element of continuity. Whether Father would have put a block on this, if he'd realised it would lead to my wanting to be an author myself, I can't say. He read only for practical purposes. When it was too late, and I had committed myself, he expressed his disgust by a silence of seven years.

However, it's possible that he had an inkling of the use of imaginative writing. I do remember the titles of the only three novels I knew him to read – Edmund Gosse's *Father and Son*, Charles Dickens's *Dombey and Son*, and Warwick Deeping's *Sorrell and Son* – one after the other when I was twelve. He must have ordered them all at once, from Paternoster Row and Son, while working out what to do with me. It was the Deeping he liked best, and the only one he shoved my way. *Verb sap*, if I'd been able to perceive it then.

Before any of this, it was first necessary that I should be born. They were in Pernambuco when Mother knew, some six years after their marriage, that she was pregnant. Father then played the joker. He instantly booked a return passage to a maternity hospital 5000 miles away in Britain. He thus deprived me of the option of being a Brazilian citizen.

Watching Aldershot being flayed by West Hartlepool we discussed this. He said he hadn't meant to go as far as that. I said I didn't believe it. He protested that he had only wanted to spare me conscription into the Brazilian army. 'You might have had to shoot Indians. You couldn't have worked on the *Guardian* after that.'

I retorted that I might have worked on *O Correio*, or *O Jornal*, or *La Prensa*. I might have been a famous Brazilian author, and ambassador to the Court of St James, or the Elysée. Latin American authors like Borges and Neruda and Marques were coming into vogue. He'd virtually condemned me to be a British author, a pebble in a mile of shingle.

It's very hard, I grumbled, for a writer to spend his first formative years in a landscape to which his countrymen are virtually indifferent, and which he therefore can't exploit. The whole boiling continent, I said, is a publishing no-no. They had this fixation on Peron, the sole dull caudillo from the time of Pizarro, and his scheming little tart. Anyone else – zilch.

Father made no reply. He studied a stricken Aldershot supporter taking a swig from a small bottle of whisky, from his overalls. 'I say,' said Father, 'look at Charlie Ox with his Bacchus!'

I ploughed on. Stefan Zweig, I said, was right in saying that Brazil is the land of the future, but here there wouldn't be a flicker of interest even in a figure like Vargas. 'The less said about Getulio the better,' said Father petulantly.

If I'd stayed on, I might have been a Latin American master, I said. Father unscrewed two cups from the Thermos, carefully wiped them and poured coffee. 'We shall probably lose three times over Christmas,' he said cheerfully, 'but as it's Christmas I'm spiking the coffee with *cachassa. Bao Noel!*' We drank and he added, 'I say, you don't seriously regret not being a Brazilian, do you?'

Not any more, I reassured him – except perhaps when watching Aldershot.

21 February 1981   **Alex Hamilton**

Index

Banks-Smith, Nancy   God sieve the Queen!   12
Dogged by Fate   173
The Queen and Gandhi's loin-cloth   195
'We're British television. Who are you?'   208

Barker, Dennis   Cashing in on The Boom   37

Bayley, John   The Master's Voice   174

Billington, Michael   Still standing   194

Blandford, Linda   86th Street: what's left and for how long?   169

Cameron, James   Who's sari now?   200
Orange lemons   218

Clouston, Erlend   The city of oil slickers   236

Cook, Stephen   Bananas   188

Cunningham, John   Part-time glory boys   211

Davies, Nick   Boys will be fathers   147

Fuentes, Carlos   Thanks to Britain   128

Gott, Richard   The writing on the wall for Reagan   123

Hamilton, Alex   A trillion and one things   56
Opening his letters   142
Messages from my father   241

Hebert, Hugh   Package flight to the knife   50
Forever Ambler   190

Hoggart, Simon   Silicon chaps   14
Getting on like a House on fire   215

249

Januszczak, Waldemar	A grand ol' soap oprey	177
	The all-round view	225
Jenkins, Peter	Thatcher's Modern England	17
	Mrs Thatcher rules, OK?	43
Keating, Frank	The end of a lovely affair	109
	Catching up with an old flyer	202
	The player's man	205
Leader	Alexander the Haigiographer	9
	Information Incorporated	49
	A wire from the shire	51
	Big Mal and the malcontents	64
	Rolling round the monde	75
	Lest we forget	135
	Baubles, bangles	140
	Tip-toe through the tappings	210
Lovell, Bernard	Preparing for the space war	230
Mackie, Lindsay	Fort Beswick and its prisoners	154
Malcolm, Derek	A short fuse from Babylon	197
'Martha'	Letters from a faint-hearted feminist 1	89
	Letters from a faint-hearted feminist 2	98
	Letters from a faint-hearted feminist 3	105
Radford, Tim	Requiem for a rodent	40
Thompson, E. P.	A show for the European theatre	110
Rusbridger, Alan	Stalking Chalkie along the prom	228
Schwarz, Walter	The moment of surrender	76
	Something nasty in the Limousin	183
Seabrook, Jeremy	The end of great expectations	29

Shrapnel, Norman	Caring clowns	139
Silver Eric	The Begin revolution	114
Stead, Jean	Toxteth people	27
Steele, Jonathan	Born-again America	100
	The Kremlin and Cold War II	117
Stuart, Malcolm	Playing soldiers	220
Taylor, Geoffrey	An ill wind in the dale	181
Torode, John	Solid Citizen	65
Toynbee, Polly	Palma days	79
	Remember forking?	149
Tweedie, Jill	Unsettling Mr Benn	60
Wainwright, Martin	Merton and The Bomb	135
Walker, Martin	Upper class fascist	222
Wavell, Stuart	The dream time as nightmare	10
	Elves at the sharp end	162
Webb, W. L.	The mouse that nibbles at freedom	68
White, John T.	A country diary: Kent 1	97
	A country diary: Kent 2	180
White, Michael	The Tory party takes freight	54
Wilson, Enid J.	A country diary: Keswick	138
Woollacott, Martin	The West's Arabian beach-head	84
	The rise of meritocracy	92

Philip Hope-Wallace

WORDS AND MUSIC

*A selection from the criticism of opera, music,
drama and literature as well as occasional pieces
written by one of the most distinguished of*
Guardian *contributors*

Introduction by C. V. Wedgwood

'This anthology covers 40 years' writing and several arts (opera,
lieder singing, theatre, ballet) besides sampling the occasional pieces
that made Hope-Wallace in some way the last of the English
essayists. When he met what he truly admired he knew how to praise
and, while praising, to make us hear. "Where we have learnt to
accept from others a desperate wailing yodel, Mme Flagstad rolls us
a note like the Atlantic sending in a breaker."'

John Rosselli, *Guardian*

'A fine representative sample of his wit and wisdom, with an
appreciative foreword by Dame Veronica Wedgwood. First and
foremost, it makes a glorious read: a bedside book insidiously
difficult to put down.'

Desmond Shawe-Taylor, *Sunday Times*

'The great set-pieces are all here, on broadcasting from Fécamp, on
the splendours and miseries of opera in the French provinces
between the wars, and on early days with the Gas, Light & Coke Co.
They are classics of written humour. He wrote about singers and
singing with supreme authority: in even the shortest notice a diva's
art is neatly, yet never patly, encapsulated. Above all, he enjoyed his
work and conveyed that enjoyment to his readers, and what this
admirable selection (introduced by Veronica Wedgwood and with
two delightful Garland drawings of the master) does is make you
laugh again and again, a small but valuable consolation for the fact
that he is no longer here to do it in person.'

Rodney Milnes, *Harpers & Queen*

COLLINS